TABLE OF CONTENTS

THE MAKING OF A BOOK

RULES FOR COMPOSITION

HINTS TO AUTHORS, EDITORS, AND READERS

TABLE OF CONTENTS

TECHNICAL TERMS AND SYMBOLS

SPECIMENS OF TYPE

TABLE OF CONTENTS

INDEXES

THE MAKING OF A BOOK

INTRODUCTION

A book, on its material side, is the visible embodiment of the subject it presents. Fitness to its subject, therefore, is the first quality of a well-made book. This involves a balance of all the elements that contribute to its total effect, including the mechanics of typography, with which we are here especially concerned.

Careful consideration should be given to making the reader's task easy, and to avoiding as much as possible all distractions from the thought to be conveyed by the text. The abnormally close spacing often attempted by the artist typographer in his effort to secure a compact page makes reading difficult and tiresome. The same result follows when no extra space is left after the closing point of a sentence. Furthermore, the omission of indention altogether in paragraphing, which is advocated by some, produces a forbidding page, and tends only to confuse the reader. On the other hand, the presence of so-called "rivers" or white lines running vertically or diagonally through a page as a result of wide spacing distracts the reader's attention. The typographer therefore must direct his efforts toward a happy medium which will produce the most readable page, with as few as possible of the abnormalities due to the mechanical difficulties encountered.

On the proportion and balance of mass and space on the type page and on the proper relation of type page to paper page depends the character of the typographical appearance of the finished work. The plan must take into account, in addition to questions involving spacing, such points as the size and shape of the type page, the proper spacing around headings, initials, and footnotes, and the placing and spacing of illustrations.

1. It is a generally accepted rule that the type page should occupy approximately one-half of the area of the paper page, and that the proportions of the two should be identical. This rule, however, applies primarily to what may be termed "library books." It is subject to considerable variation in such cases as textbooks, manuals, large reference books, pocket field books, and so on; in such books deep margins would be out of place. Quite as clearly the rule is not applicable to de luxe editions, where larger margins are often desirable. A type page measuring .71 of the paper page each way is approximately one-half of its area. In measuring a type page having no rule beneath its running head, only the body of the page should be considered; the running head, unless it is nearly or quite as wide as the type page, and the drop folio, if any, are to be placed outside the page proper. On the other hand, if there is a rule under the running head, the measurement should include the rule.

In determining the horizontal position of the type page, consider the two facing pages as a unit. Then, with the book fully open, the margins on the left and right and the space between the two pages should appear to be equal. Consideration must be given to the curve of the leaf in the back and the break of the back due to rounding and backing, which vary in books of different thicknesses. For this reason, it may be necessary to allow for slightly more space in the back than in the outer margins.

Theoretically, the vertical position of the type page should be such that it is centered on a diagonal of the

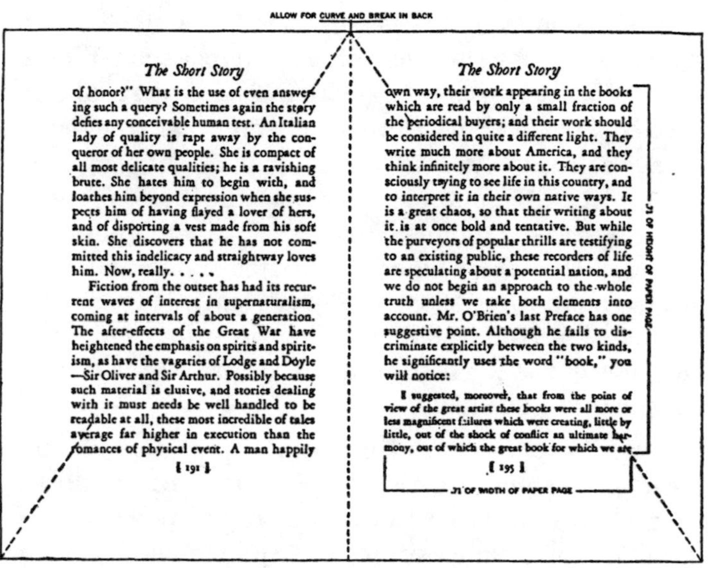

The Short Story

of honor?" What is the use of even answering such a query? Sometimes again the story defies any conceivable human test. An Italian lady of quality is rapt away by the conqueror of her own people. She is compact of all most delicate qualities; he is a ravishing brute. She hates him to begin with, and loathes him beyond expression when she suspects him of having flayed a lover of hers, and of disporting a vest made from his soft skin. She discovers that he has not committed this indelicacy and straightway loves him. Now, really. . . . .

Fiction from the outset has had its recurrent waves of interest in supernaturalism, coming at intervals of about a generation. The after-effects of the Great War have heightened the emphasis on spirits and spiritism, as have the vagaries of Lodge and Doyle —Sir Oliver and Sir Arthur. Possibly because such material is elusive, and stories dealing with it must needs be well handled to be readable at all, these most incredible of tales average far higher in execution than the romances of physical event. A man happily

[191]

The Short Story

own way, their work appearing in the books which are read by only a small fraction of the periodical buyers; and their work should be considered in quite a different light. They write much more about America, and they think infinitely more about it. They are consciously trying to see life in this country, and to interpret it in their own native ways. It is a great chaos, so that their writing about it is at once bold and tentative. But while the purveyors of popular thrills are testifying to an existing public, these recorders of life are speculating about a potential nation, and we do not begin an approach to the whole truth unless we take both elements into account. Mr. O'Brien's last Preface has one suggestive point. Although he fails to discriminate explicitly between the two kinds, he significantly uses the word "book," you will notice:

I suggested, moreover, that from the point of view of the great artist these books were all more or less magnificent failures which were creating, little by little, out of the shock of conflict an ultimate harmony, out of which the great book for which we are

[195]

paper page drawn from the inner top to the outer bottom corner. If the running head is short, the *actual* corner of the type page must be replaced by the *apparent* corner, which is determined by the trained eye rather than by mechanical means. The typographer establishes the theoretical position and then moves the page slightly until he discovers the position which affords the most pleasing effect. The accompanying diagram illustrates the method of determining the relative size and position of the paper and type pages. If the type pages in this case were lowered slightly, the result would be more pleasing.

2. In page makeup, the arrangement of type matter and illustrations should be carefully planned to give balance to two opposite pages considered as a whole. The layout of space for the illustrations is important. Where but one illustration is to appear on a page, it should be placed somewhat above the center. If it is narrower than the page and has type matter down one side, it should be placed next to the outer, rather than the inner, margin.

In case two or more small cuts fall on each of opposite pages, they may be arranged step-fashion on each page, from the upper left to the lower right. There should be several lines of type next to the top or bottom of the page. The eye is the best guide to the proper relation of such masses to the page.

3. White space on all sides of an illustration should appear to be equal. The width of such space should be governed by the general character of the page. If the page is of solid composition, the space should not be greater than the width of one line of the text type; for very compact composition, especially in a small type page, it should be even less.

If the legend consists of more than one line, it should be of the same measure as the illustration. In the case of a cut narrower than the page, centered on the full width, the legend should be of the same measure as the page. In adjusting the space above and below, such a legend should be considered as part of the illustration.

If the legend is short, it should be centered on the width of the illustration and so adjusted that the illustration shall appear to be in the center of the white space it occupies. If type must be set down the side of an illustration with an irregular outline, the type should follow the outline at an even distance from it in order to avoid leaving large white spaces.

4. A properly spaced initial letter aligns at the top with the first line of the paragraph, and at its base with the non-descending letters of the last line cut in beside it. The space below the initial governs that at the right, which should be equal to it, but the first line of type should be close to the face of the initial, unless the initial is a complete word. The high initial, which aligns at the bottom with the first line of text but extends above it, is not favorably regarded in book work, unless the whole style of the composition is ornate. Quotation marks before an initial should be omitted.

5. Equivalent half-titles throughout a book should be of the same size and type style. Similarly, equivalent headings, such as the head lines of the preface, contents, list of illustrations, introduction, chapter number (or chapter title if no number is used), appendix, notes, glossary, bibliography, vocabulary, index, should be of the same size and style.

6. The chapter title may be smaller than the chapter number or in the same size. Subtitles of less importance are set in consistently diminishing sizes. For example, in a 12-point book all the titles of the divisions beginning new pages should be in capitals of the same size as the

text. If the steps of subdivision are many, the one of first importance after the title should be 10-point caps. Under that the one of the next value should be 12-point small caps, and under that 12-point italic sideheads, 10-point small cap center heads, and so on. Scientific and mathematical books, as well as textbooks in grammar and comparative linguistics, frequently require boldface headings for ease of reference.

7. For running heads of a book, the commonest usage prescribes the book title on the verso page with the folio in Arabic numerals on the same line at the outer margin. The recto page then carries the title of the chapter or of the subject discussed in the page. There are, however, many variations from this form of running head.

8. The running head does not appear on the first page of an article in a journal or of a chapter in a book (see 21).

9. The running head and folio should not be used above a full-page illustration. Such a page, however, should be counted unless the illustration is an insert on special stock, and for the benefit of the lockup the page number should be written in by the proofreader on every proof until the page is ready for press.

THE PARTS AND THEIR FORMS

10. Every book consists of three major divisions: The *preliminaries*, including the title and other pages for identification, explanation, and preparation; the *text*, consisting of well-defined parts (chapters, sections, or other divisions) according to the natural progression of subject matter; the *reference matter*, composed of appendix, supplement, bibliography, glossary, vocabulary, index, or similar appended matter. The proper sequence of all the parts is shown in the accompanying outline. Indicators of pagination and page position are given wherever necessary:

Preliminaries

	PAGE
Series Half-Title[1]	i
Announcement or Advertising Card . .	ii
Book Half-Title	iii
Publisher's Agencies	iv
Title-Page	v
Copyright and Printer's Imprint . . .	vi
Dedication (if any)	vii
Blank	viii
Preface[2] (first use of folio)	ix
Table of Contents	recto
Errata[3]	
List of Illustrations	recto
Introduction[4]	recto

[1] Used if the book is in a series; if not, begin with book half-title as p. i.

[2] The editor's preface, if any, precedes the author's preface.

[3] Tipped in over title, or printed at end of contents.

[4] May be included in preliminaries or be the first text page, depending on context.

Text

First Half-Title (if chapters have half-titles)	recto
First Text Page[1]	recto

Reference Matter

Appendix[2]	recto
Notes	recto
Glossary	recto
Bibliography	verso or recto
Vocabulary	recto
Index	recto

The arrangement and relation of these parts, their masses and spaces, the typographical consistency of their titles, subtitles, and ornamentations—all these factors are part of the personality of a book.

THE PRELIMINARIES

11. The half-titles, title-page, and dedication page are all display matter, and should be consistent in their typographical treatment. Use no periods at the ends of lines on these pages, and reduce other punctuation to the minimum. The preliminaries are paged with Roman numerals. This paging begins with the half-title or first printed page, and, although the numerals are not printed either on that or on any other very open page, such pages are always counted as if they were numbered.

12. The half-title consists of the title only (in shortened form if necessary) on a separate leaf preceding the title-page. Half-titles are also used before each part of

[1] Chapters or similar divisions after the first usually begin either on recto or verso pages, but may begin in a very formal book on recto only.

[2] Preceded by a half-title if such style is used for other divisions of the book.

the text when it is broken into parts, and sometimes even before each chapter.

13. The full title-page follows on the next recto page after the half-title. The title-page has well been called "the door to the book." Its beauty, as well as its value, lies in its dignity and strength, and in its power to tell a whole story at once. The title of the book, the name of the author, and the name of the publishing house with its address are necessary elements of title-page composition. The publisher's insignia is usually added as an embellishment. Any further information on this page complicates the problem of the designer. The date of publication may appear in connection with the publisher's name, though it must appear on the next following page, with the copyright notice.

14. The copyright notice appears on the back of the title-page often with a historical statement giving the date of publication and the date of subsequent impressions and new editions (must be recopyrighted). The printer's imprint is placed at the bottom of this page.

15. When there is a dedication, it is placed on the recto page following the copyright notice. The page following the dedication is blank.

16. The preface contains the author's formal statement of the purpose of the book, his instructions as to its use, and his acknowledgments. It should be set in the type of the text. In early manuscript books the preface was written in italics. Such a style is still occasionally used in printed books. A book of several editions often has a preface for each edition, numbered and signed.

17. The table of contents should begin on the next recto page after the preface. It should be a complete analysis of the contents of the book, omitting the pages up to and including the table of contents and any advertisements or other matter foreign to the body of the book. It should present the chapter headings, and if subtitles are given, their relation should be shown by means of indention or grouping, or by smaller type size. Such subtitles should be set to hang indented under each chapter title; if page references are not needed, the subtitles may be run in with semicolons or dashes between them. Runovers in the table of contents should have hanging indention. (See 314.)

18. The list of illustrations should match the table of contents in general style. The titles used in the list need not read exactly like the legends under the illustrations; if the legend is long, use a shortened form that is not misleading. If the illustrations are all text figures, the figure numbers may be aligned at the left with the word "Figure" in very small type as a heading to the column.

If there are both text figures and plates, they should be numbered separately, the figures with Arabic numerals and the plates with Roman capitals. In that case they should be arranged in separate lists. The problem of the page number for plates may be solved by using "Facing Page" as a heading above the page numbers or the word "facing" in italics to the left of each page number. If part of the illustrations are paged up in the text and part are inserted, the second method will cover both kinds of reference.

If the list of illustrations is long and burdened with the names of artists and engravers, copyright credits, and so on, it is better to set the titles in caps and lowercase type with hanging indention (that being more easily read), with the credits in italics aligned at the right, next to the column of page numbers.

19. If the introduction is an integral part of the text, or if the information it contains is needed to present in sequence the meaning of the following chapters, it must begin with page 1 after the table of contents. If it gives merely historical and biographical matter for the purpose of explaining the position taken by the author toward other writers and toward his subject, it may be numbered in the preliminaries after the table of contents (or even before the table of contents if there is no preface). In that case chapter i must begin with page 1.

THE TEXT

20. The essential elements of good style are demonstrated in the typographic page. Though form is determined in every case by the nature of the manuscript, certain basic principles must be reflected in the text page of every book. The relation of running heads to text and of text to illustrations are cases in point. Type size has direct relation to the length of the manuscript, to the kind of material, and to the market to be reached in sales. There may be need to spread a brief manuscript over enough pages to give bulk; on the contrary, a manuscript may require compact type treatment in order to meet manufacturing and sales conditions.

21. As a rule, paging with Arabic figures begins with the text of the book. Here the running head is omitted and the page shortened and sunk, as on the first page of each chapter. The folio is centered at the bottom of the page, sometimes in brackets. The sink should be the same on all first pages of chapters throughout the book.

22. If a synopsis or outline precedes each chapter, it may appear at the heading of the chapter or be treated as a half-title on a separate leaf; or if chapter half-titles are used, it may be set facing the first page of the chapter on the back of the half-title.

23. Titles or subtitles of two or three lines should be centered in inverted pyramid form. When consisting of more than three lines, they should be arranged in a "flush-and-hang" paragraph. In dividing into lines, avoid the division of any word, term, or group which would result in ambiguity. This should, however, be secondary in importance to the typographical appearance.

24. Composition that is broken in its text by lines of poetry, extracts, or tables of figures, or that has many short articles separated by dashes, requires that leads be adjusted at each break to secure uniformity in appearance. In solid composition a white line or less of the text is enough to mark the distinction, but when the text is double leaded and the margins are wide, the blank should be wider proportionately. When the last line of a paragraph before a break consists of one or two words only, the white space made by the quadrats that fill this last line should be taken into consideration in adding leads at such points.

25. Poetry, quotations from other published works, letters, manuscripts, facsimiles, and similar material not part of the text are set in type one, or preferably two, sizes smaller than the text.

26. Footnotes are usually set in type several sizes smaller than the text. They should be set with plain paragraph indention with the superior reference figure separated from the first letter by a thin space (see 284 ff.).

27. The makeup often requires careful study to bring the reference and the first two lines of a footnote on the same page. Wherever it is impossible to do this, the editor or the author should be asked to change the wording or to move the reference. If the footnote is so long that it will not all go into the same page with the reference and the author cannot make an adjustment, the continuation may be carried over to the foot of the following page and be placed preceding the footnotes belonging to that page. A 3- or 4-em rule should be inserted at the left edge of the page between such a continuation and the text of the page. When a footnote must be broken in this manner, care should be taken to make the break come within a sentence in order to suggest to a reader that the note runs on to the following page. (For rules of composition, see 282–93.)

28. If many short footnotes (such as simple references to parts of a single work) occur on a wide page, set them in columns to read down. A few short references may be spaced about two picas apart to form a single line across the page.

29. The practice of using a single footnote for more than one textual reference should be avoided unless that is the only footnote on the page in question.

30. Cut-in and boxed notes should be of the same width throughout a book. They should cut in two lines below the beginning of a paragraph and should have at least two lines of the paragraph below the note. Such notes are likely to make great difficulty in paging and to cause frequent re-writing by the author.

31. Marginal notes should be separated from the text page by at least a nonpareil if the page is small and compact; by a pica if the type is large and the composition open. The first line of the note should align with a line of the opposite text.

32. A page should not begin with a short line if it is possible to avoid it, and never with a break-line ending a paragraph.

33. Avoid more than two consecutive hyphens at the ends of lines, or more than two occurrences of the same word at the beginning or end of consecutive lines. This rule should not be rigidly applied if it requires the sacrifice of good spacing.

34. Whenever it is necessary to run over type in the makeup in order to correct bad spacing or divisions, or to make or save lines to avoid bad page appearance, the proof of the runover portion must be re-read for possible new errors made in handling.

35. All legends and captions for illustrations in the same book should be treated consistently. The page lay-

out should determine the typographical requirements and whether illustrations should be identified by legends below them or by captions above. The amount of description necessary and the size of the illustrations in relation to the size of type page are factors to be considered. (For rules of composition, see 294–301.)

36. Even spacing between words is essential to insure ease of reading and to maintain uniformity in the type page as a whole. It is impracticable to adopt a standard space for all styles of type. If the type face is thin, if the individual letters are closely spaced in the words, or if the leading between the lines is very slight, the spacing between words should be correspondingly thin. On the other hand, wide type, open-spaced letters, and heavy leading call for wider spacing. It is necessary, therefore, to adopt different standards to fit different conditions.

37. By "standard spacing" is meant the ideal space between words ending and beginning with letters of the ordinary rounded form. In a perfectly spaced line, this standard space would be increased or diminished according to the shapes of the letters between which it falls, the result to be attained being an appearance of uniformity throughout the line. For example, the standard for composition such as that in the text of this book would be a 3-em space, with an en quad after colons, exclamation and interrogation points, and after periods ending sentences. Spaces next to slanting letters like *v* and *w* would be slightly less, and between straight letters like *l* and *b* slightly more than the standard. Where the

adjustment of the line to the proper length makes it necessary to increase or decrease the standard space, these same general proportions should be maintained.

38. Perfect spacing calls for the same space between words ending and beginning in similarly shaped letters throughout the entire page. In actual practice such perfection is unattainable, since the width of spacing in different lines must vary because of the necessity of breaking the lines at the end of words or syllables and spacing them all to the full-page width.

39. The rules that require uniform spacing between words sometimes conflict with other rules concerning an arbitrary division of words. Words of one syllable are rated as indivisible. To get in words like these, or long syllables at the end of the line, often compels abnormally thin spacing; or to drive them over to the next line makes wide spacing. Either alternative is objectionable. To obviate the fault, the paragraph may be overrun, but this expedient is nearly always impracticable in a narrow measure. Even spacing often has to be sacrificed for correct divisions, but the difficulty may be obviated by suggesting a slight change of wording to the author.

40. Letter-spacing for the purpose of justifying is not permissible except in forced cases of very narrow column measure, such as in tables or around cuts. Never letter-space one word in a line with other words set solid. In German text, letter-spacing is employed instead of italics.

41. In monotype and linotype composition the difficulty of even spacing is made greater by the fact that

the minimum width of the spreading, or justifying, space is fixed at about that of a 4-em space, and may be increased, but not diminished, from this width. The tendency, therefore, in composition done on these machines, is toward wide spacing. A careful operator can, however, by the sacrifice of time, overcome this difficulty. In the case of the monotype, he may omit the last letter or two of a word or syllable which he cannot get into the line, and leave them to be crowded in through thin spacing by the corrector. The linotype operator may hand-space the line before casting by substituting a number of thin spaces for the justifying spaces. Both these methods are time-consumers and therefore expensive, as indeed are all the operations tending toward correct spacing.

42. Care should be taken to avoid abrupt changes of spacing in adjacent lines, and also very open spacing next to paragraph breaks or other white space. Similarly, the spaces on both sides of short words should appear to be equal.

43. In monotype composition indentions should be such that all paragraph indentions align irrespective of the size of the type. The following indentions are a good standard for measures of 19 to 30 picas: 12 point indented 1 em 8 units; 11 point indented 1 em 10 units; 10 point indented $1\frac{2}{3}$ ems or 1 em 12 units; 9 point indented $1\frac{3}{4}$ ems or 1 em 15 units; 8 point indented 2 ems; 6 point indented $2\frac{1}{2}$ ems or 2 ems 9 units. Narrower measures should be indented proportionately less; wider, proportionately more.

In hanging indentions, in measures of less than 10 picas, indent all sizes 1 em; from 10 to 20, 11 point, 10 point, 9 point, and 8 point, 1½ ems; 6 point, 2 ems; from 20 to 30, 11 point, 10 point, 9 point, and 8 point, 2 ems; 6 point, 3 ems.

44. In ordinary reading-matter, "plain paragraphs" are always used. Where it is desired to bring into relief the opening word or words, or the number of each paragraph, use hanging indention.

45. In poetry, center the longest line and let the indention be governed by that, unless the longest line is of disproportionate length, in which case an average of the long lines should be struck. This procedure should give the whole poem a centered appearance. Where quotations from different poems of the same meter following each other in close succession vary but slightly in length of lines, it is best to indent all alike. Indent individual lines according to rhymes and length of lines. In blank verse, where the lines are of approximately the same length, they should be aligned. If consecutive lines rhyme, they should likewise be aligned. If the rhymes alternate, or follow at certain intervals, indent the rhyming lines alike; that is, if lines 1 and 3, and 2 and 4, rhyme, set the former pair flush in the measure previously determined by the longest line, and indent the latter (usually one em); follow this scheme in any similar arrangement. Indent a very short line more.

And blessed are the horny hands of toil!
The busy world shoves angrily aside
The man who stands with arms akimbo set,
Until occasion tells him what to do.

I laugh at the lore and the pride of man,
At the sophist schools and the learned clan;
For what are they all, in their high conceit,
When man in the bush with God may meet?

So nigh is grandeur to our dust,
  So near is God to man,
When Duty whispers low, "Thou must,"
  The youth replies, "I can."

      Not lightly fall
      Beyond recall
The written scrolls a breath can float;
      The crowning fact,
      The kingliest act
Of Freedom is the freeman's vote!

For rules of composition for tables, formulas, indexes, and other broken elements in the page, see 307–25, 326–32, 333–45.

REFERENCE MATTER

46. The reference matter of a book is as much an integral part of the volume as any other. It is, however, usually of secondary importance and therefore is set in smaller type. In planning it, care should be taken in the typographic treatment so that it shall not seem to be subordinate to the last chapter instead of a reference device for the whole book.

If such reference matter consists of an appendix or a bibliography only, it may be treated as the equivalent of a new chapter, beginning a new page either verso or recto if the chapters are so arranged. If the section consists of notes to the text, it is preferable to begin on a right-hand page. Glossary, vocabulary, or an index should also begin on a right-hand page, and may be preceded by a half-title even if no other half-titles are used except the book half-title.

The general appearance of an appendix, a bibliography, or notes is similar to that of the pages of text, but as a glossary, a vocabulary, or an index consists of short lines listed, and these entries are usually set in two or more columns, their composition is more difficult and their makeup requires particular care in planning. Frequently the repetition of guide lines is necessary, especially at the tops of verso pages. (For rules of composition and examples, see 333–45.)

Reference matter added after each chapter, such as a bibliography, references for further reading, or questions, should not be separated from the chapter to which it belongs. Such matter should be set a size or two smaller than the text, with a heading in caps of the same size, and run in.

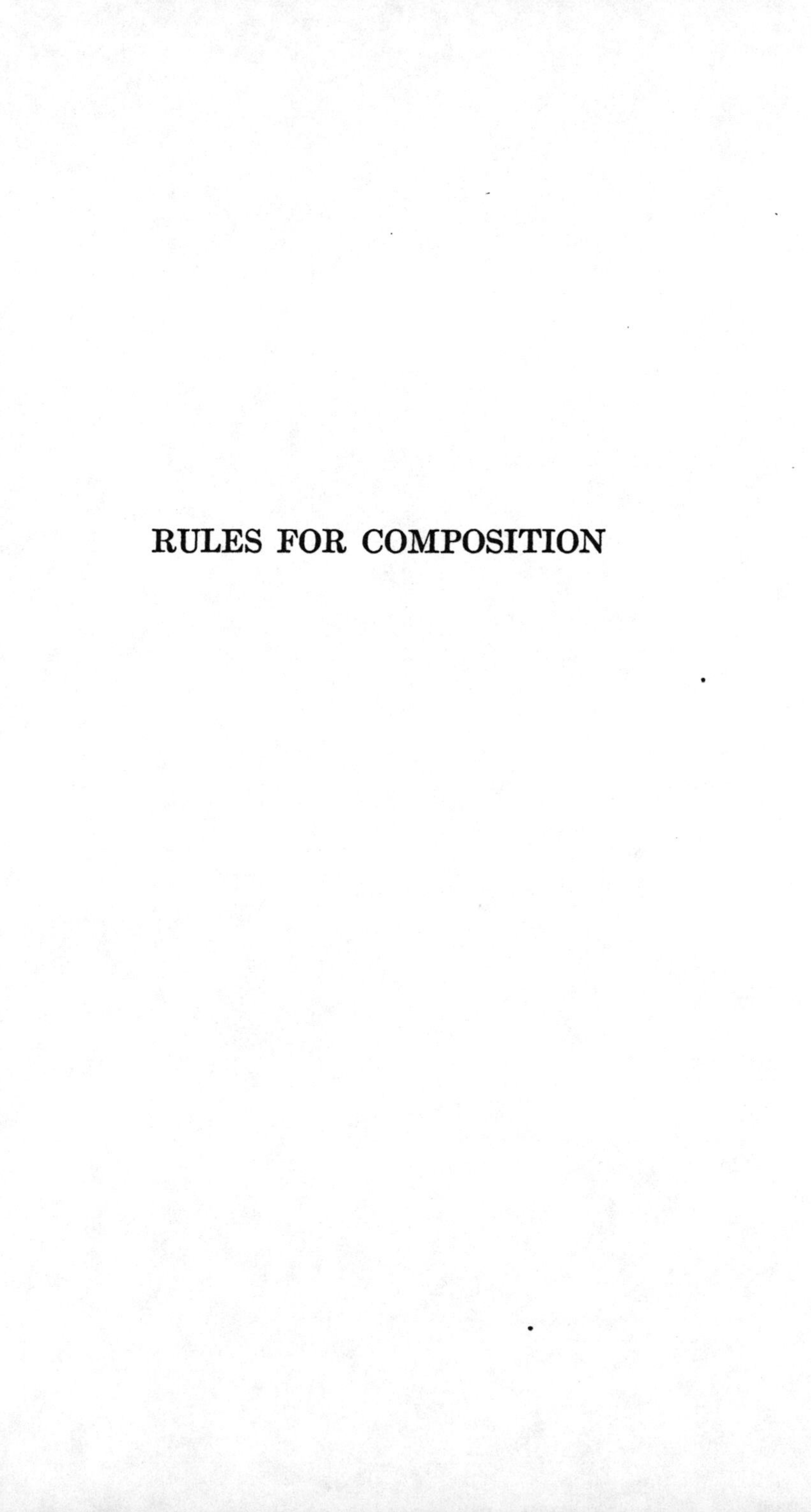

RULES FOR COMPOSITION

CAPITALIZATION

47. Capitalize proper nouns and proper adjectives in English, Latin, and Dutch text (see 82):

George	Elizabethan	bellum Gallicum
North America	French	Nederlandsche Taal

48. Capitalize proper nouns but not adjectives derived from them in French, Italian, Spanish, Norwegian, and Swedish text:

Paris	littérature française
Italia	popolari italiani
Hispanola	líricos castellanos
Copenhagen	svenska historie

49. Capitalize all nouns (both common and proper) and words used as nouns in German and Danish, but not the adjectives, except in German those derived from the names of persons:

das Neue
die französische Frage, but: die Homerische Frage
Videnskabens Fremskridt i det nittende Aarhundrede

50. In English do not capitalize words derived from proper nouns that have developed a specialized meaning:

utopia	bonanza	boycott
bohemian	paris green	italicize
philistine	china	anglicize
titanic	morocco	macadamize
platonic	roman (type)	pasteurize
quixotic	pharisaic	fletcherize

51. Capitalize epithets used as substitutes for proper names, or affixed to a name (see 56):

Holy Writ	Bloody Mary
the Pretender	Richard the Lion-hearted

52. Capitalize the particles in French names, as "le," "la," "de," "du," when they are not preceded by a Christian name or title; but do not capitalize them when they are preceded by such name or title:

Le Bossu	Réne le Bossu
La Torre	Miguel de la Torre
De Coligny	Gaspard de Coligny
D'Aubigné	Thomas d'Aubigné
Du Maurier	George du Maurier
(but: de Sitter)	

53. Set "van" in Dutch and "von" in German family names in lower-case type. Observe any variations in personal signatures:

Stephen van Rensselaer	von Tirpitz
Henry van Dyke	Hugo von Martius

54. Capitalize words that through usage in a formal union have become a part of a permanent, individual name. Shortened forms of such combinations still retain their proper-noun character and when used for the whole name should be capitalized (see 55–68).

55. Capitalize accepted geographical names:

Mississippi River	Rocky Mountains
Straits of Gibraltar	Pike's Peak

a) Capitalize in the singular only, when following the name:

Archipelago	Branch (stream)	Canyon
Borough	Butte	County[1]

[1] In Irish references: county Kildare.

Crater	Harbor	Range
Creek	Head	Reservation
Delta	Hollow	Ridge
Forest	Mesa	River
Fork	Ocean	Run
Gap	Parish (La.)	Valley
Glacier	Park	
Gulch	Plateau	

b) Capitalize in both singular and plural, when following the name:

Hill	Mountain	Spring
Island	Narrows	Peak

c) Capitalize in the singular either preceding or following the name, and in the plural when preceding the name:

Bay	Fort	Peak
Bayou	Isle	Point
Camp (military)	Lake	Sea
Cape	Mount	Strait
Dalles	Oasis	Volcano
Desert	Pass	

Exceptions:

Mere descriptive place references do not call for capitalization:

the valley of the Mississippi　　　the river Elbe

56. Capitalize special names for regions and localities, imaginary appellations, and popular formations. Clear intention of special meaning is shown in the capitalization of such forms as "Eastern peoples" (of the

Orient) and "Western customs" (of the Western Hemisphere):

North Atlantic states	the Equator
Continental Europe (or the Continent)	the Loop (Chicago)
the Far East	Eternal City
Western world	the Promised Land
the East Side (section of a city)	the Badger State
Middle West	the Levant
	the Dominion (Canada)

Exceptions:

a) Do not capitalize adjectives derived from such names, or nouns simply designating direction:

oriental customs	the south of Europe
middle western states	to the north

b) Capitalize parts of world-divisions, but lower case localities such as directional parts of states:

Northern China	Southern Italy
Eastern Persia	Upper Michigan (but: northern Michigan)
western Oregon	
East Africa	

c) Do not capitalize such words as "city," "state," "empire," etc., when standing alone, or when, with "of," preceding specific name (but: the Empire, meaning Holy Roman Empire).

57. Capitalize terms for political divisions:

United Kingdom
Evanston Township
First Ward
German Empire (*Deutsches Reich*)
French Republic (*République française*) (see 48 and 82*b*)
the Republic (United States)
the Dominion (Canada)
Eleventh Congressional District

58. Capitalize the names of thoroughfares, parks, squares, buildings, etc.

Fifth Avenue	Trafalgar Square	Théâtre Français
Lincoln Park	the White House	Lexington Hotel

Exceptions:

Do not capitalize such general designations of buildings as "courthouse," "post-office," "library," and the like, unless the context gives the single word the value of a proper name (see 54).

59. Capitalize the names of political parties, religious denominations or sects; of monastic orders and their members; of philosophical, literary, and artistic schools, and their adherents:

Republican party
Conservative party
National Liberal party
Baptist church (but:
First Baptist Church)
Roman Catholic church
Protestantism
High Church
Jew

Jesuit
Dominican
Black Friars
Epicurean
Platonism (but: neo-Platonism)
Stoic
the Symbolic school of painters
Pharisee (but: scribe)
Gentile (as a noun)

60. Capitalize the official titles of organizations and institutions:

Union League Club
State University of Iowa
Hyde Park High School
the Forty [Immortals]
Tammany Hall
Union Stock Yards

Associated Press
Typographical Union No. 16
Chicago & Alton Railroad
The Macmillan Company
Hull-House
World Court

61. Capitalize ordinals used in names of dynasties and organizations, and of individuals in a succession.

Spell out ordinals before the name, but in the case of names of individuals use Roman numerals following the name (see 171):

the Eighteenth Dynasty (but: the Ming dynasty)
the Fifty-third Congress
the Second Illinois Regiment Band
George III
Marshall Field II
Pope Pius X
Valkyrie III

62. Capitalize commonly accepted appellations for historical epochs, periods in the history of a language or literature, names of geological ages and strata, the word "age" itself being capitalized only where a failure to do so would result in ambiguous meaning:

Colonial days
Neolithic age (but: Stone Age)
Crusades
Renaissance
Commonwealth (Cromwell's)
Old English (OE—see 168*b*)
Middle High German (MHG)
Pleistocene
Lower Carboniferous
Christian Era
the Exile
post-Exilic writings (see 258*b*)
the Deluge

Exceptions:

Do not capitalize informal adjectives in such phrases as "early Algonkian," and "late Permian."

63. Capitalize names of important events:

Thirty Years' War
Civil War (American)
Battle of Gettysburg
War of 1812
Whiskey Insurrection
Franco-Prussian War
Louisiana Purchase
World War (of 1914–18)
Peace of Utrecht

64. Capitalize titles of specific treaties, acts, laws (juridical), bills, and similar documents:

Treaty of Verdun
Declaration of Independence
Magna C(h)arta
Versailles Treaty
Reform Bill (English)
Fourteenth Amendment
Sherman Anti-Trust Law
Constitution (of United States)

Exceptions:

Do not capitalize such bills as have not yet become laws, or such treaties or laws when cited otherwise than under their formal titles:

Child Labor bill
treaty at Versailles

65. Capitalize titles of honor and respect, whether religious, civil, or military, when preceding the name, and academic degrees following the name; all titles of honor or of nobility when referring to specific persons, either preceding the name or used in place of the proper name; orders (decorations) and the titles accompanying them (see 70):

Queen Victoria
former President Taft (not ex-President [see 253 n.])
General Pershing
James Brown, Doctor of Philosophy
Thomas Graham, Fellow of the Royal Geographic Society
the Apostle to the Gentiles
E. H. Wilkins, Cavaliere della Corona d'Italia
the Bishop of London
the Senator
William Randall, Knight of the Order of the Thistle
Arthur Coleman, Fellow of the Royal Society of Canada
the Pope's policy (referring to present incumbent)
Sir Valentine Chirol

66. Capitalize civic holidays and ecclesiastical fast and feast days:

Fourth of July (the Fourth)
Labor Day
Thanksgiving Day
Passover
Feast of Tabernacles
New Year's Day

67. Capitalize creeds and confessions of faith:

Apostles' Creed
Nicene Creed (see 84, 254, 258*b*)
Augsburg Confession
Thirty-nine Articles
Heidelberg Catechism
Athanasian Creed

68. Capitalize all names for the Bible and other sacred books; versions and editions of the Bible; books and divisions of the Bible and of other sacred books, Christian or otherwise (see 96*b*):

Bible
(Holy, Sacred) Scriptures
Holy Writ
Word of God
Mishna
the Upanishads
Apocrypha
the King James Version
Authorized Version
Revised Version
Polychrome Bible
Septuagint
Peshitto
American Translation
Old Testament
Pentateuch
Exodus
Wisdom Literature
Synoptic Gospels
Acts of the Apostles (the Acts)
Sermon on the Mount
Lord's Prayer
Ten Commandments (Decalogue)
the Koran
the Vedas

Exceptions:

Do not capitalize adjectives derived from such nouns:

biblical
scriptural
koranic
vedic
talmudic
apocryphal

69. Capitalize the first word of a sentence, a word standing for a sentence, and in poetry the first word of each line:

Out through the fields and the woods
  And over the walls I have wended;
I have climbed the hills of view,
  And looked at the world, and descended;
I have come by the highway home,
  And lo, it is ended.—ROBERT FROST

Exceptions:

a) In some modern English poetry only the first word of the first line (and sometimes not that, as in the following example) is capitalized. In authentic cases of such irregularity, follow copy.

if I had the lake
in my own front yard
I never would work at all
just smoke my pipe
and dream
                by the waves
                                from April
                                to frosty fall
      and in winter
I'd skate
                    from early to late
      wrapped up
      in a Paisley
      shawl   —RIQ.

b) In Greek and Latin poetry capitalize only the first word of a paragraph, not of each verse (line):

Τοῖσι δ' ἀοιδὸς ἄειδε περικλυτός, οἱ δὲ σιωπῇ
εἵατ' ἀκούοντες· ὁ δ' Ἀχαιῶν νόστον ἄειδεν,
λυγρόν, ὃν ἐκ Τροίης ἐπετείλατο Παλλὰς Ἀθήνη.
τοῦ δ' ὑπερωιόθεν φρεσὶ σύνθετο θέσπιν ἀοιδὴν
κούρη Ἰκορίοιο, περίφρων Πηνελόπεια·

Talia praefantes quondam felicia Pelei
carmina diuino cecinerunt pectore Parcae
praesentes: namque ante domos inuisere castas
heroum et sese mortali ostendere coetu
caelicolae nondum spreta pietate solebant.

70. Capitalize abbreviations for degrees and titles such as Ph.D., M.P., and F.R.G.S., initials, and designations of celestial objects (see 88), such titles to be set without space between the letters (see 92, 111). Initials of persons should be spaced. Note the rare instance of an initial letter that is *merely a letter*, not a true abbreviation. Persons having such signature forms must make known this peculiarity lest the printer use abbreviation periods. Examples of this sort are the names:

Maurice L Rothschild, W J McGee, J Harlen Bretz

71. Capitalize abbreviations consisting of one letter, except in case of units of measurement and minor literary subdivisions (see 76*a*, *b*, 92, 154):

F. (Fahrenheit)	A (angstrom units)
C. (Centigrade)	(but: p., l., n., etc.)

72. Capitalize nouns and adjectives used to designate the Supreme Being, or any member of the Christian Trinity; and all pronouns referring to the same when not closely preceded or followed by a distinct reference to the Deity:

the Almighty	the Spirit
the First Cause	Savior
the Absolute	Messiah
Providence (personified)	Yahweh
Father	Son of Man

Son
Holy Ghost
the Logos
the Virgin Mary
"Trust Him who rules all things" (but: "When God had worked six days, he rested on the seventh.")

Exceptions:

Do not capitalize such expressions and derivatives as:

(God's) fatherhood
(Jesus') sonship
messiahship
messianic hope
christological
(but: Christology)

73. Capitalize personifications:

For Nature wields her scepter mercilessly.
Everyman and Vice in the old English morality plays.

74. Capitalize the first word after a colon only when introducing a complete passage or sentence having independent meaning, as in summarizations and quotations not closely connected with what precedes. Here the colon has the weight of such expressions as "as follows," "namely," "for instance," or a similar form, and is followed by a logically complete sentence:

In conclusion I wish to say: The evidence shows that . . . .

As the old proverb has it: "Haste makes waste."

My theory is: The moment that the hot current strikes the surface . . . .

Exceptions:

Do not capitalize the first word of an indirect quotation, or the first word of a quotation which is grammatically joined to what precedes, even if such a word in the original begins a sentence. Likewise, the first word after a colon is not to be capitalized when introducing an element that is explanatory or logically dependent upon the preceding clause:

> He passed the word along that "we storm the enemy tomorrow."
>
> We have three reasons for our present economy: the nation is in debt; taxes are far too high; and other countries are threatening war.

75. Capitalize the first word in each section of an enumeration that has been formally introduced in sentence style (see 77, 178):

> His reasons for refusal were three: (1) He did not have the time for he was employed during the day. (2) He did not have the means, or, at any rate, had no funds available at the moment. (3) He doubted the feasibility of the plan which the committee had put forward.
>
> But: He objected *that* (1) he did not have the time; (2) he did not have the means, or, at any rate, had no funds available; (3) he doubted the feasibility of the plan.
>
> Brown's fourth rule is: "Proper names of every description should always begin with capitals."

Exceptions:

Do not capitalize brief items in such an enumeration when they are separated by commas:

> Three types were used: (*a*) the oral-question test, (*b*) the picture-question test, and (*c*) the performance test.

76. Capitalize a noun, or abbreviation of a noun, followed by a numeral—particularly a capitalized Roman numeral—indicating place in a sequence; also sums of money in German and French:

Room 16	Vol. I	Part IV
Ps. 20	No. 2	Plate II
Grade IV	Book II	M. 6 (six marks)
Act I	Div. III	Fr. 5 (five francs)

Exceptions:

a) In literary references do not capitalize such minor subdivisions and their abbreviations as (see 152, 155):

chapter = chap.	article = art.	note = n.
section = sec.	verse = vs.	volume = vol.
page = p.	line = l.	

b) Do not capitalize such units of measurement as:

hour = h.	pound = lb.	yard = yd.
minute = min.	ounce = oz.	foot = ft.
second = sec.		

77. Capitalize the first word of a cited speech (or thought) in direct discourse, whether preceded by a colon or a comma (see 74, 178):

On leaving he remarked: "Never shall I forget this day."

With the words, "Never shall I forget this day," he departed.

I thought to myself: This day I shall never forget [without quotation marks].

78. In resolutions capitalize the first words following "WHEREAS" (see 91) and "*Resolved*" (see 113):

WHEREAS, It had pleased God . . . . ; therefore be it
Resolved, That . . . .

79. Always capitalize the vocative "O"; capitalize the exclamation "oh" only when beginning a sentence or standing alone (see 207):

"O Lord!" "I know not, oh, I know not!" "Oh, that I were home again!" "O thou most mighty ruler!"

80. Capitalize all the principal words (i.e., nouns, pronouns, adjectives, adverbs, verbs, first and last words) in titles of English publications (books, newspapers, pamphlets, documents, periodicals, reports, proceedings, etc.) (see 84*a*); in divisions of works (parts, chapters, sections,

poems, articles, etc.); in subjects of lectures, papers, toasts, etc.; in cap-and-small-cap and italic center heads, and bold-face cut-in heads, in cap-and-small-cap box-heads in tables (see 84*b*). Capitalize references to parts of a specific work, such as Preface, Contents, Index (see 123*b*):

> *The Men Who Made the Nation*
>
> *The American College—Its Past and Present*
>
> the *Report of the Committee of Nine*
>
> "In the *Proceedings of the National Education Association* for 1907 there appeared a paper entitled, 'The Financial Value of Education.'"
>
> Such a repetition may be found in the Preface.

Exceptions:

a) In side-heads, use lower case for all but the first word and proper names. Side-heads set in caps and small caps are exceptional, but at times are used for special stressing (see 226).

b) In botanical matter only first words and proper names are capitalized. This practice may properly be followed in general bibliographies. An example may be found under the title "Literature Cited" in the *Botanical Gazette*. This style is very generally followed by librarians and others in the compilation of lists of books and publications.

81. In mentioning titles of newspapers, magazines, and similar publications, capitalize as indicated in section 80, but do not treat an initial definite article as part of the title:

> the *Chicago Tribune*, the *School Review*, the *Annual Register of the University of Chicago*

82. In foreign titles, in addition to capitalizing the first word, follow these special rules (see 47–50):

a) In Latin, capitalize proper nouns and adjective forms derived therefrom:

De amicitia *Bellum Gallicum*

b) In French, Italian, Spanish, Swedish, and Norwegian titles, capitalize proper nouns but not adjectives derived therefrom:

Histoire de la littérature française
Novelle e racconti popolari italiani
Antología de poetas líricos castellanos
Meddelelser fra norsk forening for sprogvidenskap

c) In German and Danish, capitalize all nouns but not the adjectives, except German adjectives derived from the names of persons:

Geschichte des deutschen Feudalwesens (but: *die Homerische Frage*)
Videnskabens Fremskridt i det nittende Aarhundrede
Berliner philologische Wochenschrift

d) In Dutch, capitalize all nouns and all adjectives derived from proper nouns:

Geschiedenis der Nederlandsche Taal

83. Capitalize titles of ancient manuscripts (singular MS; plural MSS) (but see 96*b*):

Codex Bernensis Cod. Canonicianus

84. In titles with the main words capitalized, capitalize all nouns forming parts of hyphenated compounds:

Twentieth-Century Progress
The Economy of High-Speed Trains

Exceptions:

a) Do not capitalize such components when other than nouns and proper adjectives (see 80):

Fifty-first Street
World-Dominion of English-speaking Peoples
Lives of Well-known Authors

b) In side-heads do not capitalize any but the first word and proper nouns (see 226).

85. In botanical, geological, zoölogical, and paleontological matter, capitalize the scientific (Latin) names of divisions, orders, families, and genera, but not their English derivatives:

Cotylosauria, but: cotylosaurs
Carnivora, but: carnivores
Cruciferae, but: crucifers
Felidae, but: felids

86. In botanical, geological, zoölogical, paleontological, and medical matter the names of species are never capitalized (see 107, 108, 109):

Cedrus libani
Felis leo
Cocos nucifera
Carex halleriana
Pterygometopus schmidti
Styrax californica
Lythrum hyssopifolia
Phyteuma halleri
Conodectes favosus

87. Capitalize the names and epithets of peoples, races, and tribes:

Kafir	Makassar	Celestials	Malay
Hottentot	Buginese	Aryans	Negroes

Exceptions:

Discriminate between tribal or racial names and mere color or localized designations:

little brown men	negroes (except in ethnic sense)
redskins	(but capitalize in sociological material)

88. In astronomical work, capitalize the names of the bodies of the planets, stars, and groups of stars (but not "sun," "earth," "moon," "stars"); designations of celestial objects in well-known catalogues:

Saturn	M 13[1]	B.D.—18°4871
Ursa Major	Bond 619	85 Pegasi
the Milky Way	N.G.C. 6165	Lalande 5761

89. Capitalize divisions, departments, titles of officers and of courses of study in the University of Chicago, in all official work dealing with its administration or curricula:

(the University), the School of Education (the School), the Department of Geography (also: the Department), the Board of Trustees (the Trustees, the Board), the Senate, the Council, University College (also: the College), the School of Commerce and Administration (also: the School), Dean of Faculties (also: the Faculty), the President, Professor of Physics, Assistant in Chemistry, Fellow, Scholar, the Van Husen Scholarship (but: the scholarship), courses in Political Economy, Autumn Quarter (but: a quarter), First Term (but: two terms; major, minor), Hall (referring to a University building).

90. In reproduction of letters, use capitals and small capitals for the name of town and state in the date line, the salutatory phrase at the beginning, and the signa-

[1] Referring to a cluster in Messier's *Catalogue of Nebulae and Clusters.*

ture and residence at the end. The writer's signature and address, if given at the end of a journal article or a preface, should be set in caps and small caps, but the date line should appear in caps and lower case. All such lines are treated as display, and punctuation is omitted at the ends of lines.

a) Place the date line with one em's indention from the right margin. If a long address precedes the date, and makes two lines, set the longest line flush to the right margin and center the other one on it.

CHICAGO, ILL., June 28, 1925

but: NAGPUR, CENTRAL PROVINCES, INDIA
January 1, 1925

b) Place the salutatory phrase flush with the left margin. This should be a separate line. When preceded by the name and address the salutatory phrase may be indented as a paragraph and run in preceding a colon with the first line of the letter (see 100, 179):

DEAR MR. SMITH:

Your letter of the first of September . . . .

Frederick I. Smith
The City Club, Chicago, Illinois

MY DEAR MR. SMITH: Your letter of September 1 . . . .

c) The signature is set with one em's indention from the right margin and in the same type as the body of the letter or article. The complimentary closing line is arranged with relation to the length of the signature (see 101):

Yours very truly,
TOM PEETE CROSS

d) Place the writer's address at the end of an article two ems from the left margin and center the date line upon the longest line of the address:

JOHNS HOPKINS UNIVERSITY
BALTIMORE, MD.
January 10, 1925

91. Use caps and small caps for the word "WHEREAS" in resolutions (see 78); for the word "NOTE" introducing an explanatory paragraph that cannot be used as a footnote (see 226); for the word "SECTION" (see 153) in reference to part of a document by number; for ascription to author of a direct, independent quotation (see 222); and for author's signature at the end of an article or preface (see 90):

WHEREAS, It has pleased God . . . .
NOTE.—It should be noticed that . . . .
SECTION I. This association shall be styled . . . .

"O brown halo in the sky near the moon,
dropping upon the sea!
O troubled reflection in the sea!
O throat! O throbbing heart!
And I singing uselessly, uselessly all the night."

—WALT WHITMAN

. . . . These essays are the records of moods and sometimes contradict each other. So much the better. The only thing I hate is prejudice. The Norman coal-heaver took me for a German: he pressed the cup of cider on me, and hailed me "Kamerad!" I would rather cut my throat than be the cause of more fighting.

JOSEPH WARREN BEACH

January 10, 1925

92. Use small capitals for the abbreviations A.M. and P.M. (*ante* and *post meridiem*), and B.C. and A.D. ("before Christ" and *anno Domini*). These should be set without a space between (see 70, 71, 155):

11:30 A.M.	53 B.C.	12:00 M.
4:25 P.M.	A.D. 1906	

THE USE OF ITALICS

93. Italicize words or phrases to which it is necessary to lend emphasis; but avoid this use of italics wherever possible because of the conflict with other meanings of the italic form and in order to avoid the displeasing appearance of italics in a roman page:

> This, however, was *not* the case.
>
> It is sufficiently plain that the *sciences of life* at least are studies of processes.

94. Italicize when necessary the first occurrence of terms with special meaning and later accepted in text as carrying such meaning:

> Little by little the conclusion gathered the force of demonstration in social science that, whatever may prove to be more particular principles of human relationships, *gradualism* rather than *catastrophism* is the universal manner of social cause and effect.

95. Italicize foreign words and phrases appearing in English text. Brief passages or single sentences in a foreign language also take italic as an alternative of reduced type (see 127):

> *De gustibus non est disputandum*, or, as the French have it, *Chacun à son goût.*
>
> Tavernier, in his review of Fräulein Sternberg's work, confirms her viewpoint and adds: *Wie Ref. an anderem Ort ausführlicher begründen will, ist Raoul in der Tat eine einheitliche Dichtung.*

Do not hyphenate foreign words when used as adjectives, nor separate their elements by line breaks (see 244*b*).

Exceptions:

a) Use roman type for foreign titles preceding proper names and for names of foreign institutions whose significance prevents any translation into English words:

Père Lagrange	the Champs Elysées
Freiherr von Schwenau	the Museo delle Terme
the German Reichstag	Gymnasium

b) Roman quote titles of articles taken from foreign-language journals (see 123).

c) Continued use of foreign words in English speech adds them to our native stock. Indicate such additions as they occur by use of roman type in place of italic. Some foreign words now incorporated in English speech in this manner are these:

addendum (pl. -da)
ad interim
ad lib[itum]
ad valorem
aide de camp
alias
Alma Mater
anno Domini
ante-bellum
a posteriori
a priori
apropos
atelier
attaché
au revoir
barrage
beau ideal
billet doux
bona fide
bon ton
bouillon
cabaret
café
camouflage
carte blanche
chaperon
chargé d'affaires
chef d'œuvre
chiaroscuro
clientèle
confrère
consensus
contra
contretemps
corrigendum (pl. -da)
coup d'état
coup de grace
crèche
cul-de-sac
datum (pl. data)
débris
début
décolleté
delicatessen
demimonde
demirelievo
demi-tasse
dénouement
dépôt (=depository)
de rigueur
dilettante
divorcée
dramatis personae

éclat
élite
en route
ensemble
entente
entrée
entrepôt
entrepreneur
erratum (pl. -a)
et cetera
ex cathedra
ex officio
exposé
extempore
façade
faïence
fête
finis
fracas
gratis
Gymnasium (German)
habeas corpus
habitué
hangar
hegira
hors d'œuvres
lacuna (pl. -ae)
laissez faire
lèse majesté
levée
littérateur
litterati
mandamus
matador
matinée
mélange
mêlée
milieu
mitrailleuse
mores
motif
née
névé
nil
nol[le] pros[equi]
nom de plume
onus
papier mâché
par excellence
parvenu
paterfamilias
patois
per annum
per capita
per cent
per contra
per se
portmonnaie
postmortem
post obit
prima facie
pro and con[tra]
procès verbal
pro rata
protégé
pro tem[pore]
protocol
queue
quondam
ragout
reconnaissance
régime
résumé
reveille
sauerkraut
savant
señor
soirée
stein
subpoena
tête-à-tête
versus (v., vs.)[1]
via
vice versa
vis-à-vis
visé
viva voce
Weltanschauung

96. Italicize the titles of books; of plays, essays, symphonies, and poems of a size to have book format; of pamphlets, published documents, newspapers, periodi-

[1] But italicize *v.* or *vs.* when standing between two opposing terms not themselves italicized (see 99) when otherwise the meaning would not be clear: Michigan *vs.* Minnesota, 3 to 0.

cals, and journals;[1] italicize the words *Journal*, *Review*, and so on, standing alone, if a part of the name of the publication. Titles of parts of published works are roman quoted (see 123). Titles of book series are roman quoted (see 121):

Spencer, *Principles of Sociology*	*Paradise Lost*
A Midsummer-Night's Dream	*The Messiah*
the *Chicago Tribune*	*Lohengrin*
the *Indianapolis Star*	*Groningen Publications*, No. 27

Report of the United States Commissioner of Education

Exceptions:

a) This rule may be disregarded in extensive bibliographical lists, in tables, or in other matter where its use would result in an undue preponderance of italics (see 80*b*).

b) Names of books of the Bible, both canonical and apocryphal, the titles of ancient manuscripts, and all symbols used to designate manuscripts should be set in roman type (see 68, 151, and 168*b*):

Psalms 53:10, D16, Mb, P, J

97. Italicize the following words, phrases, and abbreviations as used in literary and legal references:

circa (*ca.*) (about)	*op. cit.* (work cited)
et al. (and others)	*passim* (here and there)
ibid. (not *ib.*) (the same reference)	*q.v.* (which see)
	sc. (namely)
idem (not *id.*)(the same person)	*sic* (thus)
	supra (above)
infra (below)	*s.v.* (under a word or heading)
loc. cit. (place cited)	*vide* (see)

[1] *Botanical Gazette* uses italics for such titles in the text only; in footnotes, roman. Its own name it prints in caps and small caps—BOTANICAL GAZETTE.

Exceptions:

Do not italicize:

cf., e.g., etc., viz., v. or vs. (versus) (unless ambiguity would result; see note to word-list, p. 47)

98. Italicize *See* and *See also* as used for cross-reference in an index (see 334), and *for* and *read* in a list of errata. In both cases the need of distinguishing the significant words calls for a reverse of the normal practice for emphasis (see 93):

See also Sociology   *for* levee *read* levée

99. Italicize the names of plaintiff and defendant in the citation of legal causes; also the titles of proceedings containing such prefixes as *in re*, *ex parte*, and *in the matter of*, etc.:

Conolly v. *Union Sewer Pipe Co.*

In re Smith

Ex parte Brown

In the matter of the petition of Henry Robinson for a writ of habeas corpus.

100. Italicize address lines in speeches, reports, and letters (see 90):

Mr. President, Ladies and Gentlemen:

Mr. John Smith
321 Dearborn Street
Chicago, Illinois

DEAR SIR: I take pleasure in announcing . . . .

101. In signatures, italicize the title added to a person's name. If this consists of only one word, it is run into the same line with the name; if of more than one,

but no longer than the name, center the first letter under the name line and indent one em on the right. If the added title is longer than the name, center the name over the second line and set flush. These rules are, however, subject to the exigencies of special cases (see 90*a*):

ARTHUR P. MAGUIRE, *Secretary*

Yours very truly,
WILLIAM E. DEVER
Mayor of Chicago

CHARLES M. GAYLEY
Professor of English Language and Literature

102. Italicize such forms as *a*), *b*), *c*) when used to indicate subdivisions (single parenthesis if beginning a paragraph, double parentheses if run in); *a*, *b*, *c*, etc., when affixed to the number of verse, page, or other reference figure, to denote a fractional part; and *a*, *b*, when used with page numbers to indicate left and right columns of text:

Select the best reason why gold is more costly than lead:

a) It is of finer appearance.
b) It is more scarce.
c) It is used more for jewelry.
d) It is yellow.

If the health department says the drinking water is not pure, one should: (*a*) boil the water before using it; (*b*) drink sparingly; (*c*) eat vegetables and fruit.

Luke 4:31*a* p. 29*b* (page 29, right column)

103. Italicize letters used to designate unknown quantities, lines, etc., in algebraic, geometrical, and scientific matter:

$ac+bc=c(a+b)$ the lines *ad* and *AD* the *n*th power

104. Italicize letters in legends or in text that refer to corresponding letters in accompanying illustrations, whether or not they are in italics in the illustration:

At the point *A* above (see diagram)

105. Italicize references to particular letters:

the letter *u* a small *v* a capital *S*

Exceptions:

a) But use Gothic letters indicating shape:

U-shaped making a V form of an L

b) Do not italicize a letter used in place of a name in hypothetical statements, or where the initial is used alone with a dash or as a simple abbreviation:

A bought land from B without registration of title.
The news was brought at once to General M——.
Mr. G was not at home when we called.

106. Italicize *s*. and *d*. (=shillings and pence) following numerals. (The sign £ for pound sterling appears before the figure):

£1 3*s*. 6*d*.

107. In zoölogical, geological, and paleontological matter italicize scientific (Latin) names of genus and species when used together (see 85, 86):

Felis leo (but: *Felis leo* Scop.) *Conodectes favosus*
Rosa caroliniana *Phyteuma halleri*

108. In botanical, geological, and paleontological matter, italicize the names of genus and species when used together, and of genus or species when used alone:

Acer saccharum *Alternaria*
Basidiobolus *Erythrosuchus*
(but: *Viola* sp.; *Cirsium arvense* Scop.)

109. In medical text print such names in roman, avoiding italics altogether:

Bacillus typhosus B. streptococcus

110. Set in italics, in astronomical and astrophysical matter:

a) The lower-case letters designating certain Fraunhofer lines:

a, b, g, h

b) The lower-case letters used by Baeyer to designate certain stars in constellations for which the Greek letters have been exhausted:

f Tauri, *a* Herculis

111. When initials are used to express the titles of catalogues, as such, and not to designate a particular celestial object, such initials should be italicized (see 70, 88):

B.D. (*Bonner Durchmusterung*) *H.C.* (*Harvard Circular*)
N.G.C. (*New General Catalogue*)

112. In accordance with modern practice roman type is used for:

a) Symbols for the chemical elements[1] (except in the *Astrophysical Journal*)

H, Ca, Ti

b) The capital letters given by Fraunhofer to spectral lines:

A–H, and K

[1] In the *Astrophysical Journal* use italics for the chemical elements: *H, Ca, Ti.*

c) The letters designating the spectral types of stars:

A5, B4, Mb

113. In resolutions, italicize the word "*Resolved*" (see 78).

114. Italicize "*Continued*" (after a title or headline) and "*To be continued*" (at the end of an article) (see 237):

THE SCOPE OF SOCIOLOGY—*Continued*

[*To be continued*] (centered)

QUOTATIONS

115. Set within quotation marks all quotations of passages in the author's own words that are run into the text (see 95, 125, 127, 225). When quoting consecutive paragraphs of the same work, repeat quotation marks at the beginning of each paragraph and close only at the end of the last paragraph. In French and Spanish small angle marks on the lower part of the type body are used for quotation marks; in German, two primes on one type body are used, the former quote being inverted. In Spanish and French texts, long dashes and paragraph breaks may be used in lieu of quote marks to introduce successive speeches.

> "It's like being in a lighthouse," said Peyrol. "Not a bad place for a seaman to live in." The sight of the sails dotted about cheered his heart. . . . . "Tell me, patron," said Peyrol, "is there anywhere near this house a little dent in the shore with a bit of beach in it perhaps where I could keep a boat?"

> "Article I. Pact of Non-Aggression
>
> "The High Contracting Parties solemnly declare that aggressive war is an international crime and severally undertake that no one of them will be guilty of its commission.
>
> "A war shall not be considered as a war of aggression if waged by a state which is a party to a dispute and has accepted the unanimous recommendation of the Council. . . . ."

> Dit: «Quand il s'agit de la grandeur de Dieu, et les mystères de l'Evangile, il semble que l'on doive changer de maximes et de règles d'autant que toutes les actions divines sont merveilleuses ... il ne faut pas avoir recours à la vraisemblance quand les vérités se trouvent si parfaites.»

E dixeron: «Este nino sera ayna muy sesudo; e puer que el agora sabe tanto dezir; ...»—Karl Pietsch, *Spanish Grail Fragments,* I, xxix.

Daß gerade solches Bestreben, das die Nachfrage zu einer Jagd nach Ware umgestaltet, die Entwertung nur noch weiter treiben muß, kann nur den Spekulanten auf die letzte Mark gleichgültig lassen: „Mag alles zugrunde gehen, wenn nur ich selber schließlich ein Weniges übrig behalte!“

116. Quote passages from different authors, or from different works of the same author, uninterrupted by intervening original matter, even though such quotations are reduced (see 125–27).

"Hear the tolling of the bells—
Iron bells!
What a world of solemn thought their monody compels!"
—Poe, "The Bells"

"Gaily bedight,
A gallant knight,
In sunshine and in shadow,
Had journeyed long,
Singing a song,
In search of Eldorado."
—Poe, "Eldorado"

"Foreign countries have especially become acquainted with our existing misery in connection with their broad-minded assistance to our children and poor. . . . . "

"The statistics which are known regarding assistance to the poor are not exhaustive, as much goes on here under the surface; for the necessity of the present has brought good as well as much evil, in that the spirit of charity has noticeably increased in certain circles in Germany."—Kraus, *Germany in Transition.*

117. Quote a word or phrase accompanied by its definition:

"Drop-folio" means a page-number at the foot of the page.

118. Quote an unusual, technical, ironical word or phrase in the text, whether or not accompanied by a word like "so-called" directing attention to it:

Her "five o'clocks" were famous in the neighborhood.
He was elected "master of the rolls."
We then repaired to what he called his "quarter deck."
A "lead" is then inserted between the lines.
This so-called "man of affairs."

119. In translations, quote the English equivalent of a word, phrase, or passage from a foreign language:

Mommsen, *Römische Geschichte* ("History of Rome")

120. Quote the particular or unusual word or words to which attention is directed (see 94) in order to make the meaning clear:

I said "and," not "or"
the term "lynch law"
the phrase "liberty of conscience"
the concepts "good" and "bad"

Exceptions:

Do not quote in matter discussing terms where the meaning is clear:

The definition of the word God

121. Quote the titles of book series:

"The University of Chicago Science Series"
"English Men of Letters" series
"International Critical Commentary"
the series "Handbooks of Ethics and Religion"

122. Quote the titles of short poems (see 96):

Shelley's "To a Skylark"

123. Quote the titles of subdivisions (e.g., parts, books [not names of volumes, which are set in italics], chapters, etc.) of publications; the titles of papers,

lectures, sermons, articles, toasts, mottoes, etc. (see 80, 95*b*, 96):

> *The Beginnings of the Science of Political Economy*, Vol. I.
>
> *The British School*, chap. ii, "John Stuart Mill."
>
> The articles "Cross," "Crucifixion," and "Crusade" in Hastings' *Dictionary of the Bible.*
>
> The subject of the lecture was "Japan—Its Past, Present, and Future."
>
> The next toast on the program was "Our Canadian Visitor."
>
> The king's motto is "For God and My Country."

Exceptions:

a) Botanical publications do not use quotation marks for such titles in footnote references.

b) References to the Preface, Introduction, Table of Contents, Index, etc., of a specific work, should be set with capitals, without quotation marks (see 80):

> Preface, p. iii.
>
> The Introduction contains . . . .
>
> The Appendix occupies a hundred pages.

124. Quote the names of ships, the titles of pictures, and the names of art objects:

> the U.S. SS. "Oregon" Murillo's "The Holy Family"
>
> Daniel Chester French's "End of the Trail"

125. Set in smaller type ordinarily all prose extracts that will make five or more lines in the reduced type, and all poetry citations of two lines or more. An isolated prose quotation, or several short ones, may properly be run into the text if bearing an organic relation to the argument presented; but a quotation of one or two lines

standing near longer extracts in smaller type may be reduced as a matter of uniform appearance.

126. As a rule, reduce quotations from 11 point and 10 point to 9 point; from 9 point to 8 point; from 8 point to 6 point.

127. Reduced quotations should not be set within quotation marks, except in such cases as noted in 116; nor should quotation marks, as a rule, be used in connection with italics (but see 95).

Exceptions:

Foreign phrases and sentences run into English text (see 95) are set in italic and when part of a quoted conversation must also be quoted.

> Madam de Châtelet in her letters refers to De Mouhy in the following terms: "*Ce de Mouhy est un bon garçon, trop zélé et qu'il faut ménager.*"

128. Quotation marks should always include ellipses or the phrase "etc." when it otherwise would not be clear that it stands for an omitted part of the matter quoted. Perfect clearness in each case is the end sought:

> Art. II, sec. 2, of the Constitution provides that "each state shall appoint . . . . a number of electors equal to the whole number of senators and representatives . . . ."
>
> He also wrote a series of "Helps to Discovery, etc."

"Etc." here indicates not that he wrote other works which are unnamed, but that the title of the one named is not given in full; but, on the other hand:

Preaching from the text, "For God so loved the world," etc. . . . .

"Etc." here is placed outside the quotation marks in order to show that it does not stand for other, unnamed, objects of God's love.

129. Where alignment is desired, the quotation marks should be "cleared"—i.e., should be allowed to project beyond the line of alignment.

Maud Muller looked and sighed: "Ah me,
That I the Judge's bride might be.
. . . .
"And I'd feed the hungry and clothe the poor,
And all should bless me who left our door."

130. Omit beginning quotes before an initial letter:

O YE unborn inhabitants of America," said Ames, "should these alphabetical letters remain legible when your eyes behold the sun after he has rolled the seasons round for two or three centuries more you will know that in *anno Domini* 1758 we dreamed of your times."

131. Double quotation marks are used for primary quotations; for a quotation within a quotation, single marks. Go back to double marks for a third, to single for a fourth, and so on:

"Let me quote from Rossetti's *Life of Keats,*" he said. "Mr. Rossetti writes as follows:

" 'To one of these phrases a few words of comment may be given. That axiom which concludes the "Ode on a Grecian Urn"—

" ' "Beauty is truth, truth beauty—that is all
Ye know on earth, and all ye need to know,"

is perhaps the most important contribution to thought which the poetry of Keats contains: it pairs with and transcends

" ' "A thing of beauty is a joy forever." '

"And now I shall conclude my first point," he continued, "by remarking that . . . ."

SPELLING AND ABBREVIATIONS

132. In all formal typography and in straight reading-matter it is best to spell out everything that would be offensive to the eye or puzzling if abbreviated. Specific exceptions are treated in the following rules (see 152, 289).

133. Spell out titles preceding personal names, with the exception of Mr., Messrs., Mrs. (French: M., MM., Mme, Mlle), Dr., and St., which are always abbreviated, and Rev. and Hon., usually abbreviated. Abbreviate Esq., Sr., and Jr. following the name:

General Wood
Secretary of State Hughes
Ambassador White
Miss Belmont
Princess Cantacuzene
Professor Breasted
Senator Lodge
Mr. Brainerd
Messrs. White and McIntyre
Mlle Du Barry
MM. Gourgot et Saint-Cyr
Dr. Mayo
St. Andrew
Rev. Charles W. Gilkey
Hon. Frank O. Lowden
John M. Smythe, Esq.

Exceptions:

In formal matter such as announcements and invitations spell out with "the" preceding the title:

the Reverend Charles W. Gilkey
the Honorable Frank O. Lowden

134. Spell out Christian names except in copying an original signature, or in quoting from another work:

Charles M. Schwab
George D. Fuller

But in a signature because it is the author's choice:

Geo. D. Fuller

135. Spell out references in text (not parenthetical or footnote citations; see 152) to chapters, pages, lines, notes, verses, figures, plates.

The excerpt is found on page 35.

136. Spell out in isolated cases in ordinary text matter every number of less than three digits:

In 1920 there were sixty-eight cities in the United States with a population of 100,000 or over.
The admission was two dollars.
He won the fifty-yard dash.
Tithing is the practice of giving one-tenth of one's income.
The cook bought two pounds of sugar.
He spent a total of two years, three months, and seventeen days in jail. But: He spent 128 days in the hospital.
He was eighty years and four months old when he died.

Exceptions:

a) Never spell out dates or page numbers:

1925 36 B.C. pp. lx–lxvii p. 2750

b) Try to treat all similar numbers in connected groups alike; do not use figures for some and spell out others. If the largest contains three or more digits, use figures for all (see 132):

The force employed during the three months was 87, 93, and 106, respectively.

c) Dimensions, degrees, distances, weights, measures, sums of money, and like matter should be expressed in figures when appearing in mathematical or statistical text:

A board 1¼ inches thick, by 18 inches wide, by 20 feet 2 inches long.

45 miles	10°C.	45 pounds
3 cubic feet	100 bushels	$1,000
240 volts	6 meters	£3 6*s*.

137. Always use number forms for decimals and percentage:

0.257	9 per cent

Always use figures with abbreviations of such measurements as:

6 mi.	10^{M}5 (or 10.5 mag.)
2 ft. 9 in.	1100 km/sec.

138. In expressions of money, use ciphers with numbers from 1 to 10, unless in connection with fractional sums:

Articles bought for $6.00 were sold for $6.75.

The committee raised the sum of $75 (but: The committee raised sums of $15.50, $33.75, and $75.00 in three sales).

139. Spell out all numbers when beginning a sentence, even if similar numbers are figures elsewhere. If this is impracticable or undesirable, reconstruct the sentence.

Five hundred and ninety-three men, 417 women, 126 children under eighteen, besides 63 of the crew, went down with the ship.
Twenty per cent of the cost was guaranteed

140. Spell out round numbers (i.e., approximate figures in even units, the unit being 100 in numbers of 1,000, and 1,000 in numbers of more):

The attendance was estimated at five hundred (but: "at 550")
He wrote a thesis of about three thousand words (but: "of 2,700 words")

Cases such as 1,500, if spelled out, should read "fifteen hundred," not "one thousand five hundred."

141. Spell out when beginning a sentence all terms of measurement that would otherwise be abbreviated:

Number 6 is not to be used in this display.
Pi is equal to 3.1416.

142. Spell out time of day when given in ordinary reading-matter:

They called at four.

WLS broadcasts at half-past two in the afternoon.

Come to dinner at seven o'clock.

Exceptions:

Statistically, in enumerations, and always in designations of time with A.M. or P.M., use figures:

at 4:00 P.M. (omit "o'clock" in such connections)

143. Spell out references to the age of a person or an object:

eighty years and four months old; children between six and fourteen

144. Spell out numbers of centuries; of Egyptian dynasties; of sessions of Congress; of military bodies; of political divisions; of thoroughfares (see 54–68):

nineteenth century
Fifth Dynasty
Fifty-fourth Congress, second session
Fifteenth Infantry, I.N.G.
Sixth Congressional District
Second Ward
Fifth Avenue

Exceptions may occur where brevity is absolutely essential.

145. Spell out references to particular decades:

in the nineties (see 214, 216)

146. Spell out the names of months except in statistical tables or long enumerations:

From January 1 to April 15 (omit, after dates, *st*, *d*, and *th*)

147. Use the following abbreviations for the names of states, territories, and possessions of the United States

after names of towns (without space between the letters of abbreviations; see 70, 92) when mentioned in lists, signatures, and bibliographical matter:

Ala.	Iowa	Neb.	Samoa
Alaska	Kan.	Nev.	S.C.
Ariz.	Ky.	N.H.	S.D.
Ark.	La.	N.J.	Tenn.
Calif.	Me.	N.M.	Tex.
Colo.	Mass.	N.Y.	T.H.
Conn.	Md.	Ohio	Utah
D.C.	Mich.	Okla.	Vt.
Del.	Minn.	Ore.	Va.
Fla.	Miss.	Pa.	Wash.
Ga.	Mo.	P.I.	Wis.
Idaho	Mont.	P.R.	W.Va.
Ill.	N.C.	R.I.	Wyo.
Ind.	N.D.		

148. Do not abbreviate parts of geographic names (see 150):

Fort Wayne	Mount Wilson
Port Arthur	San Francisco

Exceptions:

a) In tabular matter where space must be gained or in special cases where copy must be followed exactly, the first part may be abbreviated:

Ft. Gary
Pt. Arthur
Mt. Wilson Contributions (in footnotes after the first one)
But never: S. Francisco

b) Always abbreviate (see 150):

St. Louis	Sault Ste Marie (without period)

149. Abbreviate in technical matter (such as footnote references, bibliographies, etc.), the words "Company," "Brothers," and "and" (& "short and" or "ampersand") when forming part of the name of a commercial firm:

The Macmillan Co.	Harper & Bros.
Ginn & Co.	Chicago, Milwaukee & St. Paul Railroad

Exceptions:

a) When the name of a commercial concern does not consist of personal names, the "and" should be spelled out:

The Harris Title and Trust Company
American Steel and Wire Co.

b) In text matter and in formal display such words should be spelled out. The same regard for formal appearance discredits any abbreviation of the titles of officers of a company when such titles appear alone or following the names of persons in composition of letterheads or in letter signatures:

Harper and Brothers have recently published . . . .
The Century Company announces . . . .
The extraordinary story of the South Sea Company
J. W. Wilson, Vice-President

150. Abbreviate "Saint" or "Saints" before a name (148*b*):

St. Louis, St. Peter's Church, SS. Peter and Paul

"St." should, however, be omitted in connection with names of apostles, evangelists, Church Fathers:

Luke, Paul, Augustine (not: St. Luke, St. Paul, etc.)

151. Abbreviate in exact references to Scripture passages (180, 227) the names of the books of the Bible, of the Apocrypha, of the Apocalyptic, and of versions of the Bible:

OLD TESTAMENT

Gen.	I and II Chron.	Isa.	Jonah
Exod.	Ezra	Jer.	Mic.
Lev.	Neh.	Lam.	Nah.
Num.	Esther	Ezek.	Hab.
Deut.	Job	Dan.	Zeph.
Josh.	Ps. (Pss.)	Hos.	Hag.
Judg.	Prov.	Joel	Zech.
Ruth	Eccles.	Amos	Mal.
I and II Sam.	Song of Sol. (or Cant.)	Obad.	
I and II Kings			

NEW TESTAMENT

Matt.	Gal.	Philem.
Mark	Eph.	Heb.
Luke	Phil.	Jas.
John	Col.	I and II Pet.
Acts	I and II Thess.	I, II, and III John
Rom.	I and II Tim.	Jude
I and II Cor.	Titus	Rev.

APOCRYPHA (APOC.)

I and II Esd.	Wisd. of Sol.	Sus.
Tob.	Ecclus.	Bel and Dragon
Jth.	Bar.	Pr. of Man.
Rest of Esther	Song of Three Children	I, II, III, and IV Macc.

APOCALYPTIC

En.	Asmp. M.	Ps. Sol.	Bk. Jub.
Sib. Or.	Apoc. Bar.	XII P.	Asc. Isa.

VERSIONS OF THE BIBLE COMMONLY REFERRED TO

A.V. = Authorized Version.
R.V. = Revised Version.
R.V.m. = Revised Version, margin.
A.R.V. = American Standard Revised Version.
A.R.V.m. = American Standard Revised Version, margin.
E.R.V. = English Revised Version.
E.R.V.m. = English Revised Version, margin.
E.V. = English Version(s) of the Bible.
Vulg. = Vulgate.
LXX = Septuagint.
MT = Masoretic text.

Exceptions:

But in text matter do not abbreviate references to whole books or chapters:

The story is presented in Revelation, chapter 10.

152. In parenthetical literary references, in footnotes, and in bibliographical material, abbreviate any word designating a part when it is followed by a number (see 71, 76, 132, 135, 289), and the word "following" after a number:

Vol. I (plural, Vols.)	No. 1 (Nos.)
Ps. 20 (Pss.)	Div. III
chap. ii (chaps.)	art. iii (arts.)
sec. 4 (secs.)	p. 5 (pp.)
col. 6 (cols.)	vs. 7 (vss.)
l. 8 (ll.)	n. 9 (nn.)
Fig. 7 (Figs.)	pp. 5–7 (pages 5 to 7 inclusive)
pp. 5 f. (page 5 and the following page)	
pp. 5 ff. (page 5 and the following pages)	
ed. (edd., editions)	Act II, scene 3 (not abbr.)

153. Abbreviate the word "section" (see 91) each time it is used in enumerating, except the first:

SECTION 1. The name of the association . . . .
SEC. 2. The object of the association . . . .

154. Abbreviate when following a numeral the common designations of weights and measures in the metric system, as well as the symbols of measurement in common use (see 71, 155):

1 m.	1 gm.	4 kg.	3d mag.
2 cm.	2 lb.	1 gal.	3 h-p.
3 sq. mi.	3 yd.	32° F.	5 min.

Exceptions:

In astrophysical and similar scientific matter, hours, minutes, seconds, magnitudes, etc., are expressed in tabular matter by superior letters without the abbreviating period:

$6^h17^m8^s$ $1\overset{M}{.}8$

155. Special lists of abbreviations appear elsewhere in the text (see 147, 151, 152, 154); rarer forms may be found through the Index. In the following list capital letters are used if the abbreviated forms are found only with proper names. Unless specially noted the plurals are to be formed by adding *s* to the singular abbreviation.

A, Angstrom units (no period)
abbr., abbreviated, -ion
abl., ablative
abr., abridged
acc., accusative
acct., account
A.D., *anno Domini* (in the year of the Lord) (s. caps, before the figures)
ad fin., *ad finem* (to the end)
ad inf., *ad infinitum* (to infinity)
ad int., *ad interim* (meanwhile)

adj., adjective
Adjt., Adjutant
ad lib., ad libitum (at pleasure)
ad loc., ad hunc locum (on this passage)
AFr, Anglo-French
agt., agent
A.L.A., American Library Association
A.M., *Artium Magister* (Master of Arts)
A.M., *ante meridiem* (before noon) (s. caps)
Amer., American
AN, Anglo-Norman
anon., anonymous
Apr., April
art., article
A.S., Academy of Science
AS, Anglo-Saxon
A.S., *anno salutis* (in the year of Salvation)
assoc., associate
asst., assistant
atty., attorney
Atty.-Gen., Attorney-General
at. wt., atomic weight
A.U.C., *anno urbis conditae* (year from the building of Rome, 753 B.C.)
Aug., August
A.V., Authorized Version
a/v, ad valorem
av., average
Ave., Avenue
avdp., avoirdupois
b., born; brother
B.A., Bachelor of Arts
bal., balance
bar., barometer
Bart., Baronet
bbl., barrel
B.C., before Christ (s. caps, after the figures)
B.D., Bachelor of Divinity
bdl., bundle
Bé., Baumé
bibl., bibliotheca (library)
bibliog., bibliography, -er, -ical
biog., biography, -er, -ical
biol., biology, -ical, -ist
Bk., Book
Bldg., Building
Blvd., Boulevard
bot., botany, -ical, -ist
Brit., Britannica, British
Brit. Mus., British Museum
bro., brother
B.S., Bachelor of Science
bu., bushel (both sing. and pl.)
c. (in law citations only), chapter
C., Centigrade (with numeral)
ca., circa or *circum* (about)
Cantab., Cantabrigiensis (of Cambridge)
cap., capital letter
Capt., Captain
Cav., Cavalry
cc., cubic centimeter
C.E., Civil Engineer
cf., compare
chap., chapter

Cia, *Compañia* (Company) (no period)
Cie, *Compagnie* (Company) (no period)
cm., centimeter (both sing. and pl.) (without period in scientific publications)
Co., Company; County
C.O.D., cash, or collect, on delivery
Col., Colonel
col., column
colloq., colloquial, -ly, -ism
Com., Committee; Commission
conj., conjugation; conjunction
cons., consonant
cont., continued
Corp., Corporal
c-p., candle-power
Cr., credit
cu., cubic
cwt., hundredweight
d., daughter; died
d., *denarius* or *denarii* (penny and pence)
dat., dative
D.D., *Divinitatis Doctor* (Doctor of Divinity)
D.D.S., Doctor of Dental Surgery
Dem., Democrat
Den., Denmark
Dept., Department
der., derived, -ivation
diam., diameter
dict., dictionary
dist., district
div., division
do., ditto (the same)
doz., dozen
Dr., debtor; Doctor
dr., drachma
dram. pers., dramatis personae
Dr. u. Vrl., *Druck und Verlag* (printed and published by)
D.V., *Deo volente* (God willing)
E., east; English
ed., editor; edition (plural, edd.)
EE, Early English
e.g., *exempli gratia* (for example)
e.m.f., electromotive force
Encyc., Encyclopedia
Eng., England; English
eng., engineer, -ing
esp., especially
Esq., Esquire
et al., *et alibi* (and elsewhere); *et alii* (and others)
etc., *et cetera* (and the others; and so forth)
et seq., *et sequens* (and the following) (pl., *et sqq.*)
ex., example (pl., exx.)
F., Fahrenheit; Friday
f., the following (with numeral) (pl. ff.)
Feb., February
fem., feminine (also f.)
ff., following (with numeral)
fig., figure
f.o.b., free on board
fol., folio
Fr., France; French; franc (before the numeral)

Fri. or F., Friday
ft., foot (both sing. and pl.)
fut., future
f.v., *folio verso* (on the back of the page)
g., gram (also gm.)
Gael., Gaelic
gal., gallon (both sing. and pl.)
G.A.R., Grand Army of the Republic
gen., gender; genitive
Gen., General
geog., geography, -er, -ical
geol., geology, -ical, -ist
geom., geometry, -trical
Ger., German, -y
Gov., Governor
gr., grain
gram., grammar
gro., gross (both sing. and pl.)
H., *Heft* (number [of a magazine]; part)
H.C., House of Commons
HDB, *Hastings' Dictionary of the Bible*
hdkf., handkerchief
hdqrs., headquarters
hist., historic, -ian, -ical
H.L., House of Lords
Hon., Honorable
h-p., horse-power
hr., hour (both sing. and pl.)
H.R., House of Representatives
I., Island
ibid., *ibidem* (in the same place)
IE, Indo-European (no period)
i.e., *id est* (that is)
in., inch (both sing. and pl.)
Inc., Incorporated
indef., indefinite
Inf., Infantry
inf., infinitive
infra, below (not *inf.*)
infra dig., *infra dignitatem* (undignified)
Inst., Institute, -ion
I.O.F., Independent Order of Foresters
I.O.O.F., Independent Order of Odd Fellows
Jan., January
J.D., *Jurum Doctor* (Doctor of Laws)
Jour., Journal
Jr., Junior
K, karat
kg., or kilo (no period), kilogram
km., kilometer
km/sec., kilometers per second
K.P., or K. of P., Knights of Pythias
Kt., Knight
κτλ, *καὶ τὰ λοίπα*
kw., kilowatt
L., Left (in stage directions)
l., line, (pl., ll.)
lang., language
Lat., Latin
lat., latitude
lb., *libra* (pound) (both sing. and pl.)
l.c., lower case
L.C.M., Least Common Multiple

L.H.D., *Litterarum Humaniorum Doctor*
L.I., Long Island
lit., literally
Litt.D., *Litterarum Doctor* (Doctor of Letters)
LL.B., *Legum Baccalaureus* (Bachelor of Laws)
LL.D., *Legum Doctor* (Doctor of Laws)
loc. cit., *loco citato* (in the place cited)
long., longitude
Ltd., Limited
M., *Monsieur* (plural, MM.); mark (German coin)
m., married; masculine; meter; minute
M., *meridies* (noon) (s. cap)
Maj., Major
Mar., March
masc., masculine (also m.)
math., mathematics, -ical
M.D., *Medicinae Doctor* (Doctor of Medicine)
mdse., merchandise
M.E., Mechanical Engineer; Methodist Episcopal
ME, Middle English
med., median; medical; medieval; medium
memo., memorandum
Mex., Mexico
mfg., manufacturing
mfr., manufacture, -er
Mgr, Monsignor; Monseigneur
Mgr., Manager
MHG, Middle High German
mi., mile (both sing. and pl.)
min., minute (also m.)
mo., month
Mon., or M., Monday
M.P., Member of Parliament
Mr. (not to be written out) (plural, Messrs.)
MS, manuscript (plural MSS)
M.S., Master of Science
mus., museum; music, -ical
N., north, -ern
n., neuter; noun
N.A., North America
N.A.S., National Academy of Science
nat., natural
natl., national
N.B., *nota bene* (mark well)
NE., northeast
NED, New English Dictionary (Oxford)
neg., negative
N. Lat., North Latitude
No., *numero* (number)
nom., nominative
Norw., Norwegian
Nov., November
N.P.D., North Polar Distance
N.S., National Society; New Series; New Style (after 1752); Nova Scotia
NW., northwest
ob., *obit* (he, she, or it died)
obs., obsolete
Oct., October
OE, Old English (no periods)

OFr, Old French (no periods)
OHG, Old High German
ON, Old Norse
op. cit., *opere citato* (in the work cited)
O.S., Old Series; Old Style (before 1752)
Oxon., *Oxoniensis* (of Oxford)
oz., ounce
p., page (plural, pp.); past
part., participle
pass., passive
path., pathology
pd., paid
perf., perfect
pers., person, -al
Ph.B., *Philosophiae Baccalaureus* (Bachelor of Philosophy)
Ph.D., *Philosophiae Doctor* (Doctor of Philosophy)
Ph.G., Graduate in Pharmacy
pk., peck
P.M., *post meridiem* (afternoon) (s. caps)
PMLA, *Publications of the Modern Language Association*
pron., pronoun
P.S., *postscriptum* (postscript)
pt., pint; point
qt., quart
R., Right (in stage directions)
Rep., Republican; Representative
Rev., Reverend
r.p.m., revolutions per minute
S., south; Sunday
S., *Seite* (page)
s., second; son
s., shilling (both sing. and pl.)
S.A., South America
Sat., Saturday
s.c., small capitals
sc., *scilicet* (namely)
SE., southeast
sec., second; secretary; section
Sept., September
ser., series (but see N.S., O.S.)
sing., singular
S. Lat., South Latitude
sociol., sociology
Sp., Spanish
sp. gr., specific gravity
sq., square
Sr., Senior; Señor
SS., Steamship
St., Saint (plural, SS.); fem., Ste (no period)
S.T.B., *Sacrae Theologiae Baccalaureus* (Bachelor of Theology)
subj., subject; subjunctive
subst., substantive
Sun., or S., Sunday
SW., southwest
syn., synonym
temp., temperature
Th., or Thurs., Thursday
theol., theology, -ian, -ical
trans., transitive; translated
treas., treasurer
Tu., or Tues., Tuesday
ult., *ultimo*
U.S., United States

U.S.A., United States of America; United States Army
U.S.N., United States Navy
U.S. SS., United States Steamship
usw., *und so weiter* (and so forth)
v., verb
v. or vs., *versus* (against)
vs., verse (plural vss.)
v.i., intransitive verb
viz., *videlicet* (namely)
v.n., verb neuter
voc., vocative
vol., volume
v.t., transitive verb
W., or Wed., Wednesday
wf, wrong font (no periods)
wk., week
wt., weight
yd., yard (both sing. and pl.)
Y.M.C.A., Young Men's Christian Association
yr., year
Y.W.C.A., Young Woman's Christian Association
zoöl., zoölogy, -ical

156. For extracts from modern authors whose spelling and punctuation differ but slightly from ours, if such variations do not affect the meaning, use office style. In quotations from Old English works, and in cases where the writer's method or the value of the context requires faithful rendering, follow the original copy. Titles should always be quoted exactly as to wording and spelling.

157. Form the possessive of a proper name ending in *s* or another sibilant, if monosyllabic, by adding an apostrophe and *s;* if of more than one syllable (except names ending in *-ce*), by adding an apostrophe only (see 215, 216):

Burns's poems	Jesus' birth	Berlioz' compositions
Marx's theories	Moses' law	Demosthenes' orations
Sophocles' stories	conscience' sake	Horace's odes

Exceptions:

But in the case of a proper name ending in a silent sibilant the possessive is formed by the addition of the apostrophe and *s* whether the word is monosyllabic or not:

Charlevoix's discoveries — Des Moines's population

158. Before *h* aspirate, long *u* (or *eu*), and the words "one" and "once" use "a" as the form of the indefinite article:

a hotel (but: an honor)
a harmonic rendition
a historical work
a euphonious word
such a one
a union (but: an upset)

159. The ligatures *æ* and *œ* are not used at the present day, either in Latin or Greek words or in words adopted into English from these languages. In English these words are written either with *ae*, *oe*, separately, or with *e* alone. The ligature is retained, however, in Old English and in French:

aetas; *Oedipus Tyrannus;* aesthetic; (but: *hors d'œuvre*, French); but: maneuver; medieval; Ælfric and Ælfred (Alfric and Alfred in English)

160. Differentiate "farther" and "further" by using the former in the physical sense of "more remote," "at a greater distance" (with verbs of action); the latter in the abstract sense of "moreover," "in addition":

the farther end — he went still farther — a further reason

161. The following participles retain the final *e* in the primary word (to separate vowel sounds):

agreeing
dyeing
eyeing
hieing
hoeing
shoeing
singeing
tingeing
vieing

The following participles illustrate those that omit the *e* before the terminal (the normal change):

abridging
acknowledging
aging
arguing
awing
biting
bluing
changing
encouraging
filing
firing
glazing
gluing
grudging
icing
issuing
judging
mistaking
moving
organizing
owing
trudging
truing

162. Spell:

abridgment
accouter
acknowledgment
adz
aegis
Aeolian
aeroplane
aesthetic
afterward
almanac
ambassador
amid
among
anemia
anesthetic
appareled
appendixes[1]
arbor
archaeology
ardor
armor
ascendancy
ascendent
Athenaeum
ax
aye
backward
bark (vessel)
barreled
bazaar
Beduin
behavior
biased
blessed
bowlder
burned
caesura
caliber
canceled
candor
cannoneer
canyon
carcass
caroled
castor (roller)
catalogue
caviler
center
check
chiseled
chock-full
clamor
clue
coeval
color
controller
cotillion
councilor
counselor
cozy
cue
defense
demarcation
demeanor
descendant (n.)
diarrhea

[1] "Appendices" in *Astrophysical Journal.*

dieresis
disheveled
disk
dispatch
distil
downward
draft
drought
dueler
dulness
dwelt
embitter
employee
encyclopedic
endeavor
enfold
engulf
enrol (enrolled)
ensnare
enthralment
envelope (n.)
enwrapped
equaled
Eskimo
esophagus
exhibitor
fantasy
favor
fetish
fetus
fiber
flavor
focused
formulas[1]
forward
fulfil (fulfilled)
fulness
gaiety
Galilean
gild (to cover with gold)
gipsy
glamor
glycerin
goodbye
Graeco-Roman
graveled
gray
gruesome
guarantee (v.)
guaranty (n.)
guild (an organization)
haematoxylin
hamartiology
harbor
hemorrhage
Hindu
honor
imbed
impaneled
imperiled
incase
inclose
incrust
incumbrance
indexes (of book)
indices (mathematical only)
indorse
instal (installed)
instil (instilled)
insure
intrench
intrust
inward
jeweled
Judea
judgment
katabolism
kidnaper (but: kidnapped)
Koran
labeled
labor
lacquer
leucocyte
leveled
libeled
liter
loath
lodgment
Lukan
maneuver
Markan
marshaled
marvelous
meager
medieval
meter
miter
modeled
Mohammedan
mold
molt

[1] "Formulae" in *Astrophysical Journal.*

moneyed
moneys
movable
mustache
nearby (adj.)
neighbor
niter
odor
offense
one's self
outward
paean
paleography
paleontology
Paleozoic
paneled
paraffin
parceled
parole
parquet
partisan
peddler
penciled
Phoenix
pigmy
plow (n. and v.)
practice (n. and v.)
pretense
primeval
program
quarreled
quartet
raveled
reconnoiter
refill
reinforce
rencounter
reverie
rhyme
rigor
rivaled
riveted
ruble
rumor
saber
salable
Savior
savor
scepter
sepulcher
skepticism
skilful
smolder
specter
staunch
steadfast
subtle
succor
sulphur
sumac
syrup
taboo
talc
technique[1]
theater
thraldom
thrash
timbre (of music)
today
tormentor
toward
trammeled
tranquilize
tranquillity
traveler
trousers
truncated
Tutenkhamon
upward
vapor
vendor
vigor
whiskey
wilful
woeful
woolen
worshiper

163. Differentiate between the terminations *-ise* and *-ize* as follows:

SPELL WITH *-ise*

advertise
advise
affranchise
apprise (to inform)
arise
chastise

[1] In medical work usually spelled "technic."

circumcise
comprise
compromise
demise
despise
devise
disfranchise
disguise
emprise
enterprise
excise
exercise
exorcise
improvise
incise
mainprise
merchandise
premise
reprise
revise
rise
supervise
surmise
surprise

SPELL WITH *-ize* (*-yze*)

aggrandize
agonize
analyze
anatomize
anglicize
apologize
apostrophize
apprize (to appraise)
authorize
autolyze
baptize
brutalize
canonize
catechize
catholicize
cauterize
centralize
characterize
Christianize
civilize
classicize
colonize
criticize
crystallize
demoralize
deputize
dogmatize
dramatize
economize
emphasize
energize
epitomize
equalize
eulogize
evangelize
extemporize
familiarize
fertilize
fossilize
fraternize
galvanize
generalize
gormandize
harmonize
hellenize
humanize
immortalize
italicize
jeopardize
legalize
liberalize
localize
magnetize
manumize
memorialize
mercerize
mesmerize
metamorphize
methodize
minimize
modernize
monopolize
moralize
nationalize
naturalize
neutralize
organize
ostracize
oxidize
paralyze
particularize
pasteurize
patronize
philosophize
plagiarize
polarize
professionalize
protestantize
pulverize
realize

recognize
reorganize
revolutionize
satirize
scandalize
scrutinize
signalize
solemnize
soliloquize
specialize
spiritualize
standardize
stigmatize
subsidize
summarize
syllogize
symbolize
sympathize
tantalize
temporize
tranquilize
tyrannize
utilize
vaporize
visualize
vitalize
vocalize
vulcanize
vulgarize

164. Make one word of "anyone," "everyone," "today," "tomorrow," "tonight," "cannot." Distinguish between "already" and "all ready," "sometimes" and "some time(s)," "someone" and "some one (or more) of the number." Use the form "someone else's" because it is the logical one.

PUNCTUATION

165. All punctuation marks should be printed in the same style or font of type as the word, letter, or character immediately preceding them:

"With the cry of *Banzai!* the regiment stormed the hill."
Luke 4:16*a; Botanical Gazette* **20:144.**

Exceptions:

Italic or bold-face parentheses are rarely used:

(See paragraph 6*a*) (See **12b**)

166. Double punctuation is rarely used except with quotes, parentheses, and brackets. All except ending punctuation should be dropped before a closing parenthesis. Neither a comma nor a dash is ever retained before a parenthetical element, but, if needed in the sentence, is transferred to follow the closing parenthesis. For rules regarding the use of other points with these marks, and examples, see 173, 174, 175, 177, 182, 186, 213, and 223. An abbreviating period is never omitted before a mark of sentence punctuation, except that when an abbreviation occurs at the end of a declarative sentence, the period is not doubled. When a part within a sentence needs a mark of punctuation for clearness at a point where a mark of sentence punctuation should fall, the stronger mark only is retained:

O.S.P., speaking for a study club, asks for information.
The business was organized under the name of Allen & Co.
You may well ask, "What are his qualifications?"
Who shouted, "Red apples! Ripe apples!"

PERIOD

167. A period is used to indicate the end of a declarative sentence (see 172):

The snow is falling fast.

168. Put a period after an abbreviation (see 166):

Macmillan & Co., Mr. Smith, St. Paul, No. 1, *ibid.*, *s.v.*, 10 mm., 1201 E. Main St., SE. $\frac{1}{4}$ of SW. $\frac{1}{4}$, T. 3 N., R. 69 W., Sec. 11, middle of S. line, N.NE. (north by northeast).

Exceptions:

a) Do not use a period after the chemical symbols, the format signs of books, or the phrase "per cent":

O, Fe　　4to, 8vo　　2 per cent (see 137)

b) Do not use a period after the recognized abbreviations for linguistic epochs, for titles of well-known publications in technical matter of which the initials only are given, after MS (manuscript), after letters used as names of source material (96*b*), or after Mme and Mlle in French (see 133):

IE (=Indo-European), OE (=Old English), OFr (=Old French), MHG (=Middle High German); *AJSL* (=*American Journal of Semitic Languages and Literatures*), *ZaW* (=*Zeitschrift für alttestamentliche Wissenschaft*), *CIL* (=*Corpus Inscriptionum Latinorum*), *PMLA* (=*Publications of the Modern Language Association*), 𝔊, Q (MSS).

c) British practice countenances the omission of an abbreviating period after Mr. (see 133).

169. Treat the metric symbols[1] as abbreviations:

6 cc. (cubic centimeters)　　4 sq. dm. (square decimeters)
1 mm. (millimeter)

[1] With regard to symbols of measurement note these typographical points: *Astrophysical Journal,* 12 mm (with thin space and no period); $2^{h}3^{m}4^{s}$ (superior abbreviations); *Botanical Gazette,* 12 mm., 125 ft., 9 cc. (on line, with period).

170. Distinguish between an abbreviation (a shortened form followed by a period) and a contraction (an abridged form using an apostrophe for omitted letters):

mfg., m'f'g sec., sec'y

An old style of contraction, without the apostrophe, but with the last letter set superior, is no longer in use except in copying early printed works:

w^{d} w^{h}
sh^{d} y^{e}

171. Use no period after Roman numerals, even if they have the value of ordinals, except in enumerating items (see 61 and 302):

Vol. IV Louis XVI
II. The Paleozoic Age

172. Omit the period after all display lines: after running-heads; after centered headlines; after side-heads set in separate lines; after cut-in heads; after box-heads in tables; after superscriptions and legends that do not make more than a single line of type; after items in enumerated lists; after date lines heading communications; and after signatures (see 90).

173. The period is placed inside the quotation marks. Put it inside the parentheses or brackets when the matter inclosed is an independent sentence forming no part of the preceding sentence; otherwise, outside (see 166):

Tennyson's "In Memoriam."

Put the period inside the quotation marks. (This is a rule without exception.)

When the parentheses form a part of the preceding sentence, put the period outside (as, for instance, here).

EXCLAMATION POINT

174. The exclamation point is used to mark an outcry, and also an emphatic or ironical comment. This may occur within a declarative sentence (see 166):

Long live the king! "Good!" he cried.

The speaker went on: "Nobody should leave his home tomorrow without a marked ballot in their (!) pocket."

"Don't take chances!" is a good motto for automobile drivers.

In Spanish the exclamation point is also inverted before the sentence:

¡Aquí tiene V.!

175. The exclamation point is placed inside the quotation marks or parentheses when a part of the quoted or parenthetical matter; otherwise, outside (see 166):

Then the captain shouted, "Cast off!"

In the example given ("What a piece of work is Man!") the mark is properly used.

INTERROGATION POINT

176. The interrogation point is used to mark a query or to express a doubt:

Who is the author of the new volume in this series?

The prisoner gave his name as Roger Crowninshield, the son of an English baronet(?).

Can the Bible be understood by young children? is a question involved in the plan.

In Spanish the question mark is used before as well as after the question, but the mark that precedes the sentence is inverted:

¿Que corresponde á cada uno de los siete signos indicados?

Exceptions:

a) Indirect questions should not be followed by an interrogation point:

> She asked whether he was ill.

b) A technically interrogative sentence—disguised as a question out of courtesy but actually embodying a request—does not need the interrogation point:

> Will you kindly sign and return the inclosed card.

177. The interrogation point should be placed inside the quotation marks or parentheses only when it is a part of the quoted or parenthetical matter (see 166):

> "Take hold, my son, of the toughest knots in life and try to untie them; try to be worthy of man's highest estate; have high, noble, manly honor. There is but one test of everything, and that is, Is it right?"
>
> Let us discuss the question: "Who is who, and what is what?" (But who knows "what is what"?)
>
> Were you ever in "Tsintsinnati"?

COLON

178. The colon is used to mark a discontinuity of grammatical construction greater than that indicated by the semicolon and less than that indicated by the period. It is commonly used (1) to emphasize a sequence in thought between two clauses that form complete sentences; (2) to separate a grammatically complete clause from a second one that contains an illustration or amplification of its meaning; (3) to introduce a formal statement, an extract, a speech in a dialogue. The colon often

takes the place of an implied "namely," "as follows," "for instance," or similar expression.

(1) This argument undeniably contains some force: thus it is well known that a short sentence may be made to convey two meanings by the insertion or deletion of commas.

The secretion of the gland goes on uninterruptedly: this may account for the condition of the organ.

(2) Most countries have a national flower: France, the lily, England, the rose, etc.

Lambert pine: the gigantic sugar pine of California.

(3) The rule may be stated thus: . . . . ; We quote from the address: . . . .

Charles: "Where are you going?"

George: "To the mill-pond."

Exceptions:

a) Such introductory words as "namely," "for instance," do not require a colon unless what follows consists of one or more grammatically complete clauses (see 74, 75); otherwise use a comma (see 77). "As follows" requires a colon if followed directly by the illustrating or enumerated terms or if the introducing clause is incomplete without them; but if the statement in which such a phrase occurs is complete or followed by other complete sentences, use a period:

He made several absurd statements. For example: Science and religion cannot live in the same world. Artists see all things purple.

This is true of only two nations—the wealthiest, though not the largest in Europe—viz., Great Britain and France.

The rules are as follows:

1. Place the line parallel to . . . .

A company publishing texts for use in secondary schools has the following sales procedure. Its sales amount to $1,000,000 per year.

1. All incoming mail . . . .

2. All orders are sent . . . .

3. After the order is approved . . . .

b) When the second clause is introduced by a conjunctive element leaving no break in sentence thought, no punctuation is needed (see 74).

But: He stoutly maintained that "the letter is a monstrous forgery."

179. Put a colon after the salutatory phrase of a letter and after the introductory remark of a speaker addressing the chairman or the audience (see 90*b*):

MY DEAR MR. BROWN:
Mr. Chairman, Ladies and Gentlemen:

180. Put a centered (9-unit) colon between chapter and verse in Scripture passages, between hours and minutes in time indications, and (when such style is used) between volume and page reference (see 293):

Matt. 2:5–13; 4:30 P.M.; *Botanical Gazette* 20:144.

181. Put a colon between the place of publication and the publisher's name in literary and bibliographical references (see 284*c*):

Clement of Alexandria (London: Macmillan), II, 97.

182. The colon should be placed outside the quotation marks. When matter ending with a colon is quoted,

the colon is dropped and proper sentence punctuation is added (see 166):

> Can we understand why he writes under the head of "Notes and Comments": "Many a man can testify to the truth of the old adage"?

SEMICOLON

183. A semicolon is used to mark a more important break in sentence flow than that marked by a comma, or to separate complete statements whose force is dependent upon their remaining in the same sentence:

> Are we giving our lives to perpetuate the things that the past has created for its needs, forgetting to ask whether these things still serve today's needs; or are we thinking of living men?

> This is as important for science as it is for practice; indeed, it may be said to be the only important consideration.

> It is so in war; it is so in economic life; it cannot be otherwise in religion.

> This, let it be remembered, was the ground taken by Mill; for[1] to him "utilitarianism," in spite of all his critics may say, did not mean the pursuit of bodily pleasure.

184. For enumerations within a single sentence, observe the relative values of comma, semicolon, and colon. Semicolons are to be used between the items unless these are short and simple; in a series of simple character, with little or no punctuation within the elements, comma separation is sufficient. Within each item, as between them successively, punctuation is based on desire for emphasis. If an enumerative sentence is complicated, it should be broken into two or more sentences (see 74):

> The membership of the international commission was made up as follows: France, 4; Germany, 5; Great Britain, 1 (owing to a

[1] "For" in such cases should commonly be preceded by a semicolon.

misunderstanding the announcement did not reach the English societies in time to secure a full quota from that country. Sir Henry Campbell, who had the matter in charge, being absent at the time, great difficulty was experienced in arousing sufficient interest to insure the sending of even a solitary delegate); Italy, 3; the United States, 7.

The defendant, in justification of his act, pleaded that (1) he was despondent over the loss of his wife; (2) he was out of work; (3) he had had nothing to eat for two days; (4) he was under the influence of liquor.

Presidents Angell, of Yale; Eliot, of Harvard; Butler, of Columbia; and Burton, of Chicago.

185. Use a semicolon to separate references to various divisions of the same work (see 208):

Gen. 2:3–6, 9, 14; 3:17; chap. 5; 6:15.
MLN, XXV, 26; XXVI, 31; XXX, 20.

186. The semicolon should be placed outside the quotation marks, and should follow a closing parenthesis if the context requires a semicolon (see 166):

Dr. Akenside speaks of a "horrid pile of hills"; along with this frank disapproval of mountains is a similar dislike for their concomitants, such as precipices, wildernesses, and even dense thickets.

Blair has a stream that slides along in "grateful errors"; in Falconer the light strays through the forest with "gay romantic error."

My uncle's porter, Samuel Hughes,
Came in at six o'clock to black the shoes
  (I always talk to Sam);
So what does he but takes and drags
Me in the chaise along the flags,
  And leaves me where I am.

COMMA

187. The comma indicates the smallest interruption in continuity of thought or sentence structure. The examples below demonstrate (1) minor breaks of sentence flow; (2) the offset of contrast words; (3) the fundamental difference between a defining (restrictive or limiting) element and one that is incidental to the fact (non-restrictive or non-defining); and (4) some breaks of sentence flow for logical unity of elements (see 199, 201):

(1) Here, as in many other cases, what is sometimes popularly supposed to be orthodox is really a heresy, an exaggeration, a distortion, a caricature of the true doctrine of the church. The doctrine is, indeed, laid down by an authority here and there; but, speaking generally, it has no place in the standards, creeds, or confessions of the great communions; e.g., the Apostles' Creed, the Nicene Creed, the canons of the early ecumenical councils, the Westminster Confession, the Thirty-nine Articles.

(2) Shakspere and other, lesser, poets.

(3) The books which I have read I herewith return [i.e., I return those only which I have read]. But: The books, which I have read, I herewith return [i.e., having read all, I now return them].

(4) Gossiping, women are happy; and: Gossiping women are happy.

Of these four, two Americans and one Englishman started; and: Of these, four—two Americans and two Englishmen—started.

Some boys and girls prematurely announce themselves, usually in uncomfortable, sometimes in bad, ways.

Amos, Hosea, Isaiah were the spokesmen for their people.

188. Use a comma to separate proper nouns referring to different individuals or places:

To John, Smith was always kind.

To America, Europe awards the prize of mechanical skill.

189. Put a comma before "and," "or," and "nor," connecting the last two elements in a sequence of three or more; always put a comma before "etc.":

Tom, Dick, and Harry are all here.

It may be made of copper, silver, or gold.

Neither France for her art, nor Germany for her army, nor England for her democracy . . . .

He sent for and received a catalogue listing agricultural implements, etc.

Exceptions:

Do not use a comma where such a conjunction serves to connect all of the links in a brief and close-knit phrase:

I do not remember who wrote the stanzas—whether it was Shelley or Keats or Moore.

190. Ordinarily, put a comma before clauses introduced by such conjunctions as "and," "but," "for," "or," "nor" if a change of subject takes place. Such connectives between words or phrases used in contrast or in conjunction do not require a comma.

I would not if I could, and I could not if I would.

The mistake was not confined to Europe, and the confusion of thought which it implies was world-wide.

All legitimate words should be spelled out in full in text matter, but abbreviations are often needed in book work for footnotes and tables, especially in commercial work where certain signs and forms are understood.

But: They are not intelligible to the general reader and should never be used outside the particular form of composition to which they pertain.

191. Long subordinate clauses preceding a main clause are set off by a following comma:

When he arrived at the railway station, the train had gone, and the friend who had come to bid him goodbye had departed.

As the next train was not due for two hours, he decided to take a ride about the town.

While he regretted his failure to meet his friend, he did not go to his house.

Exceptions:

a) Do not use a comma before an adverbial clause which logically completes the preceding main clause:

This is especially interesting because they represent the two extremes and because they present differences in their relations.

This is good because true.

I shall agree to this only if you accept my conditions.

b) Do not set off by a comma brief contrasting phrases introduced by "but," "if," and "though":

It is a cheap but valuable book.

I could not if I would.

He is honest though poor.

192. When following the main clause, a subordinate element is not set off by a comma unless parenthetical:

He did not go to his friend's house when failing to find him at the station.

193. Use comma punctuation to set off conjunctions, adverbs, connective particles, or phrases that make a distinct break in the continuity of thought, summarizing what has preceded, enumerating what follows, or indi-

cating an antithesis in thought to what precedes (see 178*a*, 187, 198):

Indeed, this was exactly the point of the argument.

Moreover, he did not think the plan was feasible.

Nevertheless, he consented to the scheme.

This statement, therefore, cannot be verified.

That, after all, seemed a very trivial matter.

The gentleman, of course, was wrong.

On the other hand, it is not necessary to emphasize the fact.

Exceptions:

Do not use a comma with such words when the connection is logically close and structurally smooth enough not to call for any pause in reading:

The ruse was obvious indeed.

Therefore I say unto you, Be not afraid of them that kill the body, and after that have no more that they can do.

He was perhaps thinking of the future.

194. Use no comma before "rather," "greater," etc., in such comparative expressions as:

The time-value is to be measured in this way rather than by the time-equivalent of the strata.

There is no test of patience greater than that you have mentioned.

195. Separate two or more adjectives from one another by commas if each modifies the noun alone. If the first adjective modifies the second or combination of the noun and the second adjective, no comma should be used:

Shelley had proved a faithful, sincere friend.

We were accosted by a huge white owl, who said: "To-whoo!"

They were interested in the admirable political institutions of the country.

196. A participial phrase, especially when containing an explanation of the main clause, should be set off by a comma:

Being asleep, he did not hear the door open.

Exhausted by a day's hard work, he slept like a stone.

197. Set off with comma punctuation an antithetical clause or phrase introduced by "not," if the modified element is complete without it:

Men addict themselves to inferior pleasures, not because they deliberately prefer them, but because they are the only ones to which they have access.

But: They discovered not fossils but actual growing plants.

198. For parenthetical, adverbial, or appositional clauses or phrases, use commas to indicate structurally disconnected, but logically integral, interpolations; dashes, to indicate both structurally and logically disconnected insertions (see 218); parentheses, to indicate even less essential parts of the sentence text (see 235):

Since, from the naturalistic point of view, mental states are the concomitants of physiological processes . . . .

The French, generally speaking, are a nation of artists.

The English, highly democratic as they are, nevertheless deem the nobility fundamental to their political and social systems.

There was a time—I forget the exact date—when these conditions were changed.

I (being the person least concerned) will go as soon as the car arrives.

199. Use a comma to separate two identical or closely similar words, even if the sense or grammatical construction does not require such separation (see 188):

Whatever is, is good.

What he was, is not known.

The chief aim of academic striving ought not to be, to be most in evidence.

This is unique only in this, that . . . .

200. A complementary, qualifying, or antithetical word, phrase, or clause that interrupts the sentence should be set off by commas:

Gentlemen, the present law, being of recent enactment, may not be known generally.

That, however, does not relieve from blame this defendant, who is clearly guilty.

This harsh, though at the same time perfectly logical, conclusion.

The deceased was a stern and unapproachable, yet withal sympathetic and kind-hearted, gentleman.

The most sensitive, if not the most elusive, part of child nature.

201. Two or more co-ordinate clauses ending in a word governing or modifying another word in a following clause should be separated by commas:

There lay a shallow body of water connected with, but well protected from, the open sea.

He was as tall as, though much younger than, his brother.

The cultivation in ourselves of a sensitive feeling on the subject of veracity is one of the most useful, and the enfeeblement of that feeling one of the most hurtful, things.

This road leads away from, rather than toward, your destination.

202. Interdependent antithetical clauses should be separated by a comma:

The better a proverb is, the more trite it usually becomes.

Go where a man may, home is the center to which his heart turns.

The older we grow, the more we learn.

203. Use a comma to separate two unrelated numbers (see 199):

In 1905, 347 teachers attended the convention; November 1, 1905.

204. A comma is employed to indicate the omission, for brevity or convenience, of a word or words readily understood from the context:

In Illinois there are seventeen such institutions; in Ohio, twenty-two; in Indiana, thirteen.

In Lincoln's first cabinet Seward was secretary of state; Chase, of the treasury; Cameron, of war; and Bates, attorney-general.

Exceptions:

When such constructions are smooth enough not to call for commas (and consequent semicolons), use the simpler punctuation:

One puppy may resemble the father, another the mother, and a third some distant ancestor.

205. A brief direct quotation, maxim, or similar expression should be separated from the preceding part of the sentence by a comma (see 178). A colon introduces a long, formal quotation:

God said, "Let there be light."

206. Use a comma before "of" in connection with residence, and with title or position when following the name:

Mr. and Mrs. McIntyre, of Detroit, Michigan

E. D. Burton, President of the University of Chicago

Exceptions:

Exceptions are those cases, historical and political, in which the place-name practically has become a part of the person's name, or is so closely connected with this as to render the separation artificial or illogical:

Clement of Alexandria
Philip of Anjou
King Edward of England
President Burton of the University of Chicago.

207. Use a comma after exclamatory "oh" with other words following, but not after vocative "O" (see 79):

"Oh, why did not Cerberus drag me back to hell?"
O thou most mighty ruler!

208. In literary references insert a comma between consecutive numbers to represent a break in the continuity of separate references to the same work (see 185); use an en dash to represent one continuous reference between the consecutive numbers (see 227):

pp. 4, 7–8, 10; Ezra 5:7–8; *Mod. Lang. Jour.*, IV, 123–30, 33, 36

209. Put a comma after digits indicating thousands:

1,276 115,000 10,419 4,285,995

Exceptions:

a) Astrophysical and botanical publications do not use a comma with four figures:

6225; but: 10,284

b) Do not use a comma in date or page numbers, between the constituents of dimensions, weights, and measures, or between fractional sums of money:

2200 B.C.
p. 2461
3 feet 6 inches
4 lb. 2 oz.
2 hr. 4 min.
£6 2*s*. 4*d*.
Fr. 5.12

210. In German and in Spanish a period is used instead of a comma to indicate thousands, as:

69.190.175 1.279

211. Separate month and year and similar time divisions by a comma:

November, 1905 New Year's Day, 1906

Exceptions:

Do not use a comma between month and year in display lines:

May 1915 August 1918
June 1917 May 1924

212. Omit the comma at the end of every display line, such as a signature, superscription, running head, centered head, box-head, date line (see 90).

213. The comma is always placed inside the quotation marks, but it follows the parenthesis if the context requires it at all (see 166):

See the sections on "Quotations," which may be found elsewhere in this volume.

Here he gives a belated, though stilted (and somewhat obscure), exposition of the subject.

APOSTROPHE

214. An apostrophe is used to mark the omission of a letter or letters in the contraction of a word or of figures in a number. In the case of contractions containing a verb and a negative, the negative is attached to the parent-word and no space is required between them:

ne'er	don't	the class of '96
't was	haven't	early in '22
m'f'g	't wasn't	"takin' me 'at"

215. The possessive case of nouns, common and proper alike, is formed by the addition of an apostrophe, or apostrophe and *s* (see 157):

a man's word	horses' tails	Scott's *Ivanhoe*
Jones's farms	Themistocles' era	for appearance' sake

216. The plurals of numerals (see 145), and of rare or artificial noun-coinages, are formed by the aid of an apostrophe and *s;* of proper nouns of more than one syllable ending in a sibilant, by adding an apostrophe alone (monosyllabic proper names ending in a sibilant add *es;* others, *s*):

In the 1900's	in two's and three's
the Y.M.C.A.'s	the three R's
these I-just-do-as-I-please's	all the Tommy Atkins' of England
the Pericles' and Socrates' of literature	(but: the Rosses and the Macdougals)

DASH

217. An em dash is used to denote a sudden break in thought that causes an abrupt change in sentence structure. Dashes are to be used only for striking breaks in continuity:

Do we—*can we*—send out educated boys and girls from the high school at eighteen?

The Platonic world of the static, and the Hegelian world of process—how great the contrast! "Process"—that is the magic word of the modern period.

"To be or not to be—that is the question."

218. Use dashes (rarely parentheses—see 235) to set off clauses that are both logically and structurally independent interpolations (see 198):

This may be said to be—but, never mind, we shall ignore that.

> There came a time—let us say, for convenience, with Herodotus and Thucydides—when this attention to actions was conscious and deliberate.
>
> If it be asked—and in saying this I but epitomize my whole contention—why the Mohammedan religion . . . .

219. An element added to give emphasis or explanation, or to expand a phrase occurring in the main clause through repetition of a significant word, should be introduced by a dash:

> To him they are more important as the sources for history—the history of events and ideas.
>
> Here we are face to face with a new and difficult problem—new and difficult, that is, in the sense that . . . .

220. Wherever there is added or inserted a defining or enumerating complementary element, dashes should be used preferably to mark the addition (see 235):

> These discoveries—gunpowder, printing-press, compass, and telescope—were the weapons before which the old science trembled.
>
> But here we are trenching upon another division of our field—the interpretation of New Testament books.
>
> Christianity found in the Roman Empire a civic life which was implicated by a thousand roots with pagan faith and cultus—a state which offered little.

221. In sentences having several elements as subject of the main clause, a final—summarizing—clause should be preceded by a dash:

> Amos, with the idea that Jehovah is an upright judge; Hosea, whose master hated injustice and falsehood; Isaiah, whose Lord would have mercy only on those who relieved the widow and the fatherless—these were the spokesmen.

222. Let an em dash precede the reference (author, title of work, or both) following a direct quotation that consists of at least one complete sentence, either in footnotes or when cited independently in the text. In the case of poetry the reference should be dropped a line (see 91, 125). Better practice indicates ordinary footnotes for such credit references:

"I felt an emotion of the moral sublime at beholding such an instance of civic heroism."—*Thirty Years*, I, 379.

"The green grass is blowing,
  The morning wind is in it,
'Tis a tune worth thy knowing,
  Though it change every minute."
—Emerson, "To Ellen at the South"

223. A dash should not ordinarily be used with any other point except a period (see 166, 226).

Exceptions:

When the parenthetical clause set off by dashes itself requires an interrogation or exclamation point, such punctuation may be retained before the second dash:

Senator Blank—shall we call him statesman or politician?—introduced the bill.

If the ship should sink—which God forbid!—he will be a ruined man.

224. A word or phrase set in a separate line and succeeded by elements at the beginning of each of which it is implied, should be followed by a dash:

I recommend—

1. That we kill him.
2. That we flay him.

225. In French, Spanish, and Italian a dash is used before a speech in direct discourse instead of quotation marks before and after (see 115).

—Parlons-en mieux, le roi fait honneur à votre âge.

—Le roi, quand il en fait, le mesure au courage.

—Et par là cet honneur n'était dû qu'à mon bras.

—Mi occorre da lei un piacere, signor Professore—gli disse il Sindaco, tirandolo in disparte.

—Sono ai suoi comandi.

—Ma non me lo deve negare.

—Ripeto: signor Cavaliere, lei mi comandi.

226. A dash may be used in connection with sideheads, whether the following text is run in or paragraphed. Good style calls for a period before the dash when run in (see 80*a*, 84*b*, 91):

2. *The language of the New Testament.*—The lexicons of Grimm-Thayer, Cremer, and others . . . .

NOTE.—The foregoing has been taken from . . . .

Biblical criticism in other denominations—

A most interesting article appeared in the *Expository Times* . . . .

227. Use a dash to mark the omission of the word "to" between two words or numbers (see 208):

May–July, 1906 (en dash)

May 1, 1905—July 1, 1906 (em dash)

pp. 3–7 (en dash)

Luke 3:6—5:2 (em dash)

Exceptions:

If the word "from" precedes the first word or number, use "to" instead of the dash:

From May 1 to July 1, 1906

228. In connecting consecutive numbers omit hundreds from the second number (i.e., use only two figures) unless the first number ends in two ciphers; in that case repeat the full form. If the next to the last figure in the first number is a cipher, do not repeat this in the second number. In citing dates B.C., always repeat the hundreds (because representing a diminution, not an increase) (see 208, 227):

1880–95	pp. 102–7
pp. 113–16	387–324 B.C.
1900–1906	

Exceptions:

Astrophysical Journal and *Botanical Gazette* always repeat the hundreds:

1180–1895	pp. 113–116

229. Since typographical forms do not represent exact speech but are required to give the right idea unmistakably, no part of a symbol essential to clearness may be omitted:

0°–10° C.	Not: 0–10° C.
$5.00–$10.00	$5.00–10.00
£5–£6	5–6 £

230. A 2-em dash is used (without space) following a date to indicate time as still continuing; or after a word of which the ending is to be supplied:

1876——

We ha—— a copy in the library.

231. A 3-em dash is used (with space on each side) to denote a whole word omitted or to be supplied; it is also used in bibliographies to indicate the same author as in the preceding item.

232. An em dash is often used in indexes and bibliographies (without space) before the first words of subentries, to save repeating cue words (see 341, 345*G*).

PARENTHESES[1]

233. Place between parentheses figures or letters used to mark divisions of enumerations run into the text:

The reasons for his resignation were three: (1) advanced age, (2) failing health, (3) a desire to travel.

234. Parentheses are used in pairs except that, when enumerated divisions are paragraphed, a single parenthesis is ordinarily used to follow a lower-case (italic) letter; a period is used with figures and capital (roman) letters. In syllabi and matter of a similar character, the following scheme of notation and indention should ordinarily be adhered to:

A. Under the head of . . .
    I. Under . . . .
        1. Under . . . .
            a) Under . . . .
                (1) Under . . . .
                    (*a*) Under . . . .
                        i) Under . . . .
                        ii) Under . . . .
                    (*b*) Under . . . .
                (2) Under . . . .
            b) Under . . . .
        2. Under . . . .
    II. Under . . . .
B. Under the head of . . . .

[1] For other marks of punctuation used before or after parentheses, see 166, 173, 175, 177, 186, 213.

235. Parentheses should not ordinarily be used for parenthetical clauses (see 219, 220) unless confusion might arise from the use of less distinctive marks, or unless the content of the clause is wholly irrelevant to the main argument (see 198, 218):

He meant—I take this to be the (somewhat obscure) sense of his speech—that . . . .

The period thus inaugurated (of which I shall speak at greater length in the next chapter) was characterized by . . . .

The contention has been made (*op. cit.*) that . . . .

BRACKETS

236. Brackets are used in pairs (1) to inclose an explanation or note, (2) to indicate an editor's interpolation in a quotation, (3) to rectify a mistake (such as may appear in editing a book or manuscript), (4) to supply an omission, (5) for parentheses within parentheses, and (6) for the phonetic transcript of a word:

(1) [1][This was written before the publication of Spencer's book.—EDITOR.]

(2) "These [the free-silver Democrats] asserted that the present artificial ratio can be maintained indefinitely."

(3) "As the Italian [Englishman] Dante Gabriel Ros[s]etti has said, ..."

(4) *John Ruskin.* By Henry Carpenter. ["English Men of Letters," III.] London: Black, 1900.

(5) Grote, the great historian of Greece (see his *History,* I, 204 [2d ed.]), ...

(6) repos [rəpo]

237. Such phrases as "*To be continued*" at the end, and "*Continued from* . . . ." at the beginning, of articles, chapters, etc., should be placed between brackets,

centered, and set in italics (see 114) and in type reduced in size in accordance with the rule governing reductions (see 126):

[*Continued from p. 320*]

[*To be concluded*]

ELLIPSES

238. Ellipsis marks are used to indicate the omission from quoted matter of one or more words not essential to the immediate purpose, and also to indicate illegible words, mutilations, and similar lacunae in the original material. For English text, mark such ellipses by using four periods separated by 3-em spaces (see 128). If such omission occurs after a complete sentence, do not consider the preceding period as part of the four (or three in French, see 241) ellipsis marks. A 3-em space should be used before the ellipsis as between sentences expressed (see 37):

> The point . . . . is that the same forces . . . . are still the undercurrents of every human life. . . . . We may never unravel the methods of the physical forces; . . . . but . . . .

> Quand il s'agit de la grandeur de Dieu, et les mystères de l'Evangile, il semble que l'on doive changer de maximes et de règles, d'autant que toutes les actions divines sont merveilleuses. ... Il ne faut pas avoir recours à la vraisemblance quand les vérités se trouvent si parfaites.

239. To mark the omission of a whole paragraph of prose or of a full line of poetry, insert a full line of periods separated by em or 2-em quads according to the length of the line. In no case, however, should such marks extend beyond the longest type-line.

I think it worth giving you these details, because it is a vague thing, though a perfectly true thing, to say that it was by his genius that Alexander conquered the Eastern world.

. . . .

His army, you know, was a small one. To carry a vast number of men would have been disastrous.

240. To mark the omission of letters in mutilated manuscripts or inscriptions, or lacunae in original writings, use one period for each letter lacking, with space as between words:

<table>
<tr><td></td><td>[. . . . . .]ασ[—]</td><td></td></tr>
<tr><td></td><td>[Καρκί]νος Δ|</td><td></td></tr>
<tr><td></td><td>[’Αστ]υδάμας Π|| [—?]</td><td></td></tr>
<tr><td>[Αἰ]σχύ[λος—]</td><td>[Θεο]δέκτας Π||</td><td></td></tr>
<tr><td>[Εὐ]έτης |</td><td>[’Αφα]ρεύς ||</td><td></td></tr>
<tr><td>[Πο]λυφράσμ[ων—]</td><td>[. . . . ω]ν ||</td><td>Αι</td></tr>
<tr><td>[Νόθ]ιππος |</td><td>. . . . . .</td><td>Φρ-</td></tr>
<tr><td>[Σοφ]οκλῆς ΔΠ|||</td><td>. . . . . ||</td><td>‘Ομ-</td></tr>
<tr><td>[. . . .] τος ||[—?]</td><td></td><td>Δ'</td></tr>
<tr><td>[’Αριστί]ας [—]</td><td></td><td>Ξ-</td></tr>
</table>

241. In French, Italian, and Spanish text, use three periods with no space between them, but use a 3-em space before them:

"Aux armes! ... aux armes! ... les Prussiens!"

"Je n'écris que ce j'ai vu, entendu, senti ou éprouvé moi-même ... j'ai déjà publié quelque petits ouvrages ..."

... Davanti a un nome come quello di un Agostino Palandri, si abbandona qualunque idea preconcetta; ... ma il riso, o signori, è una irriverenza indegna; è una profanazione sacrilega ... è ... oh! E io ... io me ne vado.

E este fue sienpre Dios e sera Dios; ca el non pudo aver fin en ningun tienpo. ... Aquella nascencia fue segund omne.

242. An ellipsis is usually treated as a part of the citation, and consequently should be inclosed in the quotation marks (see 128).

THE HYPHEN

243. A hyphen is used to show (1) the combination of two or more words into a single term (compound word) representing a new idea; (2) the division of a word at the end of a line, the remainder of which must be carried to the next line (see "Divisions," p. 117); (3) a part of a word (prefix, suffix, or root) (261); (4) the division of a word into syllables (262). The tendency is to omit the hyphen between compound words whenever current usage establishes a new meaning for them in union. However, many such words are better hyphenated than consolidated. The following rules are designed to cover such cases, but it must be remembered that they become invalid when common usage has made the solid form easily recognized without a chance of misinterpretation.

244. Hyphenate adjectives formed of two or more words when preceding the nouns modified:

so-called Croesus	well-known author
first-class investment	better-trained teachers
high-school course	half-dead horse
joint-stock company	English-speaking peoples
nineteenth-century progress	white-rat serum
up-to-date machinery	four-year-old boy
house-to-house canvass	go-as-you-please fashion
deceased-wife's-sister bill	the feeble-minded person

Exceptions:

a) Do not hyphenate adjectives formed of two proper names having their own fixed meaning:

Old Testament times	Old English spelling
New York subways	Scotch Presbyterian doctrines

b) Do not hyphenate foreign phrases used in an adjective sense (see 95):

a laissez faire policy — an a priori argument

c) Do not hyphenate combinations of adverb and adjective or adverb and participle where no ambiguity could result:

an ever increasing flood — highly developed species

d) Do not hyphenate adverbs or combined adjective elements used after the word modified:

He is a man well known in the neighborhood.
Pages i and ii become the flyleaf, so called.
Her gown and carriage were strictly up to date.

245. Where one of the components of a compound adjective contains more than one word, an en dash should be used in place of a hyphen:

New York–Chicago freight traffic
Norwegian–German-Jewish immigrants

246. Wherever two or more compound words have a common base, this element may be indicated in all but the last by a hyphen:

a fourth- or fifth-grade lesson — two-, three-, or fourfold
2- or 3-em quads

a) A present participle united (1) with a noun to form a new noun with a different meaning from that which would be conveyed by the two words taken separately,

(2) with a preposition used absolutely (i.e., not governing a following noun) to form a noun, should take a hyphen:

boarding-house, dining-hall, dwelling-place, printing-office (but: meeting place)

247. Compound words with "book," "house," "mill," "room," "shop," and "work" should be printed as one word when the prefixed noun contains only one syllable; should be hyphenated when it contains two; and should be printed as two separate words when it contains three or more:

handbook, schoolbook, notebook, textbook; pocket-book, story-book; reference book

boathouse, clubhouse, schoolhouse, storehouse (but: bond house); engine-house, power-house; business house

cornmill, handmill, sawmill, windmill; water-mill, paper-mill; chocolate mill

bedroom, classroom, schoolroom, storeroom; lecture-room; recitation room; but: drawing-room (sitting-room), drawing room (for lessons)

tinshop, workshop; bucket-shop; policy shop

handwork, woodwork; metal-work; filigree work

Exceptions:

a) Do not hyphenate forms using the words "store" and "fold." Either set as two words or as a compound form without space:

bookstore	grocery store	tenfold
drug store	drygoods store	fifteen fold
candy store	twofold	a hundred fold
feed store		

b) The hyphen is often omitted for the sake of appearance, or because custom has given the two words a special meaning:

check book | home work | team work
tailor shop | field work | source book

school men (to distinguish from the Schoolmen of the Middle Ages)

248. Compounds of "maker," "dealer," and other words denoting agency, compounds indicating equal participation, and compounds one of the terms of which is derived from a transitive verb should be hyphenated:

harness-maker | story-teller | hero-worship
book-dealer | office-holder | fool-killer
soldier-statesman | | clay-modeling

Exceptions:

a) A few short words of everyday occurrence that have an acquired meaning are used without a hyphen:

bookmaker | shopgirl | waterproof
dressmaker | schoolboy | workingman

b) Unwieldy combinations that could not be ambiguous should remain as two words:

encyclopedia compiler | child study training
family welfare work | civil service commission

249. Compounds of "fellow," "father," "mother," "brother," "sister," "daughter," "parent," and "foster" are hyphenated in most cases when forming the first element of a compound:

fellow-man, fellow-beings; (but: "Mr. Goodfellow"; politics makes strange bedfellows); father-love, mother-tongue, brother-officer, sister-nation, daughter-cells, parent-word, foster-son (but: godmother, lay brother, sorority sister)

Exceptions:

Words that have acquired a new meaning in combination:

fatherhood | fatherland | fellowship

250. Compounds of "great," indicating degrees in a direct line of genealogical descent, call for a hyphen:

great-grandfather great-great-grandnephew

251. Compounds of "life" and "world" require a hyphen:

life-history, life-principle (but: lifetime)
world-power, world-problem (but: World War, World Court)

252. Standard variations in the use of hyphens with some common words are shown below:

alligator skin	post-haste	post-office
business-like	postmark	postscript
childlike	postmaster	self-control
master-builder	post meridiem	selfsame
masterpiece	post-mortem	sheepskin
post card		

253. "Vice," "ex-," "elect," and "general," constituting parts of titles, should be connected with the chief noun by a hyphen:

Vice-Consul Taylor ex-President Taft[1]
the governor-elect the postmaster-general
governor-general lieutenant-governor

Exceptions:

a) In cases where the prefix has become an established part of the name, the hyphen has been omitted by custom:

vicegerent viceroy

b) Military terms are not hyphenated:

lieutenant general surgeon general

[1] But better: former President Taft.

254. A hyphen should be used with prefixes joined to proper names, to long or unusual formations, and to words in which the omission of the hyphen would make the word convey a meaning different from that which is intended (see 244, 258):

pseudo-Christianity	lying-in
un-Christian	re-democratize
pan-Hellenic	re-pulverization
pre-Raphaelite	re-cover (cover again)
ante-Nicene	re-formation (as distinguished from reformation)
lean-to	

255. Omit the hyphen from "today," "tomorrow," "tonight," "viewpoint," "standpoint" (see 164).

256. The negative particles "un-," "in-," "il-," "im-," and "a-" usually do not require a hyphen:

unmanly	illogical	indeterminate
inanimate	asymmetrical	impersonal

Exceptions:

a) Such combinations with proper adjectives retain the hyphen (see 254):

un-Christian

b) The particle "non-" ordinarily calls for a hyphen, except in the commonest words. Dictionary authority should be called upon for doubtful cases (see 254):

non-aesthetic	but:
non-subservient	nondescript
non-contagious	nonessential
non-interference	nonplus
non-membership	nonsense
non-unionist	noncombatant

257. "Quasi-" prefixed to a noun or an adjective requires a hyphen:

quasi-corporation	quasi-historical

258. The prefixes "co-," "pre-," "re-," "semi-," "demi-," "tri-," "bi-," "ante-," "infra-," "inter-," "intra-," "post-," "sub-," "super-," "supra-," and "anti-" when joined to roots do not retain the hyphen except in combination with words beginning with their terminal vowel, or with *w* or *y* (see 254):

coequal	co-operation
coeducation	co-worker
prehistoric	pre-empted
rearrange	re-enter
reunite	re-yield
semiannual	semi-incandescent
demigod	
trimonthly	tri-yearly
bipartisan	bi-weekly
bichromate	
antechamber	ante-war
inframarginal	infra-yearly
interrelation	inter-university
intrastate	intra-atomic
postgraduate	
subtitle	
superfine	
supraliminal	

Exceptions:

a) When the first vowel of the added word would form a diphthong with the terminal vowel of the prefix or suggest mispronunciation, the hyphen is retained:

ante-urban
supra-eclectic
co-author
re-use
re-read
pre-interpret
demi-equitant
pro-ally
intra-urban

b) When the added word is a proper noun or adjective retain the hyphen:

Anti-Trust Law
Anti-Saloon League
Anti-Semitic movement
ante-Nicene
post-Exilic
pre-Yostian

c) When the retention of the hyphen would indicate a change of meaning:

recreation
re-creation

d) In long and unusual formations retain the hyphen:

semi-barbarous
semi-translucent
ante-bellum
post-revolutionary

259. "Extra," "pan," and "ultra" as a rule call for a hyphen:

extra-hazardous
pan-American
ultra-conservative

Exceptions:

A few words to which usage has given a special meaning in consolidation are:

extraordinary
ultramicroscopic
Ultramontane

260. In fractional numbers, spelled out, connect the numerator and the denominator with a hyphen unless either already contains a hyphen:

The year is two-thirds gone; one-half; four and five-sevenths; thirty one-hundredths (but: thirty-one hundredths)

Exceptions:

Do not hyphenate in such cases as:

One half of his fortune he bequeathed to his widow; the other, to charitable institutions.

261. A hyphen is used to indicate a part of a word, a root, a prefix, or a suffix, as a particle or syllable not complete in itself:

the prefix *a-*; the Spanish diminutive suffixes *-ito* and *-cita*

262. Hyphens are employed to separate the syllables of a word (see 264 ff.):

di-a-gram, pho-tog-ra-phy

263. Following is a list of words of everyday occurrence which should be hyphenated. They do not fall under any of the foregoing classifications:

after-years
bas-relief
birth-rate
blood-feud
blood-relations
candle-power
coat-of-arms
cross-reference
death-rate
first-fruits
flying-fish
folk-lore
folk-song
good-will (as a business term only)
half-title
horse-power
ice-cream
infra-red
loan-word
lying-in
man-of-war
object-lesson
pay-roll
poor-law
sea-level
sense-perception
sun-god
thought-process
title-page
trade-mark
trapper-hunter
wave-length
well-being
well-nigh
will-power

DIVISION OF WORDS

264. The division of words at the ends of lines is always undesirable, but many cases occur where such divisions are unavoidable. Certain rules governing divisions should never be broken, while others are desirable but may be broken when good spacing demands it. In this chapter, therefore, rules marked with an asterisk are unbreakable rules, but those marked with a dagger are subordinate to the rules of good spacing. Section 280, referring to the division of foreign words, is an arbitrary rule and may never be broken (see rules for spacing, sections 32–42 inclusive).

*265. Divide according to pronunciation (the American system), not according to derivation (the English system):

democ-racy, not: demo-cracy   knowl-edge, not: know-ledge
aurif-erous, not: auri-ferous
antip-odes (still better: antipo-des—see 266), not: anti-podes

As far as compatible with pronunciation, divide compounds on etymological lines, or according to derivation and meaning:

dis-pleasure is better than displeas-ure
school-master, than schoolmas-ter
never: passo-ver, une-ven, etc.

* Unbreakable rule.

Good taste proscribes any division that is misleading as to meaning or pronunciation. Therefore do not divide such words as:

women	often	prayer
water	noisy	heaven

The following suffixes are also considered indivisible:

-cial	-cion	-cious
-sial	-sion	-ceous
-tial	-tion	-tious
	-gion	-geous

†266. Divide on a vowel wherever practicable. In case a vowel alone forms a syllable in the middle of a word, run it into the first line. Treat diphthongs as single letters:

physi-cal, not: phys-ical, nor physic-al
sepa-rate, not: sep-arate
criti-cism, not: crit-icism
particu-lar, not: partic-ular

Exceptions:

Words in *-able* and *-ible* should carry the vowel over into the next line:

read-able, not: reada-ble
convert-ible, not: converti-ble

*267. Two consonants standing between vowels should be separated in syllabication when the pronunciation warrants:

advan-tage	exces-sive	moun-tain
finan-cier	foun-da-tion	struc-ture
impor-tant	In-dian	profes-sor

* Unbreakable rule.

† Subject to the rules of good spacing.

†268. In present participles carry over the *-ing:*

learn-ing	re-vok-ing	whirl-ing
pic-nick-ing	chang-ing	en-tranc-ing
pranc-ing	giv-ing	cer-ti-fy-ing
dwell-ing	cat-a-logu-ing	im-pro-vis-ing
en-ter-ing	tempt-ing	tramp-ing

Exceptions:

a) When the ending consonant sounds of the parent-word belong to a syllable with a silent vowel, such consonants become part of the added syllable *-ing:*

chuck-ling	twin-kling	siz-zling
dwin-dling	han-dling	ruf-fling
ram-bling	bris-tling	gig-gling

b) When the ending consonant is doubled before the addition of *-ing*, the added consonant must be carried over:

run-ning	dab-bing	twin-ning
control-ling	bid-ding	trip-ping

†269. Do not except in extreme cases divide on a syllable with a silent vowel, or carry over a syllable of two letters.

pos-sible, not: possi-ble	di-vided, not: divid-ed
people, not: peo-ple	stricken, not: strick-en
en-titled, not: enti-tled	money, not: mon-ey
prin-ciples, not: princi-ples	losses, not: loss-es

*270. Words of two syllables pronounced as one should never be divided:

vexed	climbed	passed	helped

* Unbreakable rule.

† Subject to the rules of good spacing.

*271. One-letter divisions are never permissible. Do not divide:

enough	among	amen
able	item	again

†272. When the formation of a plural adds a syllable to a word ending in an *s*-sound, avoid dividing on the plural and thus changing the division:

cross	horse	in-stance
cross-ing	horse-man	in-stanc-ing
cros-ses	hor-ses	in-stan-ces

*273. Do not separate (i.e., put in different lines) the initials of a name, or such combinations as £6 4*s.* 6*d.*, 1406 B.C., 6:00 P.M.

*274. Do not separate parts of an equation; make a separate line and center if necessary:

$$\frac{a-y}{b}=24b+a+x-\frac{y}{2}$$

†275. Except in extreme cases do not divide sums of money or other numbers expressed in figures.

†276. In hyphenated nouns and adjectives avoid additional hyphens:

object-lesson, not: object-les-son

poverty-stricken, not: pov-erty-stricken, much less: pover-ty-stricken

†277. Avoid the separation of a divisional mark, e.g., (*a*) or (1), when in the middle of a sentence, from the

* Unbreakable rule.

† Subject to the rules of good spacing.

section which it precedes. In other words, do not allow such a mark to fall at the end of a line, but carry it over with the matter to which it pertains.

†278. Do not divide proper nouns, especially names of persons, or separate the initials of a name from the name itself, if it can be avoided with good spacing (see 273).

†279. Do not break the last word in more than two consecutive lines, leaving a row of hyphens at the edge of a page.

*280. The following are condensed rules for dividing words in the foreign languages most frequently met in proofreading. While not entirely comprehensive, they will be found to cover every ordinary contingency (see 264).

FRENCH

a) The fundamental principle is to divide as far as possible on a vowel, avoiding consonantal ending of syllables:

in-di-vi-si-bi-li-té	ta-bleau, not: tab-leau
a-ché-ter	ba-lancer, not: bal-ancer

b) Two adjacent consonants of which the second is *l* or *r* (but not the combinations *rl, lr*) are both carried over to the following syllable:

ta-bleau	per-dre	par-ler
é-cri-vain	qua-tre	hur-ler

* Unbreakable rule.

† Subject to the rules of good spacing.

c) There are as many syllables as there are vowels or diphthongs, even if some vowels be soundless:

par-lent	pro-pri-é-tai-re	fil-les
vic-toi-re	guer-re	

Exceptions:

a) A mute *e* following a vowel does not form a syllable:

é-taient, joue-rai

b) When preceding other vowels and sounded as consonants, *i*, *y*, *o*, *ou*, *u* do not form syllables:

bien	fouet-ter	yeux
é-tions	loin	é-cuel-le

GERMAN

a) The fundamental principle is to divide on a vowel as far as possible:

hü-ten, le-ben, Fa-brik

b) If two or more consonants stand between vowels, usually only the last is carried over:

Rit-ter, klir-ren, Klemp-ner, Ver-wand-te, Karp-fen

c) *sz*, *ch*, *sch*, *ph*, *st*, *th* are never separated (but see *f* below):

Bu-sze, Be-cher, Hä-scher (but: Häus-chen), Geo-gra-phie, La-sten, Ma-thilde

d) If *ck* must be divided, it is separated into *k-k:*

Deckel—Dek-kel

e) In foreign words (*Fremdwörter*), combinations of *b*, *d*, *g*, *k*, *p*, *t*, with *l* or *r* are carried over:

Pu-bli-kum, Me-trum, Hy-drant

f) Compound words are separated first into their component elements, and within each element the foregoing rules apply:

Fürsten-schloss, Tür-an-gel, Inter-esse

ITALIAN

The fundamental principle is to divide after the vowel.

a) A single consonant goes with the following vowel:

ta-vo-li-no	po-ta-re

b) Any consonant group except those noted in *c*) goes with the following vowel:

te-cni-co	mi-glio-re
a-ri-tme-ti-co	bi-so-gno
ca-sti-ghi	in-chio-stro
a-vrò	u-sci-re

c) Double consonants, the group *cq*, and groups beginning with *l*, *m*, *n*, *r* are divided:

let-te-ra	cal-do
poz-zo	den-tro
ac-qua	sem-pre

d) Two adjacent vowels are not divided:

leo-ne	miei
o-cea-no	tuoi

e) Do not divide after an apostrophe:

un'ar-te	not: un'-arte
quel-l'uomo	not: quell'-uomo

SPANISH

a) The fundamental principle is to divide on a vowel as far as possible:

ca-ra-co-les, re-ba-ño, fle-xi-bi-li-dad

b) *br, bl, ch, cl, cr, dr, ll, pr, rr, tr,* and *ñ,* being regarded as simple consonants, follow the foregoing rule; *cc* and *nn* are divided, as in English:

mu-cha-cho, ba-ta-lla, bu-lló, ba-rre-ño, ci-ga-rro; ac-ce-so, en-no-ble-cer, in-ne-ga-ble

c) The liquid consonants *l* and *r*, when preceded by any consonant other than *s*, must not be separated from that consonant except to unite parts of compound words:

ha-blar, po-dría, ce-le-bra-ci-ón, si-glo; but sub-lu-nar, sub-rayar, es-la-bón

d) Two separable consonants should be divided; *s* is always disjoined from a following consonant:

cuer-da, chas-co, pron-to; has-ta, as-pi-rar, cons-pi-rar

LATIN

a) A Latin word has as many syllables as it has vowels or diphthongs (*ae, au, oe, ei, eu, ui*).

b) When a single consonant occurs between two vowels, divide before the consonant:

Cae-sar, me-ri-di-es

c) In the case of two or more consonants, divide before the last consonant except in the combinations: mute (*p, ph, b, t, th, d, c, ch, g*)+liquid (*l, r*), and *qu* or *gu:*

om-nis, scrip-tus, cunc-tus (but: pa-tris, e-quus, lin-gua)

d) Compound words are separated first into their component elements; within each element the foregoing rules apply:

ad-est, ab-rum-po, red-e-o, trans-i-go

GREEK

a) Single consonants, combinations of consonants which can begin a word, and mutes followed by μ or ν are placed at the beginning of a syllable:

ἔ-χω, ἐ-γώ, ἑ-σπέ-ρα, νέ-κταρ, ἀ-κμή, δε-σμός, μι-κρόν, πρά-γμα-τος, γι-γνώ-σκω

Other combinations of consonants are divided:

πράσ-σω, ἐλ-πίς, ἔν-δον, ἅρ-μα-τα

b) Compound words are divided into their original parts; subject to that the foregoing rule applies:

προσ-ά-γω, παρ-ά-γω

RULES FOR COMPOSITION OF GREEK

281. The following facts about Greek accents and punctuation marks will be found useful in composition:

Every vowel or diphthong beginning a word takes a breathing. The rough breathing (῾) carries the sound of *h* (*ἑν*); the smooth breathing (᾿) has no sound (*ἐν*). The breathing is placed over the second vowel of a diphthong: *αἰ, εἰ, εὐ, αὐ, οὐ, οἰ.* All words beginning with *ρ* or *υ* take the rough breathing.

There are three accents used in Greek: acute (´), grave (`), circumflex (῀). The accent belongs over the lower-case vowel, but is justified before the capital, and over the second vowel of a diphthong (Ἕλλην, *τοῖς, τούς*).

The circumflex accent may be used only on one of the *last two* syllables; the grave may be used on the last syllable only.

The acute accent on the last syllable is changed to grave when preceding another accented word in the same clause. There is practically no other occasion for the grave accent, except on the indefinite enclitic *τὶς* used alone.

A few monosyllables which are closely connected with the word following are called proclitics and take no accent. The proclitics are:

The forms of the article *ὁ, ἡ, οἱ, αἱ*; the prepositions *εἰς, ἐν, ἐκ* (*ἐξ*); the conjunctions *εἰ, ὡς*; the adverb *οὐ* (*οὐκ, οὐχ*).

An enclitic is a short word pronounced as if part of the preceding word. It loses its accent (*'Αρταξέρξης τε*) except in case of a dissyllabic enclitic after a word with acute accent on next to the last syllable, as *'Αρταξέρξης ἐστί.*

The most common enclitics are:

τὶς; εἰμί, ἐστί, ἐστόν, ἐσμέν, ἐστέ, εἰσί; φημί, φησί, φατόν, φαμέν, φατέ, φασί; ἐστί becomes *ἔστι* at the beginning of a sentence and when it follows *οὐκ; μή; ὡς; ἀλλά; τοῦτο.* The word before an enclitic receives an added acute accent on the last syllable if it had originally the circumflex accent on the next to the last or the acute on the third from the last syllable. The circumflex on the last syllable is not changed by the addition of an enclitic.

Greek punctuation marks: The period and comma are the same as in English; the colon and semicolon are both represented by a period upside down (˙); the Greek interrogation point is the same as the English semicolon (;). The apostrophe should not be used in place of a breathing. When a final vowel is elided before a second word beginning with the same vowel, the apostrophe (') is used in its place, especially if the initial vowel of the second word has a rough breathing.

FOOTNOTES

282. For reference indexes in footnotes use superior figures in the text, placed after the punctuation marks, without space:

.... the niceties of style, which were then invading Attic prose,[1] and the variations of form ....

[1] In particular the avoidance of hiatus.

Exceptions:

In German, reference indexes are placed inside the punctuation:

Diesen Stoff hatte mir ein zufällig mir in die Hand geratenes Volksbuch vom *Venusberg* eingegeben[1].

[1] B. Wagner, *Mein Leben,* Munich, 1917.

283. In special cases such as tabular and algebraic matter, where figure reference would cause confusion, asterisks, daggers, and other symbols are used for indexes (see 303):

$F=y^2+y^3$*

* Schenk's equation.

When such symbols are used, the sequence of indexes should be:

* (asterisk or star), † (dagger), ‡ (double dagger), § (section mark), || (parallels), ¶ (paragraph mark)

When more symbols are needed these may be doubled in the same sequence:

**, ††, ‡‡, §§, || ||, ¶¶

284. Correct arrangement of footnote items is important. After the reference number or sign, which takes paragraph indention, the order of items is as follows. (For purposes of comparison all the footnotes for which indexes appear on this page are grouped together under *d*) on pp. 130 and 131.)

a) *Author's name with Christian name or initials first, followed by a comma.*[1]—After the first occurrence, the Christian name or initials may be dropped if no misunderstanding would result.[3]

b) *The title of the work or the part of a work cited.*—Give the title in full form at first occurrence[9] unless also shown in a formal bibliography set as an appendix. Omission[10] of the title of chapter or article after the first reference is permissible if book title and page reference are given. Abbreviation of a title after its first occurrence in a footnote may be either by ellipsis or by word abbreviation, or both.[13] Published titles should be in italic type.[4] Articles[9] or complete parts[8] of publications[16] should be roman quoted. Follow by a comma unless the "facts of publication" are inclosed in parentheses.

c) *The facts of publication.*—These may be given in full[4] or in partial form,[5] but should appear in the same order. For a book, follow the order: edition (if more than one), place of publication, publisher, and date. In the full form a colon is used after place of publication,[4] and commas are used elsewhere. The edition number, if given, stands within parentheses,[4] or is expressed by a superior figure following the title[6] or the volume number[14] before the punctuation. When place and date[7] only form the statement, they appear in parentheses.[2]

When citing a periodical, set the date (month or year), if given, in parentheses after the volume number.[9] If the reference is to a month, year, and page[12] only, the date may appear in its natural order with commas.[15]

d) References to volume and page.—Omit the forms "Vol." and "p." when both items are given in one reference[11] (see 289). Use Roman caps for volume number and Arabic numerals for page reference. Use a comma to separate the volume number from the page number.

[1] W. P. Ker, *Epic and Romance: Essays on Medieval Literature* (London: Macmillan & Co., 1897), p. 10.

[2] W. P. Ker, *Epic and Romance: Essays on Medieval Literature* (London, 1897), p. 10.

[3] Ker, *Epic and Romance* (London, 1897), p. 10.

[4] *A Manual of Style* (8th ed.; Chicago: The University of Chicago Press, 1925), p. 10.

[5] Maxime Du Camp, *Souvenirs littéraires* (Paris, 1882–83), II, 541.

[6] *The Works of Oliver Goldsmith*[2], ed. Gibbs (1886), 33–41.

[7] Arthur Young, *A Six Months' Tour through the North of England* (London, 1771), I, 222, as quoted in A. H. Johnson, *The Disappearance of the Small Landowner* (London, 1909), pp. 102–3.

[8] Samuel Johnson, "Observations on the State of Affairs in 1756" (1756), *Works of Samuel Johnson* (London, 1825), VI, 113–15.

[9] "Epicurism Ruinous to the State," *Gentleman's Magazine*, XVIII (1748), 270–71.

[10] *Gentleman's Magazine*, XVIII, 271.

[11] H. C. Lancaster, "The Genesis of *Ruy Blas*," *Modern Philology*, XIV (1916–17), 10.

[12] G. Lanson, "Victor Hugo et Angelica Kauffman," *Revue d'histoire littéraire*, 1915, pp. 392–401.

[13] Lanson, "Victor Hugo . . . . ," *Rev. hist. litt.*, p. 395.

[14] Mornet, *Revue des cours et conferences*, XXII[1] (1913–14), 462–63. [The superior figure attached to the volume number indicates that the reference is to the first of the two series into which the volume is divided.]

[15] H. H. Maurer, "Studies in the Sociology of Religion," *American Journal of Sociology*, November, 1924, p. 257.

[16] Breckinridge, *Family Welfare in a Metropolitan Community*, Appendix, "Statutes and Annual Reports," Sec. II, p. 861.

285. If an author's name is given in the text in connection with reference to, or a quotation from, his work, the name should not be repeated in the footnote:

. . . . This theory is questioned by Herbert, as follows:

"I cannot admit . . . ."[1]

[1] *Laws of the Ancients*, I, 153.

286. The reference mark carrying credit for a quotation should stand at the end of the excerpt. It should not be placed after a colon which precedes quoted matter. See example for section 285.

287. Where references to the same work follow each other closely and uninterruptedly, use *ibid.* instead of repeating the title. Thus *ibid.* takes the place of as much of the previous reference as should be understood by a reader as he sees the new reference following this abbreviation:

[1] Spencer, *Principles of Sociology*, chap. iv, p. 128.

[2] *Ibid.*, p. 129.

[3] Barnes, "Charles Sumner," *Journal of Political Economy*, XXXV, 427.

[4] *Ibid.*, XXXVI, 495.

a) If the reference[1] is to precisely the matter covered by a reference not immediately preceding,[2] use *loc. cit.* (the place cited), or *op. cit.* (the work cited), according to the exact meaning intended. *Op. cit.* is not used to repeat the title of a journal,[3] when the reference is to another author, but may be used in reference to the same author's work[4] in a periodical, or to his book:

[1] *Loc. cit.* [if exactly the same place is cited], or

[2] Smith, *op. cit.*, p. 290.

[3] R. D. McKenzie, "The Ecological Approach to the Study of the Human Community," *American Journal of Sociology*, XXX, 287.

[4] *Op. cit.*, p. 288.

288. For tables, whether ruled or open, all footnotes should be in 6 point and should invariably be placed at the foot of the table and not at the foot of the page (see 321). For reference indexes in such cases use symbols and not superior figures (see 283), and double the signs needed in excess of those in the type font.

289. Ordinarily, omit the abbreviations "Vol." and "p." in parenthetical or footnote references[2] to particular passages. Use Roman numerals[1] (capitals) for Volume, Book, Part, Division (except in reference to ancient classical works, when lower-case Roman numerals should be used) (see 290); use Roman numerals (lower-case) for chapter and pages[1] of introductory matter (Preface, etc.); and Arabic numerals for number (*Heft*) and text pages.[4] When confusion might arise, use "Vol.," "p.," etc., in connection with the numerals; but where the reference is to a page, unaccompanied by fur-

ther details, the abbreviation "p." or "pp." must be used[3] (see 76, 132, 152, 155):

[1] Miller, *French Revolution* (2d ed.; London: Abrahams, 1888), II, Part IV, iii.

[2] S. I. Curtiss, "The Place of Sacrifice among Primitive Semites," *Biblical World*, XXI (1903), 248 ff.

[3] P. 63; pp. 27–36.

[4] Fraser, *The Golden Bough*[5], I, 27 [superior figure within punctuation indicating number of the edition].

290. In classical references use no comma between author's name and the title of his work, and no comma following the title unless "Vol.," "p.," or some kindred symbol is used. In all references to divisions of classical or ancient works, use periods in place of commas, reserving the comma to indicate a succession (of pages, etc.):

[1] Cicero *De officiis* i. 133, 140.

[2] *De div. per somn.* 1, p. 463*a*.

291. The practice prescribed for classical references is frequently desired by authors with respect to English references, and may with equal propriety be followed:

[1] W. W. Greg *Pastoral Poetry and Pastoral Drama* (London 1906) 114.

292. In work set on the linotype machine, footnotes should be numbered consecutively through each article in a journal, or through each chapter in a book, to save resetting in paging (see "Hints to Authors and Editors," p. 167). Monotype footnotes[1] are renumbered on each page, in makeup.

[1] *Botanical Gazette* numbers its footnotes consecutively throughout an article.

293. *a*) In botanical and other scientific material, especially the *Botanical Gazette* and the *Astrophysical Journal*, the following styles have been adopted, which conform to current practice of scientific societies:

Botanical Gazette—

[1] Livingston, B. E., (1) On the nature of the stimulus which causes the change in form of polymorphic green algae. Bot. Gaz. 30:289–317. 1900.

[2] ———, (2) The heredity of sex. Bull. Mus. Comp. Zoöl. 40: 187–218. 1903.

Astrophysical Journal—

[1] "Revision of Wolf's Sun-Spot Relative Numbers," *Monthly Weather Review*, 30, 171, 1902.

[2] *Astrophysical Journal*, 10, 333, 1899.

b) Law publications have a special style of footnote order and of abbreviation. References to the British statutes are cited as follows: regnal year in Arabic numerals, name of sovereign, comma, lower-case c. (law abbreviation for chapter) with Arabic chapter number:

[1] Act of 8 Anne, c. 19.

[2] 1 Eliz., c. 18.

LEGENDS AND CAPTIONS

294. The legend of a full-page cut without a figure number, if consisting of not more than one line, may be set in caps two or three points smaller than the text type. Such a line should be centered below the cut. The description should be set in lower case of the same size in a plain paragraph. If the page is small, the identifying legend may be set in small caps; or if the page is large and the identifying legend very long, it may be set in caps and small caps.

A MOUNTAIN FASTNESS OF THE DHAMMA
Diamond Mountains, Korea, with shrine of Kwanyin

CHILD'S DRAWING OF A CAVE AND TREES

BRITISH EAST INDIAN TROOPS AT OUR DISPOSITION FOR EXCAVATING THE GROUND PLAN OF THE TEMPLE IN THE ANCIENT FORTRESS OF DURA

295. For a numbered figure the whole legend may be set in lower case in a plain paragraph with the figure number in caps and small caps run in with a period and a dash:

FIG. 6.—So-called Laurentian layered gneiss and amphibolite on Grondine Point, Georgian Bay. This exposure is typical of the Huronian and Keweenawan complex near Killarney.

296. For illustrations of small size, the legends appear better in smaller type. All the legends should be of

the same size in the same work, but sometimes 6-point looks better than 8-point type (see 35).

ILLINOIS RIVER FROM SUMMIT OF STARVED ROCK

The Illinois River Valley was a favorite route of travel for the Indians, the early explorers, and the early settlers. Joliet, Marquette, La Salle, and Tonti all traversed the region shown in this scene.

297. Credits and copyright legends, if short, should be set in very small italic type, at the lower left of the illustrations very close to the edge.

298. In cases of adaptation or redrawing of illustrations, or where many credits must be given, put such credits in parentheses following the legend and description, and in the same type as the legend:

FIG. 48.—Outline polar view of an armadillo quadruplet egg after the completion of the process of twinning. (After Patterson.)

299. Display legends (all caps, or caps and small caps) even if longer than one line take no periods:

FIG. 57.—COLLAR, NECKLACE, AND PECTORAL ORNAMENTS OF THE LADY BITHNANAIA

300. Descriptive paragraphs of more than one line are punctuated in the same manner as text (see illustration for 298).

301. Captions serve as identification marks above such material as maps, tables, and charts. Set captions in caps, or in caps and small caps (see 320). A key to a chart or a scale of miles for a map is usually included in the illustration itself (see 35, 361, 364, 372).

MISCELLANEOUS SPACING

302. After Arabic and Roman numerals at the beginning of a center head an em quad should be used and at the beginning of paragraphs denoting subsections, a period and an en quad should be used. Cap-and-small-cap and small-cap headings in type such as used in this book should be spaced slightly wider than a 3-em space, and cap headings with an en quad; in more condensed types, these spaces should be correspondingly reduced.

303. A thin space should be used after §, ¶, and similar signs followed by figures, and after figures followed by f., ff., and the metric symbols (see 70, 142, 154, 282, 283).

304. In American and English sums of money no space is used between the symbols and the numerals following (see 209).

$395	8c.	£5 6*d.*
$1,000,000	6*s.*	£8 4*s.* 2*d.*

305. Scripture references should be spaced thus (use 9-unit colon):

II Cor. 1:16–20; 2:5, 3–12

306. Between letters forming products, before superior figures or letters indicating powers, and before inferior figures or letters, no space should be used:

$$\mu_x^2 = \Sigma m^2(v^2z^2 - 2vwyz + 2w^2y^2)$$

TABLES

307. Tables having only two columns should be set open (without rules); those of three or more are to be ruled, except in such a case as the following table. All continuations of tables should be of the same dimensions, even if blank columns are necessary, and columns with identical headings in such tables should stand parallel to one another.

TABLE I

No.	Thickness		Total Thickness	
	Feet	Inches	Feet	Inches
8. One layer of gray limestone......	4	0	2	9
7. Layer similar to one above......	2	2	6	9
6. Massive light-gray layer. No fossils noted....................	3	0	4	7
5. Shale parting....................	..	1	1	7
4. Grayish limestone...............	..	9	1	6
3. Bluish shales....................	2	3	0	9
2. Limestone, hard and fossiliferous.	5	4	8	6
1. Grayish to bluish shales.........	3	2	3	2

308. In 12-point, 11-point, and 10-point matter, open tables should ordinarily be set in 9 point leaded. Table I is set in 9 point leaded. Ruled tables in 12-point, 11-point, and 10-point matter are set in 8 point solid (Table II). In 9-point matter, both open and ruled tables should be set in 8 point solid (Table III). In 8-point matter, open tables should be set in 6 point leaded; ruled tables, in 6 point solid. In 6-point matter,

both open and ruled tables should be set in 6 point solid (see Tables IV and IX).

TABLE II

Method	π	No. Stars
I. From variable stars................	0″00008	2
II. From Kapteyn's luminosity-curves:		
C.I. −0.39 to −0.20............	.000005	17
C.I. < −0.10..................	.000007	53
C.I. < −0.10 (Pv. mag. < 15.30)...	.000009	23
C.I. −0.10 to −0.01............	.00003	33
All colors......................	.00005	495
III. From Russell's data for absolute magnitude:		
C.I. < −0.10..................	.00005	53
All colors......................	0.00010	495
Provisionally adopted mean.........	0″00003	....

309. For columns representing totals, averages, percentages, and generalizations, italic and black-face figures may be used if desired to set off the various classes of results (Table III).

TABLE III

District	Members of Family Groups		Lodgers		Total
	Number	Percentage	Number	Percentage	
Stockyards.....	6,348	*73*	2,383	*27*	**8,731**
Jewish.........	813	*79*	220	*21*	**1,033**
Bohemian......	1,183	*95*	....	....	....
Polish.........	12,657	*96*	574	*4*	**13,231**
Italian.........	2,249	*73*	835	*27*	**3,094**

310. Captions for the columns of open tables and box-heads for ruled tables should ordinarily be set in 6 point. Column heads of open tables should be in

6-point caps and lower case, unless subheads are used; in the latter case caps and small caps are to be used for the upper head (Table I). In ruled tables with box-heads of several stories, the upper story (primary heads) should be set in caps and small caps (Table IV). In such tables put the lower (secondary) in caps and lower case:

TABLE IV

MEAN ANOMALIES

CHARACTERS OF STATIONS	MEAN ANOMALIES			
	With Regard to Sign		Without Regard to Sign	
	Hayford; Depth, 113.7 km.	Bouguer	Hayford; Depth, 113.7 km.	Bouguer
Coast stations	−0.009	+0.017	0.018	0.021
Stations near coast	− .001	+ .004	.021	.025
Stations in interior, not in mountainous regions	− .001	− .028	.019	.033
Stations in mountainous regions, below sea-level	− .003	− .107	.020	.108
Stations in mountainous regions, above sea-level	+ .001	− .110	.017	.111
All stations (except the two Seattle stations)	− .002	− .036	.019	.049
All stations	−0.003	−0.037	0.020	0.050

311. In a long column of numbers, zero preceding a decimal may be omitted from all sums excepting the first and the last; with these the cipher must be given. Other digits must always be given. The decimal and the first decimal figures must not be omitted even if they are the same figures in each place throughout the table (see Tables II and IV). A similar usage is permitted for designations such as plus or minus signs (Table XI). Degrees and dollar signs must be repeated at the top of each column and after every break of column, such as total rules and cut-in heads (see Table II).

312. Where caps and small caps are used in box-heads, the heading for the "stub" (i.e., first column) should be set in caps and small caps. Cut-in heads should not cut through the stub (Table V) unless ambiguity would result. In such a case the cut-in heads should be set in small caps (see Table XII). Subheads for the stub may be set in italics, or in caps and small caps with a colon, and the lines below each should be indented (Table V).

TABLE V

THE DISTRIBUTION OF EACH GROUP IN ENGLISH IN GRADES 6-2 TO 11-2 INCLUSIVE

CLASS INTERVALS	GRADES					
	6–2	7–2	8–2	9–2	10–2	11–2
	Junior High-School Group					
First Year:						
95–100	42	33	38	23	19	15
90– 94.99	6	17	54	40	24	23
85– 89.99	65	72	54	62	53	53
80– 84.99	54	54	44	52	71	78
	Non-Junior High-School Group					
Second Year:						
95–100	29	30	43	19	19	19
90– 94.99	6	10	9	32	22	13
85– 89.99	80	77	91	67	44	47
80– 84.99	58	66	51	59	83	84

313. In ruled tables there should be a space of at least two leads between the horizontal rules and the matter inclosed. If practicable, put at least the equivalent of an en quad (of the type in which the body of the table is set), between the perpendicular rules and the matter inclosed (Table V).

314. In open tables (such as tables of contents and lists of illustrations) 9-unit leaders one and one-half ems apart may be used between the columns (see p. vii and examples below). In more compact open tables (as indexes), and in the stubs and blanks of closed tables, use period leaders to guide the reader's eye across a space to the right word or number (Tables VI and VIII) (see 317, 318).

SPACES BETWEEN NINE-UNIT LEADERS

(For Eight Point)

Nine-unit leaders with 9 units between . . . .
With 18 units between . . . .
With 27 units between . . . .
With 36 units between . . . .

(For Nine Point)

Nine-unit leaders with 9 units between . . . .
With 18 units between . . . .
With 27 units between . . . .
With 36 units between . . . .

TABLE VI

EPOCH 1923.66

e....................................	0.038
T (after light-minimum)..................	1.506 days
ω....................................	277°.5
K....................................	44.1 km
γ....................................	+16.9 km
a sin i..............................	1,736,000 km

315. An en leader is to be used in all tables to indicate a decimal point. Align all columns of figures by the decimal points. Align dollar signs, plus and minus signs, degree marks, and other indicators (Tables IV, VII,

XI). Align all digits at the right. Dissimilar items must each be centered on the column (see Table VI).

BALANCE SHEET FOR DECEMBER

Assets		
Cash	$1,500.00	
Notes receivable	100.00	
Accounts receivable	2,940.00	
Merchandise inventory	3,500.00	
Office furniture	450.00	
Delivery equipment	640.00	
Total assets		$9,130.00
Liabilities		
Notes payable to merchandise creditors . .	$ 200.00	
Accounts payable	1,300.00	
Total liabilities		1,500.00
Proprietorship		$7,630.00

316. Where space must be saved in a crowded table, set long box-headings broadside (i.e., vertically) so as to read up from the bottom of the text page (Table VII).

TABLE VII

DISPERSIONS ORIGINALLY PROPOSED

MATERIAL	NUMBER OF PRISMS	ANGLE OF PRISMS	TRANSMISSION OF PRISMS	DEVIATION OF PRISMS AT λ 4200	ANGULAR DISPERSION AT Hγ	LINEAR DISPERSION AT Hγ — Focal Lengths of Cameras: 381 mm	711 mm	965 mm
O 118.....	1	60°	.768	50° 0′	8″.51	63.6	34.1	25.1
O 118.....	1	63	.756	54 40	9.86	54.9	29.4	21.7
Ordinary...	2	63	.603	109 20	19.72	27.4	14.7	10.8
Flint......	3	63	.503	164 0	29.58	18.3	9.8	7.2

317. To express a blank in ruled columns of figures use leaders across the full width of the column (Tables III, VIII) except in "Remarks" column (Table IX). Center the figures in the column. If the number of digits is uneven, center on the majority of items and align all at the right.

318. Descriptive matter in a column of a ruled table should be centered, with runovers indented, and should be aligned on right and left. Drop down the result to align with the end of such matter (Tables VIII, IX).

TABLE VIII

	Brine	Sea-Water*		Brine	Sea-Water
K	1.37	1.11	HCO_3	0.20	....
Na	34.99	30.59	Cl...........	55.95	55.29
Mg..........	0.55	3.73	I............	Nil	....
Fe...........	....	....	Si...........	0.03	....
Al...........	0.01	....	Percentage of		
SO_4..........	4.88	7.69	salinity....	7.29	3.30

* Mean of seventy-seven analyses by W. Dittmar.

TABLE IX

Name	Observed Temperature		Remarks
	C.	F.	
Daisy Geyser.........	86°.9	188°.4	Surface drainage
Brilliant Pool.........	89.3	192.7	
Punch Bowl Spring....	93.8	200.8	12 feet diameter, bubbling on edge. Silica
None................	93.4	200.2	Bubbling spring 2 feet diameter, 50 feet southwest of Punch Bowl Spring
Black Sand Pool......	92.9	199.3	40 feet diameter, quiescent
None................	85.3	185.5	Quiescent spring, 400 feet east of Black Sand Pool. At bottom of hole
Spouter..............	93.3	199.9	25 feet diameter. Bubbling violently
None................	93.0	199.4	Bubbling spring 12 inches in diameter, 30 feet from Spouter
Rainbow Pool.........	71.7	161.0	
Old Faithful Geyser...	93.4	200.1	Temperature of steam at depth of about 10 feet. No variation in temperature could be detected over an interval of about 40 minutes

Exceptions:

Where the table is divided into groups separated by blank lines, a better appearance is secured by aligning all results with the top line of the group (Table X[1]).

TABLE X

EFFECT OF ETHYLENE (1:1000) UPON RESPIRATION OF LEMONS

LOT NO.*	TREATMENT	CARBON DIOXIDE (MG.) RESPIRED†			
		Start	First day	Second day	Fourth day
821..........	Ethylene added at start, discontinuing at end of second day	8.0	21.5	29.7	23.0
832..........	Ethylene added at start, continued throughout	8.2	15.9	21.2	31.6
849..........	Ethylene added end of second day	6.8	8.2	9.7	26.7
841..........	Check; no ethylene	7.7	12.0	8.7	9.0

* These numbers also represent the weight in grams of the sample used.
† Milligrams per hour per kilogram of fruit.

319. Double rules should be used at the top of all tables and as divisions between sections of a table set side by side when the stub is repeated or the table is doubled to save space (Table VIII). In broadside tables, continued on the opposite page where the heading is not repeated, use a single rule. Repeat the heading in such cases on each even page (see 307). When a table showing totals, such as those used in bookkeeping, must be broken at the end of a page, the balance must be added up and appear in the last line of the first part with the index "Carried forward." The same balance must be repeated in the top line of the new page with the index

[1] This table shows style used in botanical publications, especially the *Botanical Gazette.*

"Brought forward." Supplied indexes of this kind are set in italics. The figures remain in roman.

320. The table number (Table I), or the descriptive title of an unnumbered table (see below), should be set in caps in the type of the body of the table and should not exceed the width of the table. If a descriptive title follows the table number, it should be set in caps and small

SYSTEMATIC VARIATION FROM HOMOGENEITY IN $\Delta\lambda'$

Region	Group	$\Delta\lambda$	$\Delta\lambda'$	$\Delta\lambda'$ Group *c*5, *d* *minus* $\Delta\lambda'$ Group *a*, *b*
4200–4300.......	*c*5, *d*..... *a*, *b*......	.159 .163	.165 .164	+0.001
5000–5100.......	*c*5, d..... *a*........	.165 .178	.173 .180	− .007
5100–5200.......	*d*........ *a*........	.155 .170	.168 .172	−0.004

caps of the same type (see Tables X, XII). Avoid long captions set in capitals by numbering the tables in order. This method is to be used even though there are only a few tables. When 6-, 8-, and 9-point tables are used in the same work, set the headings of all in 8 point.

321. Footnotes to a table should be set in 6 point (see 288) with paragraph indention and should not exceed the width of the table (see Tables VIII, X). When tables containing footnotes run over several pages, repeat the footnotes on the even pages. Notes to a table that consist of general explanations without indexes to specific places are set in type the size of the table in plain paragraphs at the end of the table.

322. Means, averages, and totals should be indented in the stub, but the total rule should close only the columns, not the stub (Table XI).

TABLE XI

Group	c'_1	c'_2	c'_3
	km/sec.	km/sec.	km/sec.
I..............	+14.4± 1	− 4.0± 1	−10.9± 1
II..............	−44.8± 1	7.5± 1	3.1± 1
III.............	15.6± 1	15.5± 1	1.3± 1
IV, V...........	11.1± 0.8	8.9± 0.8	5.0± 0.5
VI, VII.........	13.5± 3.4	28.5± 2.6	5.2± 2.4
VIII............	−26.4± 5.3	−31.6± 4.2	− 2.4± 4.6
Mean IV–XII..	−11.6± 0.8	....	− 5.0± 0.5

323. Use the brace to preserve relations of groups (Tables XII, XIV, and the table under sec. 320). Set braced matter solid, but separate the braces by leads.

TABLE XII

Distribution of Stars in Eight Clusters

Plate (Exp.)	Ring	Sectors				Mean
		15°	45°	165°	195°	
N.G.C. 5024, Messier 53						
102 (180m).......	0*.....	....	344	....	....	325
	I......	385	384	362	376	370
	II.....	200	182	189	200	196
	III....	100	92	94	106	97
	IV.....	44	28	34	42	38

*Radius of central area .05.

324. *a*) Genealogies, pedigrees, charts showing organization or relationship, and similar subdivided or

grouped matter may be graphically represented by means of braces or rules. Several illustrations of such usage are given in Tables XII, XIV, and XV.

TABLE XIII

CHARLES THE GREAT (XII) OF SWEDEN

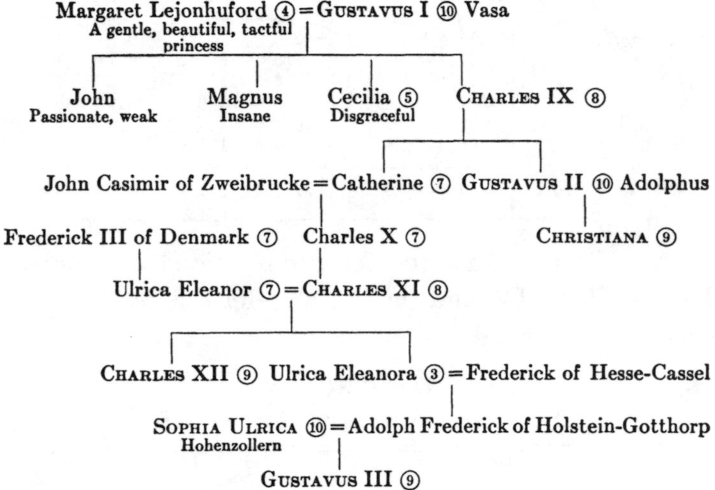

b) Chemical formulas and combinations are shown by a similar use of rules and other symbols:

$$CH_3C(:\overset{+}{N}H_2)OCH_3+\overset{+}{H}+\overset{-}{O}H\rightarrow \underset{H}{\overset{H}{HC}}—\underset{OCH_3}{\overset{NH_3}{C}}—OH\rightarrow \underset{H}{HC}{=}\underset{OCH_3}{C}—OH+\overset{+}{N}H_4$$

c) Any graphic presentation which requires the use of curved lines or unusual shapes not easily set in type should be drawn by an artist and reproduced in a zinc. Letters may be set in type and pasted on a sheet on which the drawing may then be completed.

d) The brace should be placed close to the matter inclosed and the line leading to the matter embraced should align exactly with the point of it.

TABLE XIV

		Thickness	
		Feet	Inches
Homewood (sandstone) formation			
Mercer "group"	Mercer iron-ore shales	0 to 20 }	6
	Mercer limestone	0 to 1 }	
	Mercer coal	0 to 2 }	
	Mercer shales	30	
	Mercer iron ore		2 to 6
	Mercer limestone	0 to 3	
	Mercer coal	0 to 4	
	Mercer iron-ore shales	0 to 30	
Upper Connoquenessing sandstone			

TABLE XV

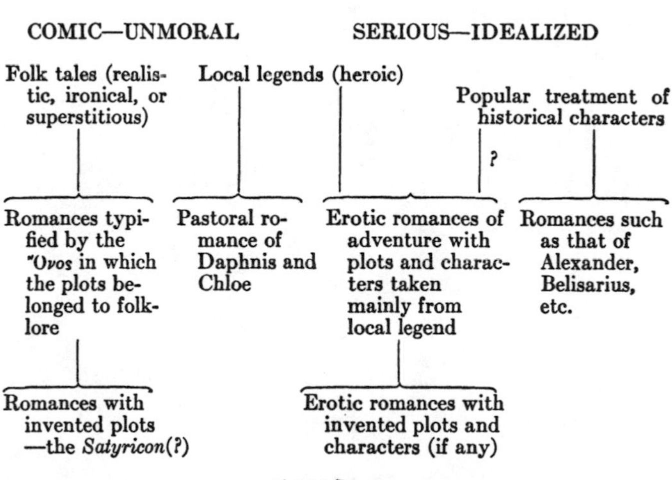

325. Vertical rules may be omitted in closed tables in such special cases as are illustrated in Table XVI:

TABLE XVI

CALCULATED NUMBERS OF STARS IN THE INTERVAL $M=\frac{1}{2}$ BRIGHTER THAN m

M	m								Limiting log ρ
	2.0	3.0	4.0	5.0	6.0	7.0	8.0	9.0	
−5.5....	1	2	3	9	19	34	55	82	4.3
4.5....	1	4	12	30	67	135	136	406	4.1
3.5....	2	8	27	76	191	429	867	1580	3.9
2.5....	4	14	48	150	419	1049	2352	4745	3.7
1.5....	5	18	68	236	735	2050	5126	11494	3.5
−0.5....	5	21	71	260	895	2787	7776	19446	3.3
+0.5....	4	17	70	240	883	3041	9468	26408	3.1
1.5....	3	13	51	204	696	2558	8810	27430	2.9
2.5....	2	8	32	127	504	1717	6309	21729	2.7
3.5....	1	4	17	67	267	1061	3620	13303	2.5
4.5....	1	2	8	31	121	480	1909	6512	2.3
N_m	29	112	412	1447	4864	15609	47603	137376	
log N_m ..	1.462	2.049	2.615	3.160	3.687	4.193	4.678	5.138	
O.−C....	+0.133	+0.074	+0.033	+0.005	−0.013	−0.018	−0.014	+0.005	
Mode....				−0.5	−0.1	+0.4	+0.8	+1.2	

FORMULAS

326. Formulas are usually set in 10 point. In text matter smaller than 10 point they may be set in 8 point. They should be centered on the page. Mathematical symbols[1] should be set without space on either side except when standing betweeen terms that are in brackets or parentheses. In such cases use a thin space on either side of the symbol. When the sentence ends after the formula, use a thin space before the period.

$$\nu_\theta=\nu_0/(1+2a\ \sin^2\tfrac{1}{2}\theta)$$

$$\left(\frac{m\beta c}{\sqrt{1-\beta^2}}\right)^2=\left(\frac{h\nu_0}{c}\right)^2+\left(\frac{h\nu_\theta}{c}\right)^2+2\frac{h\nu_0}{c}\cdot\frac{h\nu_\theta}{c}\cos\theta$$

Expressing u in terms of the moment of inertia of the molecule I, this equation becomes

$$u_r=\frac{n^2h^2}{8\pi^2I}\ .$$

327. Similar mathematical signs are to be aligned when formulas are set in columns:

The electron..................	$e=(4.774\ \pm0.005)\times10^{-10}$
The Avogadro constant........	$N=(6.062\ \pm0.006)\times10^{23}$
Number of gas molecules per cc. at 0° C. 76 cm............	$n=(2.705\ \pm0.003)\times10^{19}$
Kinetic energy of translation of a molecule at 0° C..........	$E_0=(5.621\ \pm0.006)\times10^{-14}$
Change of translational molecular energy per ° C.........	$\epsilon=(2.058\ \pm0.002)\times10^{-16}$

[1] A list of symbols in common use and their names may be found on p. 216.

328. Superior and inferior figures, letters, and characters should be on the same body as the type of the text matter and must be set close to the quantity to which they belong:

$$P(\log T_0)d(\log T_0)=\frac{h}{\sqrt{\pi}}\,e^{-h^2(\log T_0-B)^2}d(\log T_0)$$

329. The rule that separates the numerator from the denominator should be exactly as long as the longer term. Both should be centered:

$$h\nu_0=h\nu_0-mc^2\left(\frac{1}{\sqrt{1-\beta^2}}-1\right)$$

330. Where double-line formulas are run into the text matter, an effort should be made to eliminate white space by removing leads; but the standard length of type page should not be reduced in so doing.

> The dispersion in v certainly increases with M: but this does not necessarily imply a change in the dispersion in log v, since by the sixth formula, $\frac{1}{2h_v^2}=\overline{(\log v-\log \underline{v})^2}$. Thus, if the velocities of all frequencies increase in the same ratio with increasing M, the value of h_v will be independent of M.

331. The abbreviations sin, log, cos, tan, cot, cosec, mod (for sine, logarithm, cosine, tangent, cotangent, cosecant, modulus) should remain in roman in all formulas. They are to be set without abbreviating periods:

$$\sin x=2\sin\frac{x}{2}\cos\frac{x}{2}$$

332. Parentheses, brackets, summation signs, and integral signs that inclose fractional expressions must be

of exactly the same height as the tallest expression included plus dividing or vinculum rules. Pairs of such brackets and parentheses must be of the same size:

$$\int \frac{dx}{x^4\sqrt{1+x^2}} = -\int \frac{\frac{zdz}{(x^2-1)^{\frac{3}{2}}}}{\frac{1}{(x^2-1)^2}\cdot\frac{2}{(x^2-1)^{\frac{1}{2}}}} = -\int (x^2-1)dz$$

$$\int \frac{xdx}{(a+bx)^2} = \frac{1}{b^2}\left[\log\,(a+bx) + \frac{a}{a+bx}\right] + C$$

$$\lim_{n\to\infty}\left(\frac{2x+1}{x+3}\right)$$

$$\lim_{n\to\infty}\sum_{k=1}^{n}\frac{1}{k(k+1)} = 1$$

$$\begin{vmatrix} 4, & 7, & 7 \\ 5, & -4, & 2 \\ -2, & 5, & 1 \end{vmatrix} = 0$$

$$\sqrt{\frac{x-1}{x-7} + \frac{(3x+5)^2+1}{(x-7)^4}}$$

INDEX (TYPOGRAPHICAL FORMS)

333. In indexes of proper nouns and other alphabetical lists the following rules for alphabetical order should be observed:

a) Names beginning with M', Mc, Mac, or St., Ste, whether the following letter is capitalized or not, should be listed as if the prefix were spelled Mac, Saint, Sainte. Within a group of such names maintain proper alphabetic sequence of the main elements:

Machiavelli
M'Intyre, Henry
McIntyre, James
MacIntyre, Thomas
Mack, Joseph

St. Louis
Sainte Beuve
Salt Lake City
Sault Ste Marie

b) Compound names should be listed under the first part of the name. List the other parts of the names in their respective alphabetical position and give cross-references:

Campbell-Bannerman, Sir Henry
Stratton-Porter, Gene
Watts-Dunton, Theodore
Porter, Stratton, Gene. *See* Stratton-Porter

In the case of hyphenated names adopted gratuitously, as in the case of a married woman adding a maiden name to a married name, ignore the name preceding the hyphen and list under the letter of the true name, with a cross-reference for the name preceding the hyphen.

c) Names with prefixes should be listed under the main element wherever the prefix is still a separated element in form and in meaning. The examples of words from various languages illustrate this principle. Naturalized names with prefixes should be treated according to the rules for the language adopted:

Hoffmann, von; Lima, de; Ponte e Horto, da; Santos Pereira Jardin, dos

English: À Becket; De Quincey; De Morgan; D'Israeli; MacDonald; Van Buren

French: Du Moncel; La Rochefoucauld; Le Sage; Du Pin; Du Bocage; but: Rosny, de; Bouille, de; Allard, de

Italian and Spanish: La Lumia; La Farina; Lo Gatto; but: Farina, da; Rio, del; Torre, della

Prefix compounded with the name: Vanderkinde, Zurlauben, Dechambre, Vanderhoeck, Delacroix

In the case of the exceptions noted above, the first letter of the prefix governs the alphabetical position of the name.

d) In Spanish, *ch, ll,* and *rr* are individual letters and are so treated in an index.

e) Names in German spelled with the umlaut *ä, ö, ü,* should be listed as if the umlaut were spelled out (*ae, oe, ue*):

Müller, A. Mufola, C. Muller, B.

f) Names having two parts or names of firms connected by "and," "&," "y" (Spanish), "et" (French), "und" (German), or "e" (Italian) should be listed according to the first letter of the name preceding the connective:

Smith & Evans (under "S")
Gomez y Pineda (under "G")

Loubet et Meunier (under "L")
Duncker und Humblot (under "D")
Sandrone e Vallardi (under "S")

g) In an index of general terms the alphabetical arrangement should be according to the first principal word (i.e., adjective, noun, verb, adverb; not the article, conjunction, or preposition):

Numbers: beginning a sentence, 73; in connected groups, how treated, 74; consecutive treatment of, 113, 119; round, 73; use of dash in consecutive, 119

334. Good cross-references are of vital importance in an index. For instance, if "Mankind" is indexed under that catchword, "Human beings," "Race," "People," when added in their own alphabetical places, should be followed by the cross-reference:

See Mankind

Cross-references may also be employed to save duplication: for instance, when "Child welfare" is listed under "C," the entry under "W" should read:

Welfare, child, *see* Child welfare

335. An index that is little more than a full table of contents, with one page reference to each item, may be set full measure and leadered out to the page number (see A and B. Examples of styles are shown on pp. 159–62). If space allows, for clearness, let each subdivision occupy a separate line (see C). Indexes of short lines, such as chapter and verse references, are set in double columns or in more if the page arrangement is adapted to such style. The type should be two or three points smaller than that of the body of the book.

336. An extensive index should be set in double column. A page number follows its entry, with a separating comma. Runovers should be solid, indented one em, with 2 points between entries and with a quad line between alphabetical changes of initial letters. If the page is very narrow and space is precious, the runovers may be indented one en instead of one em (see D). When indented subdivisions run over to the top of a verso page, the main catchword should be repeated with a continuation line (see G). Index letters may be centered above each block belonging under that letter.

337. There are various ways to classify specific references, if it seems necessary, by using special typography. For instance, in a book containing bibliographies, page references to the bibliography may be set in italic or in bold-face type, but such usage should be explained in a bracketed note under the heading of the index. References to sections or illustrations may be in bold-face, and to pages in light-face type (see E). Also, book or section may be expressed in Roman numerals (bold-face or italic) and page references in Arabic figures in ordinary roman face (see J).

338. Various systems of punctuation are used, but the simplest is the best. Always use a comma between a catchword and the page number. In case a single reference includes consecutive pages, use an en dash between the first and last page numbers. Subentries with their page numbers may be run in with semicolons between; in such instances the main catchword is followed by a colon.

339. Occasionally an index requires subentries under subentries. Double indention is then necessary, or special side-heads may be used. If such special side-heads are used, they may be set in caps and small caps or in italics with or without a colon or a dash; never both (see B and G).

340. If several subdivisions of entries are necessary, the main entries may be indicated by setting in bold-face, small caps, or italics. Care should be taken, however, that the style chosen does not conflict with any other meaning of the same form of typography (see F, note).

341. Another device to obviate the necessity for double indention or repetition of a catchword is the use of an em dash to take the place of the first word of a subject as in bibliographies (see G). This index is arranged according to sequence instead of alphabetical order.

342. In a mixed index of subjects and authors it is sometimes desired to bring out authors' names. Such names may then be set in caps and small caps (see H).

343. Beware of confusing identity by indexing individuals of different families under the same surname. The same rule applies to subjects that would be confused by similar treatment.

344. Ordinarily the appearance of the index page will be better if the first word of each general entry is capitalized; but in some cases, such as in the index to a grammar or the vocabulary of a book in a foreign language, all catchwords should appear in exactly the same form as on the text page (see I and J). Here, of course, the

form is too important to be lost in the niceties of typography. The same usage should prevail in the reference list of a dictionary or glossary. Instructions for preparing an index may be found in section 389.

345. Examples of various kinds of indexes that show the typographical usage required are here given. The heading of each block of examples is lettered to correspond with references in the foregoing rules. It is to be remembered that the value of any index lies in its service for quick reference, and by that test author, editor, and compositor may answer all questions of technique and style:

A. CONTENTS TYPE OF INDEX

B. CONTENTS TYPE WITH SUBDIVISIONS

C. INDEX WITH ENTIRELY SEPARATED LINES

masque, 86
mass, 30, 50, 51, 53, 131, 133, 137, 186
Massenet, J., 262, 163
mauresca, 78
Mayer, C., 227
mazurka, 176, 177, 238
medieval dramas, 75
  music, 28–47

milk, boiled, 187, 355
  bottled, 184
  certified, 184–85
  clean, 153, 157, 185
  condensed, 101, 161, 185
mirage, 185
  desert, 185
  distance, 191

D. STYLE FOR AN EXTENSIVE INDEX

Explanation: of technical terms, 251–94; use of brackets for, 173

Expositions, capitalization of names of, 17

"Extra," compounds with, 209

Extracts, rules for punctuation of, 112

Eye, as a guide, 128; measurement proved, 130; portions of, 136; training, 171

Foreign languages: division of words in, 231; English translation accompanying word, phrase, or passage cited from, to be quoted, 78; sentences and passages quoted from, how to treat, 59, 85; words and phrases borrowed from, incorporated into English, how to treat, 59

Foreign titles of publications, capitalization of, 42

E. INDEX WITH SPECIAL TYPOGRAPHY

[References to definitions of terms or characteristics of plants and animals are in italics; illustrations are in bold-face type; other references in ordinary type.]

Basalt, **19**, *75*, 76
Beach association, 115, **119**
Bearberry, 124, *125*
Bee, carpenter, 219
Beech, **204**
  water, 137, *138*, **140**, 205, 206, 270
Beechfern, 210, **213**
Birds:
—Bittern, American, 240, **243**; least, *240*
—Blackbird, redwinged, **242**, 243
—Cardinal grosbeak, **270**, 271
—Kingbird, 156, **157**

Bloodroot, *Sanguinaria canandensis*, *128*, 150, **276**
Blue Island, 36, 78, **85**, 86
Bluffs, **2**, 259, **260**
Boneset, *Eupatorium perfoliatum*, *201*, 203, **207**
Butterflies, *see Lepidoptera*

Cactus, *Opuntia Rafinesquii*, **98**, 99, *132*
Chalk, *71*
Chicago, Lake, see Lake Chicago; site of, 50, 52, 57, **64**
Clover:
—Bush, 27, **29**

INDEX

F. INDEX SHOWING DOUBLE SUBENTRIES

G. THE USE OF THE DASH

[1] Here it would be better to use caps and small caps to avoid two uses of italics.

H. SPECIAL STYLE IN MIXED INDEX

I. STYLE FOR A GRAMMAR OR A FOREIGN-LANGUAGE BOOK

[All references are to sections except as otherwise indicated. Japanese words are in bold-face type.]

J. SPECIAL PHILOLOGICAL STYLE

HINTS TO AUTHORS, EDITORS AND READERS

HINTS TO AUTHORS AND EDITORS

PREPARATION OF MANUSCRIPT

346. In submitting copy an author may rely on the judgment of his publisher with regard to format and typographical style. Vexation and delay are the usual results of interference with one who is a specialist in book-making. If the author has an idea he wishes carried out, he should talk it over with the publisher in order to get proper help on the details. If on the other hand he is willing to leave the work entirely to the publisher's judgment, he should ask for a dummy with a few pages set showing the type, margins, stock, binding, and stamping. He may then make suggestions before giving his approval. This method is far more satisfactory than costly experimenting with the proof. If an author will try to visualize type style before putting copy into final typewritten form, he will aid his publisher by producing intelligently arranged manuscript.

The rules and suggestions contained in this *Manual of Style* are intended to help authors and editors to prepare manuscript in such a manner. The entire book should be studied with care. The more closely copy conforms to the style in which it is to be set, the less work will be left to the copyreader in editing.

347. Manuscripts should be typewritten, double spaced, or be written in a perfectly clear hand in ink. The former is preferable for many reasons. Original

copy should always be furnished, not a carbon or a mimeographed copy. A duplicate copy of manuscript should always be kept by the author for possible reference needs and likewise as protection against loss of the original.

348. The sheets should be of uniform size, preferably $8\frac{1}{2}\times 11$ inches. Only one side of the paper should be used. Manuscripts should never be rolled. They should be placed flat in a box or envelope, and if sending by mail, one should be sure that the container is tough enough not to wear through. The package should be carefully marked with the author's return address, and properly insured or registered.

349. The sheets should not be sewed or tied together, but should be fastened only with clips or pins, which may be easily removed. When an addition or an insert is to be made, the sheet should be cut and the insert pasted in the proper place. No fliers should be attached, for they may be torn off. Nor should parts of sheets be pinned on: they may become unfastened and misplaced. Each new chapter should begin at the top of a sheet, and the pages belonging to that chapter should be clipped together separately. Liberal margins should be left at the top and at the left-hand side of the sheet. Such space is needed by the copyreader or printer for directions for setting.

350. All pages should be numbered consecutively. Any change of pagination through insertion or omission must be indicated unmistakably. Full pages only should be inserted, and each should be placed *after* the sheet on

which new matter is to be run in. Thus, "Insert A" on a numbered manuscript page has reference to "A" on the next page, a full-sheet insert that bears the true page number followed by a letter. If four sheets, for instance, are inserted after page 40 of a manuscript, make a marginal note on page 40 "Insert 40A–40D" and number the inserted pages 40A, 40B, 40C, 40D.

Where used, mark such inserts both at point of insertion ["Insert A" here] and in brackets above the copy ["Insert A"]. If the result is illegible, retype the entire page, adding a full insert sheet if necessary. Only brief inserts of a word or two or a sentence should be attempted on the margin.

351. Quotations and footnotes may be single spaced as a sign that they are to be set in smaller type. Footnotes should be designated by separation from the text by lines running entirely across the page, or by use of a different-colored typewriter ribbon. They should never be run into the text in copy, whether in parentheses or otherwise. The word in the text to which the note refers should be followed by a superior figure corresponding to that preceding the note. Cite references according to the standard rules (see 282–93).

352. Since it is impossible to foresee how the notes will happen to come out in the makeup, it is inadvisable to number them in manuscript from 1 up on each page. The best way is to number them consecutively throughout a journal article or in a book by chapters. It is important to remember that in matter set on the linotype machine the slightest change calls for the resetting of a

whole line. Bear in mind that the change, by omission or addition, of a single number involves the resetting of the whole first line of each succeeding note to the end of that series, as well as the line in the text bearing the reference to the note. This difficulty is not encountered in matter set on the monotype or by hand, where the change of a number amounts simply to substituting one figure for another. This is done in makeup.

Study the sections on "Footnotes" (see 27–30, 282–93) in this book, and make your footnote copy agree with the rules there given.

353. Do not abbreviate references to publications, expecting the printer to spell out the full form. Even if footnotes are so numerous that it seems best to abbreviate repeated references to the same work, spell out the exact title the first time it is used and abbreviate consistently all later references. If there are many such instances, a list of abbreviations may well appear in the preliminary pages.

354. Tables and illustrations should be numbered in separate series consecutively through an entire article or book (see 320). Do not number them separately in each chapter or section.

355. For numbering chapters, tables, plates, charts, inserted maps and graphs use Roman numerals. Arabic numerals are used for text illustrations.

356. Legends are properly titles. They usually are not complete sentences and are not to have sentence punctuation. A description following the title line is punctuated the same as the text (see 294–301).

357. Differentiate between a synopsis and an abstract. The former should be the outline of what follows in the chapter or book division. An abstract, on the other hand, is a connected résumé of contents.

358. Copy for title-pages, preface, table of contents, list of illustrations, and so on, should be submitted with the manuscript. Copy for indexes should be compiled from the extra set of page proof furnished for that purpose, and should be delivered to the printer soon after final approval of all pages preceding the index. Delayed publication is often due to the author's tardiness in supplying the index (see 203 ff.). For proper forms of index see 333–45.

COPYRIGHTS

359. In case of quotation or abstract from the copyrighted work of any other author, it is necessary for the writer to obtain permission from both author and publisher, and in addition to see that proper credit is given in the form prescribed by the publisher.

360. The publisher usually attends to securing the copyright on the completed book either in his own name or in that of the author, as mutually agreed upon. If your own publisher cannot supply the necessary information, secure an official statement of copyright law and procedure by making application to the Register of Copyrights, Washington, D.C.

ILLUSTRATIONS

361. The first question to be considered in regard to illustrations for a book, is whether the figures shall be distributed in the text or aggregated into plates. Since

the decision of this question has a distinct bearing on the mechanical makeup of the book, it should be made only in consultation with the printer or publisher. If a rough (eggshell) paper is desirable for the text, on account of its lightness and bulking properties, only coarse line-drawings can be used unless the illustrations are put in as plates. The presence of fine line-drawings and half-tones in the text calls for the use of a highly finished, heavy, and non-bulking paper.

When its use is feasible, the text figure (i.e., one inserted into the type page) is usually preferable, because it can be placed at the point of greatest service to the reader. In scientific works, however, plates are preferable when a series of figures must be before the eye at one time, or when some figure must be referred to at many points in the text.

When it has been determined whether text figures or plates are to be used, the mode of reproduction must be selected, for it is necessary to adapt the copy to the method.

Where text figures are used, it is obvious that a printing block, or cut, of the same nature as the type itself must be provided. Such blocks are: wood engravings, wax engravings, zinc etchings, and halftones. The following hints for the preparation of copy for these various processes will be found useful (see 362–72).

362. *Wood engravings* are particularly adapted to the illustration of machinery, furniture, wearing apparel, and similar subjects. They are also well adapted to the reproduction of geometrical figures in mathematical

textbooks. In the production of wood printing blocks everything depends upon the engraver, who must himself be an artist, since much of the design is cut with a graver by hand. While almost any kind of copy can be used by a competent engraver, photographs or finished drawings and paintings are preferred.

363. *Wax engraving* is the best medium for reproducing maps, charts, and geometrical figures. Any copy which shows the correct outline of the subject in such form that it can be transferred to the wax plate by photography or tracing can be used. Such copy will prove much less expensive than the usual haphazard pencil sketches which leave all the details and much of the form for the engraver to puzzle out. Accurate drawings, either in pencil or ink, are needed.

364. *Zinc etchings* will reproduce any drawing or print with solid black lines or dots on a white background. It is even possible, by the use of color filters, to pick out one or more from a number of colors with reasonable fidelity. The printer should, however, be consulted in such cases before the copy is finally submitted. In preparing copy for zinc etching, bear in mind that gradations of tint cannot be reproduced, and that therefore the lines of the design must be in solid color, regardless of their thickness. Only india ink should be used and gray or broken lines should be avoided. In making drawings on cross-section paper, as in plotting out graphs, a blue-lined paper should be selected, for blue does not photograph. If it is desired to show the cross-lines in the illustrations, a paper lined in black should be selected.

Care should be taken that the lines are not ragged or broken. If the figures are to be lettered, different degrees of reduction should be taken into account so that the lettering on all the figures will be reproduced in the same size. Where parts of zinc-etched figures are to be shaded, the shading can often be put in to advantage with Ben Day tints. Consult the printer on this point.

365. *Halftones* are adapted to the reproduction of photographs, wash drawings, and paintings, either in black and white or in colors. Engravers prefer glossy photographic prints, for these give better results than dead-finished or mat prints. It should be remembered that at best the halftone is but an approximation of the original, and that only the most favorable conditions of all the elements of copy, engraving, ink, paper, and presswork can bring the final result to anything near the original subject. The author should, therefore, use every effort to furnish his printer the best possible copy from which to work. Halftones are sometimes specially designated as "hand-tooled," when, by the use of a graver, they are given the appearance of woodcuts, or "highlight" when the light parts are entirely cut away. The finishes of the edges are designated as "square," "lined," "vignetted," or "outlined." Combinations of line and halftone cuts are frequently made by stripping the two kinds of negatives together on one plate.

366. Through the use of plates, a much wider range of methods of illustration, including those mentioned above, is possible. The processes which may be added are: gelatine plates (heliotype, albertype, collotype,

etc.), lithography (including photolithography and offset printing), photogravure, steel and copper engraving, rotagravure, and three- and four-color halftones. Since all these are in a large degree dependent on photography, the copy should permit an exact reproduction in all respects except as to size.

367. *Gelatine plates* and *photogravure,* made by two very different processes, give perhaps the most faithful reproduction of photographic subjects. The former is not particularly expensive, and is especially well adapted to scientific work where detail is important.

368. *Lithography,* in its modern adaptation to the offset press, has come into much more general use than formerly. By the offset process straight black-and-white subjects may be photographically reproduced with great fidelity, and much finer drawings copied than by zinc etching. By it, also, photographs and paintings are reproduced in black and white or in colors. Lithography on stone—the original process—while now little used commercially, remains the most accurate process known for the reproduction of subjects in color. It is, however, very expensive, and much depends on the skill of the lithographic artist. In the case of all the lithographic processes, the original copy should be prepared exactly as it is finally to appear.

369. *Steel* and *copper engravings* and *rotagravures* are used chiefly for portraits and landscapes. Copy should be provided in the form of photographs or paintings.

370. *Process work* is the common name for three- and four-color halftones, by which subjects in color can be

reproduced in close approximation. It is well adapted for many illustrations of this character. Compared with the cost of lithography, process work is much cheaper. An exact original copy should be provided for this method.

371. The printer should be consulted in every case with reference to the best method of reproduction.

372. *Lettering* on cuts should be of uniform size, large enough to reduce with the lines of the cut and still be in correct proportion to the illustration itself. Parts of a compound figure consisting of separate units should be lettered *A*, *B*, *C*, etc. (italic); sections in each component part should be lettered *a*, *b*, *c*, etc. When several series of letters are necessary on the same plate, be careful that there is no confusion of meaning. If possible, each letter on the cut should be explained at length in the description; otherwise, in the text. Lettering on the margin of the cut is better set in type. Such cuts, however, should be ordered trimmed flush and anchored, to admit of placing the type close up to the face of the illustration.

ESTIMATING MANUSCRIPTS

373. The most accurate method of estimating the amount of space a given manuscript will occupy when set in type is to determine the number of characters—letters, points, and spaces—that the manuscript contains, and to divide that total by the number of characters in the type page it is desired to use. In the case of typewritten manuscript, this computation is very simple. Nearly all typewriting is in either "Pica" or

"Élite" type—the former ten and the latter twelve characters to the lineal inch. It remains, therefore, only to find the total number of lines and the average length of line in inches, and to follow that step by a simple computation. If the manuscript is divided into chapters, each chapter should be figured separately, to provide for the partially blank pages at the beginning and the end. Partially blank lines at the close of paragraphs should be counted as whole lines. To the total of all chapters should be added the pages occupied by the preliminary pages, the index, and any illustrations.

Suppose, for instance, a chapter of fifty pages of Élite typewriting, with thirty seven-inch lines to the page, to be printed in a type page $4 \times 6\frac{1}{2}$ inches in size, composed in 11-point Oldstyle No. 31, leaded with two points. There would be 84 characters to the line, times 30, times 50=126,000 characters. Eleven-point Oldstyle No. 31, with 2-point leads, averages 100 characters to the square inch, or 2,600 to a page of $4 \times 6\frac{1}{2}$ inches. Dividing 126,000 by 2,600 gives 49 pages for the chapter.

In computing hand-written manuscript, choose pages of average density for word-counting, in order to arrive at a basis for the number of characters on a page. A considerable variation will be found among the different pages of this class of manuscript, and the author will need to use added care in his method of estimating.

The process is simplified by use of the data in this book under "Specimens of Type." Statements given there of the number of characters to a square inch of each style and size of body type are for authors and editors in estimating manuscripts. First determine the number of type characters (letters and spaces between words) on a manuscript page; then use the statistical data.

READING OF PROOFS

374. All proofs should be read and returned promptly. As soon as copy is in galley form the publisher sets up his schedule for the completion of the work, based upon the date of release for publication and an allowance of ample time for each operation. It is rarely possible to speed up these operations without sacrificing somewhere the quality of the product. After the publication date has been set and all the machinery of advertising and sales put in motion, it is imperative that no unnecessary delay be incurred in any part of the work. If the author holds the proof unduly, he will throw into confusion all the careful plans of his publisher, and sacrifice quality of workmanship or specially timed sales—perhaps both.

375. It is best to return proofs complete, with everything supplied and in order for paging up. This saves not only the author's time but the printer's also.

In case a work consists of a large number of pages, or is so complicated as to require intricate corrections, running type around cuts, or careful revision before paging, it may be advantageous to the makeup to return a few chapters at a time, in their proper order. In such instances care must be taken to keep material ahead, so that the printer need not wait for galleys at any time.

376. In marking proof sheets use the standard proofreader's marks (see p. 189). Make all marks on the margin opposite the line in which correction should be made,

and if several belong to a single line, put them exactly in the order of their occurrence.

377. Be careful to answer all queries on the proofs. Do not erase the proofreader's marks or queries. If you approve a suggestion made, cross out the question mark and let the correction stand. If you do not approve, cross out the whole question, or answer in full. Delays and errors may result from failure to attend to such queries. Cross-references, especially, should be checked by the actual pages, for no one but the author can say with certainty to what page he intended to refer.

378. All changes made by the author, whether in type or in the arrangement of paragraphs or illustrations, including the time spent in the re-reading by copy of subsequent proofs caused by the overrunning of matter, are rated as author's alterations and are at the publisher's expense. On the other hand, actual changes from manuscript when carried to an extreme react upon the author by compelling payment for all alterations above an agreed maximum. The percentage of total cost that is to be allowed for corrections will be reported to an author by his publisher; if the amount allowed is not stated in the contract, the author should inquire regarding the facts.

379. An author should realize that returning galley proofs to his printer implies that he will make no further changes of matter in his text. Single words or even phrases of equal spacing may be substituted thereafter, but only under real necessity. Changes made in type are expensive. To omit a word or to add one in the body of

a paragraph may cause the resetting of all of that paragraph following the point of change. If the alteration is in galley proof, the expense stops with the paragraph reconstruction; if, however, the change is made in the page proof, it may further involve repaging the entire article or chapter. Make your manuscript as perfect as possible before delivering it to the printer. Read your galley proof as carefully as possible, as corrections in succeeding stages add to the cost. Corrections in plates should be avoided, not only because they are expensive, but because they are likely to injure the plates.

380. The original manuscript should always be returned with the galley proof, in order that the proofreader may refer to it, should any question arise. Each successive set of proofs should be accompanied by the previous marked set, which is always used in computing the cost of alterations properly chargeable to the author. No change should ever be made in manuscript which has been set or in proof that has been corrected and a later proof pulled.

The author should retain a duplicate set of proofs bearing all corrections, as protection against loss of the sheets in transit to his printer. Frequently the last manuscript sheet sent out with proof will contain matter that is to be set on the next proof sheet beyond that lot. In that event hold back the unfinished manuscript sheet to read against the page proof bearing the unread matter. In the same manner hold over the last sheet of page proof having matter beyond the manuscript in that lot. Note any holdover of this sort on the last page returned to the printer.

381. Corrections of general character and those regarding proof that has passed from your hands should never go with proof being returned to the printer. Report such items, carefully defined, by letter; moreover, keep a copy of the letter for check against the final page proof.

382. When returning part or all of the final page proof, send a letter to your publisher indicating that such pages are ready for printing. This procedure will hasten the printing process in the manufacture of a large book.

383. An extra set of page proofs is always sent to the author for indexing (358). As the index cannot be set to advantage until all page numbers can be supplied exactly, it is best to begin compiling the index as soon as the first pages come from the printer. Copy for the index should be sent to the printer immediately upon the return of the final page proofs (see 333–45 and 384–89).

INDEXING

384. Every book that may be used as reference or authority merits a good index, i.e., one which enables the reader or student to locate readily the subject or item he seeks. The usefulness of a book often depends wholly on its index. To make one of real merit, however, is a technical operation of some difficulty. One unfamiliar with the subject is apt to make serious errors. For this reason the publisher usually requires each author to make his own index or to arrange to have it done under his own supervision. The error in this arrangement is in

supposing too often that an author knows how to make an index properly. For typographical style of index, see 333–45.

385. The treatment required, both editorially and typographically, varies with the kind of book and the use to which the index is to be put. Some books and some subjects are indexed more easily than others. A book of sermons or lectures, a collection of poems, a yearbook, or a work of argumentation, complete only in its sequence, will require a much simpler index than that needed for a scientific work, for a book of unrelated facts, statistics, or ideas, needed frequently for reference.

386. A collection of addresses or sermons could very well be indexed by principal words in titles of chapters, by subtitles, by proper names, and by subjects. This form need not be much more complicated than a very full table of contents. The items of such an index should not be consecutive, however, without regard to alphabetical order of the subentries; neither should it be laden with long entries to indicate any conclusions or the progression of thought. The index, unlike the text, is not *read;* it is *referred to*, and only those catchwords actually needed are read at any one time.

387. The best usage in all indexes is to arrange entries and subentries alphabetically. A book of poems, if large and consisting of works of many classes, may require a subject index, an author index, and an index of first lines. These will all be fairly simple and will need little subdivision. A comparative study of literary

manuscripts or a book of the Synoptic Gospels may need also a reference index, listing in numerical order the chapters and verses studied. A scientific work that is invariably used for reference and for authority requires a full general index including both subjects and proper names; also, it may have its references divided into a subject index and an author index.

388. The indexing of complex and involved subjects requires a thorough knowledge of the subject matter, as well as a technical knowledge of the typographical form that best expresses it. Suppose, by way of example, that the work or passage to be indexed is one covering the several processes of photo-engraving, a complex and intricate subject. If each process is treated separately in the text under its appropriate title, the work of indexing will be comparatively easy. But if all the various processes are covered by paragraphs more or less general, and without special segregation of subjects, every item must be searched out and put into its part of the index. Without such discrimination a casual glance at the index may fail to indicate that some particular branch of the subject is treated at all. Superficial indexing may cause a failure to use the book.

389. The simplest way to prepare an index is by means of slips or cards. The 3×5 size is easy to handle. First read over the whole book carefully, underlining in blue pencil all words to be indexed, whether as general entries or as subentries. If marking for a professional indexer, underline the subentries in red pencil, and note in the margins in blue the catchwords under which they

should be indexed. In this operation the full program of the index is developed clearly.

When the entire book has been so marked, enter the items on cards. Each entry with its page number is written on a separate card. Next sort the cards into stacks in alphabetical order. Then arrange them in a card file or in a box enough larger than the cards to allow plenty of room for rearranging.

When all the marked words and expressions have been transferred to cards, perfect the alphabetical arrangement and combine the subentries in alphabetical order under each main entry. Wherever there are a number of page references for one item, such figures should appear in numerical sequence. The entire series of card entries may be typewritten on sheets, with carbon copy, for the convenience of the printer in setting. Be careful to show capitalization, punctuation, and indentions.

Verify all items by checking the markings of the text manuscript against the carbon copy of the index manuscript. A good method is to cross out every item as found until all have been checked.

Verify page references if possible in the galley proof of the index and leave the details of paging to the publisher. Waiting for the return of page proofs of an index may seriously hamper the presswork and the completion of the volume.

HINTS TO COPYREADERS

BOOK COPY

390. Read the specifications very carefully. Do not neglect to re-read them often in the course of editing if there is any doubt as to what is wanted.

391. Look through all the copy and check the headings and subheadings with the table of contents. If there is no table of contents, make one.

392. Examine the dummy. Visualize the completed book with all its parts (see 10–46).

393. If the preliminaries are incomplete, supply those missing or else insert blank sheets in their place while waiting for the author to supply them.

394. If copy for cuts is attached, mark their places, identify the copy so that no mistake can be made, see that the sizes are marked, and detach them to send to the engraver after the legends have been edited. They should not be sent, however, until all the copy has been edited and descriptions in the text have been checked with lettering or references on the copy for the illustrations.

395. Read the preface to get the purpose of the book in mind. Then proceed to edit the copy for the machine operator and the proofreader.

396. "Editing" is a very broad term. It implies a careful and critical literary survey of the context; yet

this type of editing is not permitted to the copyreader unless special instructions give such freedom. Not a single word of the author's meaning may be changed. However, contradictions, duplications, obvious errors of fact, incomplete statements, or incorrect sentences are to be queried (see 408). If, after reading a portion of the text, the copyreader finds carelessly written copy, he should immediately take up the question with the publisher's editor and get exact instructions before proceeding farther.

397. Primarily, the copyreader's task is to prepare the copy for composition by marking the measure, the sizes of type for text, quotations, footnotes, headings, subheadings, tables, legends, etc.; to apply the adopted rules of typography; and to check the author's consistency in his use of capitalization, citation, spelling, punctuation, and his sentence structure. At every step it is necessary that the copyreader imagine the printed page before him. Simplicity and exactness of typographical expression are of the greatest importance. Expense also must be considered, and mechanical difficulties must be foreseen and forestalled. Quality must never be sacrificed. Consequently a nicety of judgment must be exercised constantly. Read everything as if you were the author. If the copy is not perfectly clear, or if you have reason to doubt its correctness, look up the point or query it to the publisher's editor.

398. For standards of typographical form refer to this *Manual of Style*. The copyreader is expected to be thoroughly familiar with its rulings and to use them, un-

less expressly instructed in copy to use a contrary style. For spelling and divisions use *Webster's International Dictionary* unless the *Manual of Style* makes an exception. The latter is final authority.

399. Do not query a misspelled word in ordinary text. Look it up if you are not certain, and thereby learn it for future use. The proofroom library is for your convenience. Never query style to the author. If you cannot be sure what style should be used, confer with the editor. Do not allow book matter to be put in type with questions of style unsettled. Do not leave it for the operator to decide which of several forms is the intended one, nor for the proofreader to make it consistent after it is set.

400. Verify all days and dates and check them so that the proofreader may know you have done so.

401. Co-ordinate all headings and subheadings; check the sequence of all numbered headings; supply missing letters when abbreviations must be spelled out. Take special care with proper names.

402. Check the copy for cuts for sequence, size, possibilities of reproduction, identification. Edit the captions or legends, mark the lettering or marginal figures that should be set in type, and the places where cuts are to appear. Number text figures in Arabic and plates in Roman numerals, and hand the copy to the proper person to order the engravings.

403. Observe the rules for tabular work (see 307–25). Do not leave copy in tables inconsistent. Double the stub if necessary to widen or shorten the material.

Keep footnotes to tables in their correct sequence. The author rarely attempts any arrangement of such notes.

404. Mark the different sizes of type so prominently that the operator will recognize them at a glance. Leave the ordinary text unmarked; indicate reductions by a red line along the left margin; indicate footnotes by a blue line similarly placed.

405. Familiarize yourself with the names given in the *Annual Register* and the Press *Catalogue*. There is no excuse for misinterpreting or misspelling the name of a member of the Faculty or the title or name of the author of a book published by the house for which you work.

JOURNAL COPY

406. Read the composition ticket for any special instructions. See that the copy is slugged with the name of the author and the name of the journal. If copy is for a minor division of a journal, so designate on the manuscript.

407. Keep the last journal beside you for ready reference. Verify the sizes of type by the specifications. Mark the measure in the upper left-hand corner of the first sheet of copy, and below a separating line give the size of type to be used for the text.

408. Keep the style of the journal for which you are editing. Each has peculiarities of its own. Study the preferences of each editor as evidenced by the way he answers queries, the changes he makes, the condition of his copy. One editor may expect you to do as a matter of course what another would consider an unwarranted interference if suggested.

HINTS TO PROOFREADERS

409. Various printing offices differ in their methods of handling proof. In fact there may be different requirements on different jobs in the same office. One job may require more care, closer punctuation, and more reading than another. An author may be glad to pay for the added time spent on his work, or the nature of his material may make extra care imperative. Newspaper copy and trade journal matter are usually given one reading, and that a very fast one, sometimes without a copyholder. Fine magazines and book work require three or four readings. Technical books are frequently read as many as eight times or even more, each time with great care.

410. The proofreader acquires speed only through practice and training. He must have the ability to think quickly, a ready judgment, and a thorough knowledge of the subject—all of which may be acquired only through study and experience. He has an important service to render in any printing operation.

411. College or university education is the best preparation for proofreading, but added to this must be a thorough knowledge of printing; of faces and sizes of types, symbols, spaces, furniture; of all the materials needed in the composition of printed matter, whether machine- or handset; and some understanding of composition and the processes of plating, presswork, and bind-

ing. The reader must be able to tell at sight whether a lead is too thick or too thin, and to discriminate between a thick space and a thin space. He must be able to detect a change of type face, even of a single letter of Modern mixed with Old Style, or vice versa. He must be able to tell whether a lockup is square and must know type that is off its feet ever so slightly.

412. Proofreader's marks vary somewhat, but all sets of marks have the same general intent. They are simply symbols adopted for expediency, to save writing out instructions that take time and space. The marks now in common usage are shown and defined on page 189.

413. All marks should be made in the margin on the same line as the error, and if there is more than one correction in a line, they should appear in their order separated by a slant line (i.e., *cap/wf/tr/*); if there are many, both margins may be used for marks.

414. Guide lines should be used only when the material is of narrow measure without margins, or if corrections are too numerous to be marked in ordinary manner. Such guide lines, if used, should never cross each other.

415. Proof should be marked in ink, and no erasures should be attempted. If it is necessary to change marks once made, they should be crossed out.

416. Broken letters should be ringed, not blotted out; also letters to be transposed should be ringed, not marked through.

HINTS TO PROOFREADERS

PROOFREADER'S MARKS

	Delete and close up	en|	En dash
	Reverse	;|	Insert semicolon
	Close up	(:)	Insert colon and en quad
#	Insert space	(.)	Insert period and en quad
¶	Paragraph	?|	Insert interrogation point
□	Indent one em	(?)	Query to author
[	Move to left		Use ligature
]	Move to right	(sp)	Spell out
⊔	Lower	tr	Transpose
⊓	Elevate	wf	Wrong font
∧	Insert marginal addition	bf	Set in **bold face** type
V∧	Even space	rom	Set in roman type
×	Broken letter	ital	Set in *italic* type
	Push down space	caps	Set in CAPITALS
	Straighten line	sc	Set in SMALL CAPITALS
‖	Align type	lc	Set in lower case
	Insert comma		Lower-case letter
	Insert apostrophe	stet	Let it stand
	Insert quotes	no ¶	Run in same paragraph
=|	Hyphen	ld>	Insert lead between lines
em|	Em dash	hr #	Hair space between letters

GALLEY READING

417. Accuracy is the first requirement in galley reading; the next is to carry out faithfully the copyreader's intention in typography. If the copy has not been edited, the proofreader's task is much more difficult. It then requires thinking quickly, exercising careful judgment, and weighing the cost of change against the values of appearance and correctness. Contradictions, duplications, errors of fact, anachronisms, imperfect sentences, solecisms, barbarisms, and so on are to be detected by the reader and pointed out. Such corrections are very costly if made in the type; therefore most printing houses whose work must be of good quality employ editors and copyreaders to prepare their copy before passing it to the compositor. When this is not done, the proofreader must assume such responsibility.

If the copy has been edited, the galley reader has but to prove that the printer has interpreted the copyreader's marks correctly. This task is not an easy one under the best conditions.

The best galley reading consists of two operations—a preparatory silent reading for purely typographical errors, and a reading with the copyholder for accuracy, sense, and all other possible errors of consistency. In preparatory reading the proofreader should note the condition of the copy so that he can time the first reading to a speed that will insure perfect accuracy.

418. Particular care should be taken with proper names, figures, and scientific terms. If copy is not perfectly clear, or if there is reason to doubt its correctness,

the copyreader or the publisher's editor should be consulted. In case there is still doubt, a query to the author should be carried on the proof.

419. In asking questions of the author or editor, make the point perfectly clear. A simple query mark is not always enough to draw attention to the point at issue. Queries on the manuscript must be transferred to the first reading and so on to all sets of proofs sent out until they are answered. Discretion should be used in making queries. The author will be thankful for any sensible suggestion but will resent trivial criticisms. Anything that is obviously wrong should be corrected, for the proofreader will be justly blamed for such an error. He should never follow copy blindly, though he may be required to reproduce it exactly.

420. Style should never be queried to the author. The *Manual of Style* is the guide; if there is room for doubt, the matter should be referred to the editorial department.

421. The proofreader should never fall into the error of thinking that an author's or editor's O.K. relieves him of all or any part of his responsibility. Authors and editors depend on the proofreader to see to it that the typographical requirements have been met, and that the adopted style has been used.

422. The first mention of a figure or plate must be marked in the margin as a guide for placing the cuts when the galleys are returned for makeup.

423. The reader should never permit himself to be stampeded. Speed may be necessary, but accuracy is even more important. In unavoidable cases of "rush" the reader must do his best in the time allotted, but he should let it be understood that he disclaims any further responsibility.

SIGNING AND SENDING PROOFS

424. After the reading is completed the galley proof should be signed in the upper right-hand corner with the initial of the proofreader above that of the copyholder. This signature is carried on all subsequent galley proofs. In case copyholding and revising are done by two different people, on the revised proof the copyholder's initials should follow the reader's above a line with the reviser's initial below. This will save time in tracing proofs and will insure the giving of credit where it belongs.

425. The number of proofs wanted should be marked on the first readings before they are sent to the corrector. The required number must be ascertained from the specifications, the composition ticket, or from special instructions on the copy.

TRAINING A COPYHOLDER

426. Each reader should help to train his own copyholder to be increasingly efficient. The copyholder should be allowed to see what the proofreader marks, and as time permits he should be told why certain things are marked. As he learns the "local style" of the journals and special publications, he will repay his teachers by finding errors, inconsistencies, and deviations from style, and thus will save time for the reader.

427. The proofreader should never shield himself behind his copyholder. The responsibility is the reader's, and decisions are for him to make. If he doubts the copyholder's version he should consult the copy for himself.

428. The proofreader should not read to the copyholder except in special cases in order to rest him after long, close work, and then he should proceed slowly and very distinctly. The copyholder's eye and ear are not trained at first to follow copy with insertions and special editing as fast as a proofreader can read printed matter. Nor should the proofreader suggest to the copyholder the reading of a word or phrase which he has difficulty in making out from the manuscript. If he cannot decipher the manuscript, the reader must be the arbiter.

429. The proofreader should never let a miscalled word or sound pass without challenge. The proof may be wrong, even if he suspects the copyholder has misinterpreted or miscalled. With training, the copyholder learns to enunciate perfectly and to be more and more dependable.

430. The reader should teach the copyholder to make himself useful during the time he is occupied with silent reading by putting copy or galleys in order, by looking up spellings or divisions, by returning proofs for filing, and by studying the *Manual of Style*.

431. As soon as the copyholder has mastered his oral duties he should be taught to revise and to transfer house corrections on duplicate proofs. The proofreader may

raise the efficiency of his own work appreciably by taking a little trouble to help the copyholder learn all phases of his work (see 436).

PAGE READING

432. The page reader first arranges his material in complete sets in the order of their paging. Then he revises the author's alterations and any house corrections that may be left on the galley proofs, by comparing them with the page proofs, and by checking each line or marking it with a dot, so that none shall be overlooked if the revision should be interrupted. Runovers must be read with a copyholder.

After this careful revision, the reader next checks the table of contents by pages, verifying the wording of chapter titles and subtitles and supplying the page numbers. By this method any discrepancy or omission may be detected at once and rectified. In like manner the list of illustrations should be verified.

At this time the job ticket and the specifications should be constantly consulted, for the page reader's particular duty is to *prove* that the instructions of the author and publisher have been carried out.

433. Sometimes, in order to save time, the page reader begins his work before the printer has completed the makeup, receiving more chapters as the paging is completed. In such a case, of course, the revising is done by chapters or sections. It is more advantageous, however, to do it all before beginning the actual page reading, because the author's preferences, or objections, if any, and his general point of view may be revealed by

his corrections as well as by his attitude toward the first reader's queries on the proof.

434. Every word should be read carefully, the sequence and footnotes checked, and all the rules of good practice in paging carefully observed. See 2–46 and all the rules for composition (47–345).

435. The running-heads and folios of each article or chapter should be read as a separate operation after the reading of pages has been finished. The reader should sign the first page and verify number of pages and plates in each article or chapter and the total number of pages in the finished product, including preliminaries. He should report uneven forms at once. All half-titles, blank pages, inserts, and so on, should be numbered and indicated; likewise all necessary queries should be copied on every set of proofs.

436. When pages are ready to go out they should be placed neatly in sets, pinned together at the top, and returned to the record clerk to be recorded and sent. Dirty or over-inked proofs should never be sent out; nor should proofs go to the author with unreadable spots caused by type being off its feet or by failure of the proof-press roller to ink the type properly. The copyholder can be trained to inspect the proofs and to procure duplicates of any that are not readable. The author cannot be held responsible for anything wrong in a poor proof.

437. This is the last chance for queries to the author. Unfilled page references must be queried here and all

references to charts, maps, plates, inserts, and figures must be verified or queried.

438. When a page is unduly short, it is the duty of the page reader to suggest to the author that it be increased in length. The approximate number of words needed should be asked for on the proof. Likewise a page that is too long must be adjusted by the author, unless there is some other legitimate way of meeting the difficulty.

Plates must be marked to face the first mention or description, and it is the reader's duty to assure himself that such insertion will not cause difficulty in binding. The best usage prescribes the insert as a right-hand page facing the verso page. If, in a scientific publication, the value of illustrations would be lost if they were so treated, they may be allowed to face the exact reference, whichever page it falls upon. In case two such references fall on opposite pages, the inserts must be printed on both sides of the sheet; otherwise the second reference must be moved by the author. Under no circumstances should two blank pages be bound facing each other.

In case references to several plates occur on the right-hand page permission must be secured from the author to move the references or to place the inserts facing the next following page.

HINTS TO COPYHOLDERS

439. The copyholder should cultivate a low, soft, clear reading voice. Only his own proofreader should hear him. Remember that, from the proofreader's point of view, the small words are as essential as the big ones. Get them all in—and get them in correctly.

440. Enunciate plural *s*'s distinctly. Try to perfect your enunciation so that you can read an entire galley without error.

441. Regulate and equalize your speed. Do not race at a breakneck pace through typewritten copy and then thread your way slowly through the mazes of handwritten manuscript.

442. Do not keep guessing at a word. Look at it closely; consider the context. Do not speak it until you have made it out—or at least have made the very best guess of which you are capable.

443. Give your reader a chance to make his corrections. Slow up the moment he puts his pencil to the paper. This will save going over the same ground twice. Repeat cheerfully what the proofreader has not understood.

444. Evolve your own system of signals. Do not, for instance, waste time by saying "in italics" for every word or letter so treated. Instead, raise your voice, or tap the table with your pencil once for each word, or do

both. Such a code is to be established between yourself and your reader.

445. Read to your proofreader every instruction, editorial mark, and stet-mark carefully. Learn the job number and *read it for every galley*.

446. Consult the job ticket or the specifications for the number of proofs wanted and the name and address of the person to whom they are to be sent, before having proofs corrected, so that the number wanted may be marked for the printer.

447. Be careful in transferring marks. A mark in the wrong place means two errors uncorrected in place of one corrected. Each set of proofs must carry every mark. Copy all queries and makeup instructions on the galley proof and indicate the insertion of tables, figures, charts, etc., where they are first mentioned.

448. In sending out proofs see that everything is there. Arrange the copy and proof sheets neatly and consecutively.

449. The manuscript should accompany the galley proof; the foul proof (author's marked galley proof) should accompany the page proof. In case no galley proof has been sent the manuscript should accompany the page proof.

450. Fasten your pins in the center at the top. If pinned diagonally in the left-hand corner, any directions written there may be covered up.

451. Return every evening to the file or the bookcase any volume that may have been taken out for reference

during the day. Return all proofs ready for filing at least once a day so that the files may be kept as complete as possible.

452. A copyholder who has no assistance from a file clerk must care for the disposal of his material in the proofroom. He must likewise note the contents on each envelope of proof going out of the shop; this item is to appear in the lower left-hand corner of the envelope as an identification in case it is necessary to trace the package in the mail.

TECHNICAL TERMS AND SYMBOLS

GLOSSARY OF TECHNICAL TERMS

ALTERATIONS.—Changes from manuscript made in proof by the author or editor. It is the custom of the printer to charge for making such changes.

BEARERS.—Strips of metal or wood, type high, placed around the type page to protect it in the molding of electrotype or stereotype plates.

BEN DAY PROCESS.—A process for producing a variety of shaded tints by the use of gelatine films, particularly in connection with engraving plates by zinc etching; named after the inventor, Benjamin Day.

BEVEL.—The sloping edge of an electrotype or stereotype plate, by which the plate is attached to the base while being printed. Also the edge of a halftone block about one-eighth of an inch in width, used for tacking on to a wood base. The bevel is included in all cases in computing the measurement of a plate or cut for the purpose of fixing the price.

BLIND STAMP.—A design on a book cover, stamped or tooled without the use of ink or gold leaf.

BOOK CLOTH.—The sized or glazed cloth made from cotton or linen (or both) used for book covers, and made in a large variety of weights, finishes, colors, and patterns.

BOOK PAPER.—Paper used principally in the manufacture of books and magazines as distinguished from news print, writing, and cover papers.

Bronzing.—Printing with an appropriate size and applying bronze powder while still wet to secure the effect of printing in gold, silver, aluminum, etc.

Buckram.—A heavy linen book cloth much used for library bindings or for binding of large, heavy edition books.

Caption.—The heading of a chapter, the title above an illustration, or matter used in similar cases.

Colophon.—A design placed in former times at the end of a book giving the information now usually included on the title-page.

Deckle Edges.—The untrimmed edges of paper as it comes from the machine, or the rough natural edges of handmade paper.

Dummy.—An unprinted or partially printed or sketched sample of a projected book, pamphlet, book cover, or other material to suggest the final appearance of the completed work.

Edition.—The first printing of a book, or any subsequent one that is different from a previous printing. Subsequent printings without change are designated as *impressions.*

Electrotypes.—Metal printing plates cast from a wax matrix of type or illustrations, on which has been deposited by electrolysis a copper, nickel, or steel shell, which thus forms a hardened metal face on the soft lead backing. Used in place of the original type and cuts for printing a large or subsequent impression of a book.

End Papers.—The folded sheets tipped or sewed to the first and last signatures of a book, one leaf of which is pasted down to the inside of the front and back covers.

FORMAT.—The form, size, and style of a book.

FORWARDING.—In book binding, the processes between sewing and casing in, such as rounding and backing, putting on headbands, reinforcing backs, etc.

HEADINGS.—A *center-head* is a headline placed at equal distances from both margins of the page or column.

A *side-head* is a headline placed at the side of the page or column. It may be set either as a separate line, in which case it is usually set *flush* with the margin of the type page, or *run in*, i.e., in a continuous line with the paragraph to which it belongs. Side-heads are set in italic, small caps, or bold-face.

A *cut-in head* is a head placed in a box cut into the side of the type page. It is usually set in different type from the text, and as a rule is placed under the first two lines of the paragraph.

A *box-head* is similar to a cut-in head with a rule around it; or it is a head for a column in a ruled table.

A *running head* is a headline placed at the top of each page of a book, usually giving the main title of the work on the left-hand (*verso*) page, and the title of the chapter or other subdivision on the right-hand (*recto*) page.

A *marginal head* is one set in the margin opposite the beginning of the paragraph to which it refers.

IMPOSITION.—The process of arranging the pages of a form so that when printed and folded they will fall in the proper order in the signatures.

INSERTS.—Illustrations or type matter not printed in the regular signatures but tipped in between pages.

LEADING.—The term *leading* refers to the vertical spacing between lines, paragraphs, etc. A *lead* is a thin strip of metal of the length of the line, being 1, 2, or 3 points thick. Ordinarily the word *lead* used alone means a 2-point lead, and *leaded matter* therefore refers to matter in which there are 2 points between the lines. A *slug* is a strip of metal 6 or 12 points in thickness, to be used where wider blank spaces are necessary. Spacing material of greater thickness than 12 point is known as *furniture,* and is ordinarily made in multiples of 12 points.

LINOTYPE.—A typesetting machine invented by Ottmar Mergenthaler, and developed about 1880. By use of a keyboard, matrices of various letters and signs are arranged and spaced out automatically in lines. The line of matrices is then brought in contact with molten type metal in which the entire line is cast in one "slug." This machine is primarily, because of its speed, a newspaper machine. It is also, however, much used for cheaper grades of book and magazine work and general printing. The *Intertype* is the same kind of machine manufactured by a rival company under another name.

LOGOTYPE.—Two or more connected letters cast on the same body, such as *œ*, *fi*, etc. Also referred to as a *ligature.*

MAKEUP.—The arranging of type lines and illustrations into page form is called *makeup.*

The *folio* is a page number, usually placed at the outside of the running head at the top of the page. This is sometimes put at the bottom of the page, and is then known as a *drop folio.*

A *half-title*, or *bastard title*, is the abbreviated title of a book placed on a separate page preceding the full title page, or the title of a part or chapter preceding such part or chapter on a separate page in the body of the book.

MAKE-READY.—The operation of putting the type form on the press and getting it ready for printing. It includes the leveling-up of the impression so that all parts will print clearly. This process requires a varying amount of time, from a comparatively short period for plain type forms to many hours where halftone illustrations are involved.

MARGINS.—The white space around the printed page. The proper balancing of the width of margins has much to do with the pleasing effect of a book page.

MEASUREMENT.—The printer's unit of measurement is the *point*, practically one seventy-second of an inch (actually .013837 of an inch). The standard of measurement, however, is the *pica*, or 12 points (one-sixth of an inch). This is often referred to as an *em*, the qualifying word *pica* being understood. Thus the length of the type line is spoken of as "18 ems" (meaning 18 picas = 3 inches), or a block of spacing material is referred to as "6×6 em furniture" (= 1 inch square). To the layman this use of the word *em* is liable to be confusing, because the literal meaning of the word is a lineal measurement equal to the point size of the type in question, i.e., a 6-point em is 6 points, and 8-point em is 8 points, etc. To one familiar with printing practice, however, the different usages of the term are so clearly understood as to avoid confusion.

MONOTYPE.—A composing machine invented by Colbert Lanston and developed about 1890. In this machine a band of paper, which is perforated on a keyboard, operates a casting machine by bringing the single matrices in contact in the proper order with a mold, so that the letters are cast one at a time and arranged in lines automatically spaced to the proper length. This machine is in general use for the better class of book and magazine work. Since each letter is cast separately, corrections are made much more easily than on the linotype.

PAPERS.—Book papers are known as *laid* or *wove*, these names referring to the formation as determined by the weave of the screen on which the fibers are gathered in the process of manufacture. *Laid paper* shows a regular pattern of lines close together in one direction and crossed at right angles at greater intervals in the other. *Wove paper* shows the wire marks at uniform distances in both directions. The following are the names by which different finishes of book paper are known:

Calendered paper has been run through heavy steel rolls, known as "calender rolls," to give it a smooth surface; spoken of as "S. & S.C." or "Super," meaning "sized and super-calendered."

Coated paper is machine-finish paper which has been coated with clay, used principally for printing halftone engravings. It is made with a dull, semi-dull, or glossy surface according to the amount of calendering to which it is subjected.

Eggshell paper presents a fine-grained surface, and is commonly used in book printing where bulkiness is desired.

English-finish paper has a smooth, even finish imparted by running through felt-covered calender rolls. It is much in favor for school textbooks, since it is of a sufficiently smooth surface for halftone printing and yet has a dull finish that is less fatiguing to the eyes than glossy paper.

Machine-finish paper is a paper that comes from the machine in a completed condition. It is moderately smooth, between the S. & S.C. and the eggshell finish. It is known to the trade as "M.F."

PARAGRAPHS.—There are two kinds of ordinary paragraphs. A *plain paragraph* has the first line indented, and the other lines flush. A *hanging paragraph*, or *hanging indention*, has the first line set flush and all others indented.

PROOFS.—A *galley proof* is a printed impression of the type as it is locked in a long, shallow, metal tray known as a *galley*. Such proofs are taken for reading by the proofreader, and the correction of errors is made while the type remains in this form. After corrections have been made on a galley, a *revised proof* is taken for checking them up. This process may be repeated until the final revise to be sent to the author is identical with the manuscript.

A *page proof* is an impression of the type after it has been read by the author and has been made into page form.

A *foundry proof* is a proof taken of the type page after it is locked up for the casting of book plates. The black border on such proof is made by the *bearers* in which the type is inclosed in locking up.

A *plate proof* is a proof taken of the completed plate for final comparison before printing.

Ream.—The number unit on the basis of which paper is handled. In most cases it is 500 sheets. Some manufacturers of fine ledger papers and handmade book papers still adhere, however, to the old ream of 480 sheets. The weight per ream is ordinarily the basis on which the price is fixed; for instance, 25×38–80# @ 8c per pound = $6.40 per ream.

Rules.—Strips of brass or type metal, type high, by the use of which lines of various characters are printed (see specimen p. 332).

Run In.—To set without paragraphs in order to save space, or to insert new matter without making a new paragraph. Matter run along the side of a cut narrower than the type page is said to be "run in around cut."

Serif.—A short, light line projecting as a finish from the main stroke of a letter.

Set.—The horizontal dimension of type. It is expressed in units on composing machines, and generally is spoken of as "condensed" or "extended," "thin" or "fat."

Signature.—A sheet of a book as folded ready for sewing. It is usually 16 pages, but may be only 8 pages if the paper stock is very heavy, or 32 or 64 pages if the paper stock is very thin.

Sizes of Books.—The designations of book sizes in general use are survivals of a practice introduced in the early days of printing, when the size was determined by the number of folds in the sheets used; thus octavo (8vo) meant a sheet folded into eight leaves. The varying sizes of paper necessarily made these designations indefinite. The following descriptions represent the approximate dimensions of the common sizes: 32mo, $4\times5\frac{1}{2}$ inches; 18mo, $4\frac{5}{8}\times6\frac{1}{8}$ inches; 16mo, $4\frac{3}{4}\times7\frac{1}{8}$ inches; 12mo, $5\frac{1}{4}\times7\frac{3}{4}$ inches; crown 8vo, $5\frac{1}{2}\times8$ inches; 8vo, 6×9 inches; royal 8vo, $6\frac{3}{4}\times9\frac{1}{2}$ inches; 4to, 10×12 inches; folio, 13×15 inches.

Spacing.—By *spacing* is meant lateral spacing between words, sentences, or columns, and paragraph indentions. The meaning of technical names for spaces and methods of spacing depends on whether "foundry" type (i.e., type cast for hand composition) or machine-set type is in question. An *em quad* is a block of metal the top of which forms a square. A 12-point em quad is thus 12 points square. The term *em* is often used, the qualifying word *quad* being understood, in any given size of type, as a unit of measurement. Thus in 8-point matter "indent 2 ems" means that the line should be indented 16 points. Two- and 3-em quads are multiples of the foregoing in one block of metal, and are used for spacing out the last lines of paragraphs or filling other blank spaces. Spaces smaller than the em quad are *en quads*, *3-em*, *4-em*, and *5-em spaces* equaling one-half, one-third, one-fourth, and one-fifth of an em, respectively. A *hair-space* is a very thin space, usually about one-half of a point in thickness.

In *monotype* composition a variable unit of measurement is used, and therefore the spacing material is less uniform than in the case of foundry type. The system is too complicated for a full explanation here. There are

18 units in a quad, which, while approximately an em quad, may be more or less according to whether the type face is "fat" or "thin." There is also a *9-unit*, a *6-unit*, a *5-unit*, and a *4-unit space*, equaling approximately an en quad, a 3-em space, a 4-em space, and a 5-em space, respectively. These are all fixed spaces, and vary only with the variation of the *set* (meaning width) of the type face. The *justifying space*, by which the line is spaced out to the proper width, is normally a 5-em space, and is automatically expanded in the casting machine to lengthen the line to the width of the page.

In the case of the *linotype* machine the system is again different. There are three fixed spaces, varying according to the width of the type face with which they are used, but approximately the *em quad*, the *en quad*, and the *4-em space*. The *justifying space* is normally approximately a 4-em space, and may be spread to somewhat larger than an en quad.

STEREOTYPE.—Printing plates cast from a paper matrix made by beating tissue paper into the face of type matter, backing it up with powdered chalk, and drying it by baking. Used in printing books in the same manner as electrotypes.

SWASH LETTERS.—Any letters of peculiar or unusual character introduced into a font of type for ornamental purposes.

TYPE SIZES.—Previous to the adoption of the point system, which became general about 1878, type sizes were known by distinguishing names. The sizes to which these names referred lacked uniformity among different type founders, particularly in different countries, and this confusion led to the immediate popularity of the point system, which originated in France and was developed in the United States. Following is given the different smaller sizes of type, with their present and former designations:

	Former Name
This line set in 18 pt.	Great Primer
This line is set in 14 point -	English
This line is set in 12 point - - -	Pica
This line is set in 11 point - - -	Small Pica
This line is set in 10 point - - - -	Long Primer
This line is set in 9 point - - - - - - -	Bourgeois
This line is set in 8 point - - - - - -	Brevier
This line is set in 7 point - - - - - -	Minion
This line is set in 6 point - - - - - - - - -	Nonpareil
This line is set in 5 point - - - - - - - - - -	Pearl

The designation of type by points refers to the vertical size of the piece of metal on which the type face is cast, and has no definite reference to the size of the type face itself. While all the different styles of 12-point faces, for instance, are approximately of the same size, there is, as will be seen by reference to the type specimens in the back of this book, considerable variation. The designation "12 point," as referring to a particular type face, means that it is ordinarily cast on 12-point body. In monotype and linotype composition, the size of the body is often increased to enlarge the space between the lines without the necessity of inserting leads for that purpose. Thus a face ordinarily cast on 10 point may be cast on 12 point to give the appearance of 2-point leading.

Type Styles.—The type in common use in books and all classes of ordinary reading matter is known as *roman.* While all roman types are essentially the same in form, there are two fairly well-defined divisions or styles. The older form is called *Old Style,* and is characterized by strength and boldness of feature, with strokes of comparatively uniform thickness, and with an absence of weak hair-lines. The serifs are rounded, and the contour is clear and legible. Caslon, one of the first of such letters cast in England, and still in general use, is an example of old-style type. The other style is known as *Modern,* and is characterized by heavier shadings, thinner hair-lines, and thin and straight serifs. The *Bodoni* shown in the type specimens is a recent copy of the original modern letter cut by Bodoni. While a few type faces may combine certain characteristics of the two styles, it is usually easy to classify any particular face as *old style* or *modern.*

Aside from the *roman* there are four other general classes, known as *italic, script, gothic,* and *text.*

The slanting letter mainly used for emphasis and display is known as *italic.* It is cut to match all roman type faces, and a font of roman type for book and magazine work would be considered incomplete without a corresponding font of italic.

Script types are imitations of handwriting. Their use is limited to the printing of announcements, invitations, and stationery.

Gothic is perfectly plain, with lines of uniform thickness, and without serifs. It is sometimes known as *block-letter.*

Text is a survival of the first types cast, and was originally an imitation of the hand lettering which prevailed before movable types were invented. It is often known as *black-letter*.

A *font* is a complete assortment of a given size of type, including capitals, small capitals, and lower case, together with the figures, punctuation marks, logotypes, and the commonly used signs and accents. Many special signs and accents are available, but are not included in the regular font. The *italic* of a given face is considered a part of the equipment of a font of type, but is spoken of as a separate font.

Body type is a common name for type used for reading matter as distinguished from display type, which is used for advertisements, title-pages, headings, etc.

Wrong Font.—A type of different face from that of the font in which it accidentally appears.

LIST OF SYMBOLS

In almanacs, arithmetics, dictionaries, gazetteers, and technical books, abbreviations are not a fault but a positive merit where they save needed space.

—DE VINNE

$+$	Plus
$-$	Minus
$\times$	Times
$\cdot$	Multiplied by; single bond of affinity
$\div$	Divided by
$=$	Is equal to
$\equiv$	Is identical with
≑	Is approximately equal to
$\neq$	Is unequal to
$>$	Is greater than
$\ngtr$	Is not greater than
$<$	Is less than
$\nless$	Is not less than
$\geqq$	Is greater than or equal to
$\leqq$	Is less than or equal to
$\pm$	Plus or minus
$\propto$	Varies as
:	Is to; divided by
::	As; equals
$\therefore$	Hence; therefore
$\because$	Since
∞	Infinity; indefinitely more
o	Infinitesimal; zero
$\sim$	Difference between; cycle
$\sqrt{\ }$	Square root; radical
$\overline{\ }$	Vinculum (above)
( )	Parentheses
[ ]	Brackets; concentration symbol; used to inclose dimensional expressions
{ }	Braces
$\int$	Integral
f	Function; fugacity
∺	Geometrical proportion
∹	Difference between
$\doteq$	Approaches
|	Bar; single bond of affinity (between letters)
/	Solidus; shilling
$\cong$	Is congruent to
··	Minus
Σ	Sum
!	Factorial product
D_x $\left(\text{or } \frac{d_x}{d}\right)$	Derivative
D_x^{-1}	Anti-derivative
D	Diameter
d	Differential
∂	Partial differential
M	Modulus; mass; molal; molecular weight

LIST OF SYMBOLS

m	Molality
g	Gravity; acceleration
⌃	Intersection of sets; equivalent conductivity
⊕	Direct sum; the earth
♁	The earth
⊖	The earth
☌	Conjunction
□	Quadrature
☊	Descending node
☋	Ascending node
☍	Opposition
⊙	Sun; sun's longitude; Uranus
ℂ	Quintile
✱	Sextile; assumed (in etymology)
△	Trine; triangle; an evergreen plant
◬	Triangles
a	Mean distance; angular acceleration; coefficient of thermal expansion; degree of dissociation
a	Right ascension; activity
β	Celestial latitude; coefficient of compressibility; specific heat constant
γ	Activity coefficient; surface tension
φ	Apparent molal volume; fluidity
ϑ	Freezing-point lowering
δ	Declination; variation; difference
Δ	Finite difference; distance; double bond; increment; diffusion coefficient
ϵ	Dielectric constant
η	Viscosity
θ	Angle (plane); temperature C. above ice point
L	(l or ϵ) Mean longitude in orbit
λ	Wave-length; longitude; molal freezing-point lowering
+	North
−	South
ν	Longitude of ascending node; number of ion molcculcs formed by dissociation of a molecule; frequency
q	Perihelion distance
T	Time; temperature (absolute)
ϕ	Angle of eccentricity; geographical latitude
♈	Aries, the ram
♉	Taurus, the bull
♊	Gemini, the twins
♋	Cancer, the crab
♌	Leo, the lion
♍	Virgo, the virgin
♎	Libra, the scales
♏	Scorpio, the scorpion
♐	Sagittarius, the archer
♑	Capricornus, the goat
♒	Aquarius, the waterman
♓	Pisces, the fishes
~	Tilde
^	Circumflex accent
¯	Macron
˘	Breve
¨	Dieresis
¸	(ç) Cedilla

‸	Caret
....	Ellipsis; leaders
´	Acute accent
\`	Grave accent
᾿	Smooth breathing
῾	Rough breathing
○	Circle; circumference
Ⓢ	Circles
∠	Angle
∡	Angles
▭	Rectangle
‖	Parallel to
⊥	Perpendicular to
≚	Equiangular
°	Degrees of arc; degrees of temperature (°. decimal)
′	Minutes of arc (′. decimal); prime
″	Seconds of arc (″. decimal)
h	Hours (h. decimal)
m	Minutes of time (m. decimal)
s	Seconds of time (s. decimal)
d	Days (d. decimal)
M.	Absolute magnitude
mg.	Magnitude
π	3.1416 (3.14159265+); longitude of perihelion
e	2.7182818+; charge on electron; eccentricity
μ	Micron; magnetic permeability; mean angular motion in time; ionic strength; Joule-Thomson coefficient
$\mu\mu$	Micromicron
$\sqrt{}$	Radical
$\sqrt[3]{}$	Cube root
^{2}	Power (set superior, as x^2)
$_3$	Set inferior (as x_3)
Φ	Farad; magnetic flux
κ	Magnetic susceptibility; constant
ρ	Specific resistance; density
σ	Stefan's constant (radiation)
ω	Ohm; longitude of perihelion; frequency; angular velocity; molecular magnetic rotary power; solid angle
Ω	Microhm; relative molecular magnetic rotary power
⇆	Electrical current
→	Direction of flow
J	Radiance
K	Kelvin (absolute) temperature scale; specific inductive capacity
L	Conductance
N	Rydberg constant; number of molecules in a mol
R	Resistance; gas constant; Rydberg constant; Réaumur
Z	Impedence
X	Reactance
Λ	Equivalent conductance (Λ_0, at infinite dilution)
N/	Normal solution (N/$_{10}$, tenth normal solution)
N—	Nitrogen bound
O—	Oxygen bound
$\propto$	Degree of dissociation
S	Entropy

LIST OF SYMBOLS

Γ_0,	(Γ_1, Γ_2, etc.) Coefficient for heat capacity
⬡	Benzene nucleus
′	Valence (in chemistry)
+	Unit charge of electricity
ψ	Pseudo; luminous flux
‾	(Above letter) Indicates acid
sin	Sine
cos	Cosine*
tan	Tangent*
sec	Secant*
cosec	Cosecant*
cot	Cotangent*
log	Logarithm
mod	Modulus
⌒	Arc
#	Number; in German, *Seite*
$	Dollars
¢	Cents
£	Pounds sterling
@	At
%	Per cent
a/c	Account of
℅	Care of
B/L	Bill of lading
⅌	Per
&	Ampersand
*	Asterisk
¶	Paragraph mark
§	Section mark
☞	Index

†	Dagger
‡	Double dagger
℞	Recipe; ā or āā of each same quantity†
℔	Pound
O	Pint
♏	(Minim) drop
℥	Ounce
ʒ	Drachm
℈	Scruple
C	Gallon
O	Pint
f℥	Fluid ounce
fʒ	Fluid drachm
①	Annual plant; Ceres
②	Biennial plant; Pallas
③	Juno
④	Vesta
♃	Perennial herb; Jupiter
♆	Neptune
♄	Saturn
♂	Male or staminate flower; Mars
♀	Female or pistillate flower; Venus
☿	Perfect or hermaphrodite flower
F_1	First generation
<	Derived from (in etymology)
⟨ ⟩	Broken brackets (MS supplied)
⌜ ⌝	Broken brackets
ʿ ʾ	Hebrew breathings

* The following variations built on the symbol for "sine" are also true of cos, tan, sec, cosec, and cot: $\sin^{-1}$ = antisine; sinh = hyperbolic sine; $\sinh^{-1}$ = antihyperbolic sine.

† Quantities always lower case. If quantity ends with *i* it is written with j, as in vij (= seven)

ARABIC, ROMAN, AND GREEK NUMERALS

Arabic	Roman	Greek	Arabic	Roman	Greek
1	I	α′	24	XXIV	κδ′
2	II	β′	30	XXX	λ′
3	III	γ′	40	XL	μ′
4	IV	δ′	50	L	ν′
5	V	ε′	60	LX	ξ′
6	VI	ϛ′	70	LXX	ο′
7	VII	ζ′	80	LXXX	π′
8	VIII	η′	90	XC	ϙ′
9	IX	θ′	100	C	ρ′
10	X	ι′	200	CC	σ′
11	XI	ια′	300	CCC	τ′
12	XII	ιβ′	400	CD	υ′
13	XIII	ιγ′	500	D	φ′
14	XIV	ιδ′	600	DC	χ′
15	XV	ιε′	700	DCC	ψ′
16	XVI	ιϛ′	800	DCCC	ω′
17	XVII	ιζ′	900	CM	ϡ
18	XVIII	ιη′	1000	M	͵α
19	XIX	ιθ′	2000	MM	͵β
20	XX	κ′	3000	MMM	͵γ
21	XXI	κα′	4000	MV̂	͵δ
22	XXII	κβ′	5000	V̂ (or ↁ)	͵ε
23	XXIII	κγ′			

SPECIMENS OF TYPE

Bruce Old Style

Monotype No. 31

A POPULAR OLD-STYLE LETTER SUITABLE FOR GENERAL BOOK AND MAGAZINE PRINTING ❧ ❧

MATRICES FOR ALL THE REGULAR AND HUNDREDS OF SPECIAL CHARACTERS AND ACCENTS ARE ON HAND AND ANY ADDITIONAL ONES CAN BE FURNISHED ON SPECIAL ORDER

Cast in 6, 7, 8, 9, 10, 11, *and* 12 *point*
Roman and italic

Monotype Bruce Old Style

Six Point, One Point Leaded

DURING THE PERIOD OF ROMAN HISTORY identified with Julius Caesar there were customs in manuscript making that are interesting in their suggestion of modern newspaper methods. In fact, Caesar is credited with having been the founder of the newspaper.

He introduced the daily publication of the news of the Roman senate and people, a radical change from the previous custom of issuing yearly news-letters known as the *Annals*. The acts of the senate were reported by trained writers known as *tabularii*, or inscribers of tablets, and were revised and edited before publication by a senator appointed to that duty. Abbreviated forms of writing were used in "reporting," a sort of short-hand which enabled the scribe to write as rapidly as a man could speak. Caesar himself wrote his letters in characters which prevented them being read by his enemies.

The "Acts of the Senate" grew into a diary of general news, known as the "Acts of the City," and it is likely that the educated slaves in the families of public men were called into service to duplicate copies for circulation.—EDMUND G. GRESS, *The Art and Practice of Typography*.

Characters to square inch, 250; solid, 290

Seven Point, One Point Leaded

NUMBERED CHAPTERS OR CHAPTER headings in some form have been approved guide-posts for a reader ever since books were written. For this purpose the Roman numeral still keeps its prominent position, but largely because its letters are broader and plainer than the thinner characters of Arabic figures. Numerals of Roman letters mate neatly with the capital letters that precede them in the line. The modern practice of beginning a chapter with a fresh leaf, with a broad margin at its head, and of ending that chapter with a blank that shows its finish at the end of its last page, was also known in the fifteenth century.

For many years it was customary to have one chapter follow its predecessor without any intervening lane of white space, as must still be noticed in all compact modern editions of the Bible. This huddling of print, without a rest for the eye in the form of blank space, made study fatiguing and the print repelling.

Early writers of fine manuscript books were more considerate, and provided blank space for added decorations of borders, center bands, initial letters, or illustrative miniatures. Initial letters were most frequently employed, for they permitted an infinite variety of ornamentation.—THEODORE LOWE DEVINNE, in *Historic Design in Printing* by HENRY LEWIS JOHNSON.

Characters to square inch, 200; solid, 230

Monotype Bruce Old Style

Eight Point, Two Point Leaded

WITHIN THE FIRST DECADE following the invention of printing, three wonderful Bibles had been produced, two of which are commonly, but perhaps erroneously, attributed to Gutenberg, and the third indisputably the work of Fust and Schöffer. The first is known as the 42-line or Mazarin Bible, because it is printed 42 lines to a page and a copy was found in the library of Cardinal Mazarin. The second is known as the 36-line Pfister, or Bamberg Bible, because printed 36 lines to the page and because Pfister of Bamberg at a later date acquired and used the type. The third edition of the Latin Bible is the finest production of the three, and constitutes the first dated issue. —MADDOX, *Printing, Its History, Practice, and Progress.*

Characters to square inch, 144; solid, 180

Nine Point, Two Point Leaded

MEMORIES OF THINGS that have deeply stirred the imagination are the seeds from which invention springs. The art of printing from movable types was foreshadowed by the brick stamps of the ancient Babylonians, yet it is none the less honor to Gutenberg, who conceived the invention and made the first practical application of the principle, that some germ of the principle itself was known and in use centuries before him.

To present ideas visibly by the use of written or printed characters has been deemed the noblest and most beneficial invention of human ingenuity.

"With the art of writing," said Carlisle, ". . . . of which printing is a simple, an inevitable, comparatively insignificant corollary, the true reign of miracles for mankind commenced."—FREDERIC W. GOUDY, in *Monotype.*

Characters to square inch, 125; solid, 150

TEN-POINT
BRUCE OLD STYLE
with
MONOTYPE GREEK

Two Point Leaded

The word chosen to represent *princeps* was ἡγεμών, "leader." But ἡγεμών did not have the uncompromising meaning of "a leading citizen of a free state" which was suggested by *princeps*. Even in classical Greek it had been used of military commanders. The regular Greek equivalent for *imperium Romanum* was ἡ ἡγεμονία τῶν Ρωμαίων. Moreover ἡγεμών was coming to be the common word in Greek for "provincial governor," and a provincial governor certainly did not bear to the provincials over whom he ruled the relation of a *primus inter pares*. To an ordinary Greek, therefore, there would appear no inconsistency in attributing absolute powers to οἱ ἡγεμόνες τῶν Ρωμαίων. In fact, the only difference between the word *princeps* and its equivalents, and the words δεσπότης or τύραννος which a Greek could readily discern was the distinction between a "king" and a "tyrant."[1]

It was not so difficult for the Greeks to discover an equivalent for *imperator*. In the early days of the Roman domination in the East, the Greeks sometimes simply transliterated *imperator* as ἰμπεράτωρ. But they soon realized that they had a term in their own language which made the mere transliteration of the Latin term unnecessary, viz., the word αὐτοκράτωρ. The Greeks of classical times were familiar with στρατηγοὶ αὐτοκράτορες and πρεσβεῖς αὐτοκράτορες. By the former phrase were meant commanders intrusted with discretionary powers, such as commanders sent on distant expeditions like the Sicilian expedition of 416 B.C.; the latter was the ordinary Greek for "ambassadors plenipotentiary." The Roman provincial governors might be said to combine the functions of στρατηγοὶ αὐτοκράτορες and πρεσβεῖς αὐτοκράτορες. On the one hand, they were the com-

[1] Cf. Philo *in Flaccum* 105: ἔνιοι γὰρ καὶ ἐπὶ Τιβερίου καὶ ἐπὶ τοῦ πατρὸς αὐτοῦ Καίσαρος τῶν διεπότων τὰς ἐπικρατίας τὴν ἐπιμέλειαν καὶ προστασίαν (*principatum*) εἰς δυναστείαν καὶ τυραννίδα μεθαρμοσάμενοι, κ. τ. λ.

Characters to square inch, 100; solid, 120

Monotype Bruce Old Style

Eleven Point, Two Point Leaded

IT WOULD BE BEYOND the truth to say that the principles which underlie all old work are the same. These principles are as diverse as the temperaments and characters of the races among whom they were developed. The Egyptians loved mystery and symbolism; the Greeks carried the refinement of form to perfection; the Romans reveled in richness; the Byzantines indulged in a brilliance of color that is yet always barbaric; the Arabs gave themselves up to the subtle interweaving of intricate detail; the artists of the Gothic period combined religious sentiment with energy of executions; and those of the Renaissance returned to the symbolism that runs through Egyptian ornament, the purity of line that characterizes Greek detail, or the sumptuousness that belongs to Roman scrollery. Inasmuch as all nations and all ages differ, their expression in ornament differs, and inasmuch as all nations and all ages are alike, they express themselves alike in their everyday art.—LEWIS F. DAY, in *Historic Design in Printing* by HENRY LEWIS JOHNSON.

Characters to square inch, 83; solid, 100

Monotype Bruce Old Style

Twelve Point, Three Point Leaded

EXACTLY AS THE CHISEL of the Roman sculptor and the pens of the Mediaeval and Renaissance scribes largely determined the characteristic details of their letters—the omnipresent and potent influence of the tool upon design, which has a horrid example in the steel nib and writing of to-day—so did the new vogue of engraving, with its fine tool, allowing for infinite precision and delicacy of the finest lines, have a profound effect upon the letter-shapes of the late 18th century. In captions to engraving, in maps and in engraved copy-books were now displayed the letters with stiff perpendiculars, horizontal serifs and extreme contrast of thick and thin lines; and letters "open," "outline," or "shadowed." Fournier (1760), Bodoni (1780) and the Didots (1800) cast such letters as type; and the "modern" type-faces had arrived.—FRANCIS MEYNELL, *Typography*.

Characters to square inch, 66; two point leaded, 74; solid, 82

Caslon Old Style

Being a close reproduction of the original Caslon series as cut by William Caslon in 1720

Cast in 6, 7, 8, 9, 10, 11, 12, 14, 18, 22, 24, 30, 36, 42 and 48 point. In roman and italic

THE whole history of type-founding shows no more brilliant and lasting achievement than the type produced by William Caslon of London, in 1720, which we now call Caslon Old Style. Thousands of type faces have had their day and been lost in oblivion in the five hundred years since typography was born, but this face has had an ever increasing popularity since it was first cut.

The following alphabets illustrate the characters in the various sizes. All regular accents are on hand, and any special accents may be secured on special order. On account of the long ascenders and descenders, it is necessary to cast the 7-, 8-, 9-, 10-, and 11-point sizes on 1-point larger bodies.

A B C D E F G H I J K L M N O
P Q Q R S T U V W X Y Z & Æ Œ
A B C D E F G H I J K L M N O
P Q Q R S T U V W X Y Z Æ Œ
a b c d e f g h i j k l m n o p q r s t u v w
x y z 1 2 3 4 5 6 7 8 9 0 ff fi fl ffi ffl $ æ œ ct
ſſ ſ ſi ſl ſſi ſſl ſb ſh ſk ſt

A A B B C C D D E E F F G G
H H I J J K K L L M M N N
O O P P Q Q R R S S T T U
V V W W X Y Y Z & & Æ Œ
a b c d e e f g h i j k k l m n o p q r s t u v v w w x
y z z 1 2 3 4 5 6 7 8 9 0 ff fi fl ffi ffl $ æ œ ct gy
ſſ ſ ſi ſl ſſi ſſl ſb ſh ſk ſt

Small Caps in 6 to 36 point

Swash letters available in 14 to 48 point — *Quaint characters in 14 to 48 point roman and italic*

Caslon Old Style

Six Point, One Point Leaded

CASLON'S WORK MARKS A TURNING-POINT IN ENGLISH TYPE-FOUNDING. HE WAS BORN IN 1692 AT CRADLEY, WORCESTERSHIRE, and in the parish register his baptism is entered as "child of George Casselon by Mary his wife." Tradition has it that the surname was originally Caslona, after an Andalusian town, when in *1688 William Caslon's father came to England. Caslon as a lad was apprenticed to an engraver of ornamental gun-locks and barrels in Lon-*

Characters to square inch, 250; solid, 290

Seven Point, One Point Leaded

CASLON'S WORK MARKS A TURNING-POINT IN ENGLISH TYPE-FOUNDING. HE WAS BORN IN 1692 AT CRADLEY, Worcestershire, and in the parish register his baptism is entered as "child of George Casselon by Mary his wife." Tradition has it that the surname was originally Caslona, after an *Andalusian town, when in 1688 William Caslon's father came to England. Caslon as a lad was apprenticed to an engraver*

Characters to square inch, 200

Eight Point, One Point Leaded

CASLON'S WORK MARKS A TURNING-POINT IN ENGLISH TYPE-FOUNDING. HE WAS BORN IN 1692 AT Cradley, Worcestershire, and in the parish register his baptism is entered as "child of George Casselon by *Mary his wife." Tradition has it that the surname was originally Caslona, after an Andalusian town, when in*

Characters to square inch, 164

Nine Point, Two Point Leaded

CASLON'S WORK MARKS A TURNING-POINT IN ENGLISH TYPE-FOUNDING. HE WAS BORN in 1692 at Cradley, Worcestershire, and in the parish register his baptism is entered as "child *of George Casselon by Mary his wife." Tradition has it that the surname was originally Caslona, after*

Characters to square inch, 118; one-point leaded, 135

Eleven-Point Monotype Caslon

TWO POINT LEADED

CASLON'S work marks a definite turning-point in English type-founding. He was born in 1692 at Cradley, Worcestershire, near Halesowen in Shropshire, and in the parish register of Halesowen his baptism is entered as "child of George Casselon by Mary his wife." Tradition has it that the surname was originally Caslona, after an Andalusian town, when in 1688 William Caslon's father came to England. Caslon as a lad was apprenticed to an engraver of ornamental gun-locks and barrels in London. In 1716, he set up a shop of his own there, where he did silver-chasing and also cut tools for bookbinders. John Watts, a partner of the second Tonson, was accustomed to employ him to cut lettering for bindings—and sometimes punches for type. About 1720, William Bowyer the elder is said to have taken Caslon to the James workshop, to initiate him into letter-founding; and Bowyer, his son-in-law Bettenham, and Watts eventually advanced money to enable Caslon to set up a foundry of his own. The only good foundries there were those of the Oxford Press, of Grover, and of James. In the same year the Society for Promoting Christian Knowledge engaged Caslon to cut a font of Arabic of English size, for a Psalter and New Testament for Oriental use—ultimately printed respectively in 1725 and 1727.—D. B. UPDIKE, *Printing Types; Their History, Forms, and Use.*

Caslon Old Style

Ten Point, Two Point Leaded

CASLON'S WORK MARKS A TURNING-POINT IN ENGLISH TYPE-FOUNDING. HE was born in 1692 at Cradley, Worcestershire, and in the parish register his baptism is entered *as "child of George Casselon by Mary*

Characters to square inch, 96; one point leaded, 108

Eleven Point, Two Point Leaded

CASLON'S WORK MARKS A TURNING-POINT IN ENGLISH TYPE-FOUNDING. He was born in 1692 at Cradley, Worcestershire, and in the parish register *his baptism is entered as "child of George*

Characters to square inch, 78; one point leaded, 84

Twelve Point, Two Point Leaded

CASLON'S WORK MARKS A TURNING-POINT IN ENGLISH TYPE-founding. He was born in 1692 at *Cradley, Worcestershire, and in the*

Characters to square inch, 70; solid, 80

Fourteen Point

CASLON'S WORK MARKS A TURNING-POINT IN ENGLISH TYPE-founding. He was born in 1692 at *Worcestershire, and in the parish reg-*

Caslon Old Style

Eighteen Point

CASLON'S WORK MARKS the turning-point in English type-founding. He was born in 1692 at Cradley, Worces*tershire, and the parish register*

Twenty-two Point

CASLON'S WORKS mark a turning-point in English type-founding. *He was born in 1692 at*

Twenty-four Point

CASLON'S WORK marks a turning-point in English type-found*ing. He was born in the*

Caslon Old Style

Thirty Point

CASLON TYPE marks a turning-point in English type-founding. In *Caslon's work much*

Thirty-six Point

THE WORK of Caslon was a real turning-*point in English*

Caslon Old Style

Forty-two Point

CASLON'S
work marks
the turning
point in type

Forty-eight Point

CASLON
type faces
mark a turn

A modern adaptation of the Caslon
in the form of a bold-face
useful for display work
of all kinds

Available in 6, 8, 10, 12, 14, 18, 24, 30, 36, 42
and 48 point. Roman and italic

Caslon Condensed

Available in 6, 8, 10, 12, 14, 18, 24, 30
36, 42, and 48 point

American Caslon

Six Point

CASLON'S WORK MARKS A DEFINITE TURNING-POINT IN ENGLish type-founding. He was born in 1692 at Cradley, Worcestershire, near Halesowen in Shropshire, and in the parish register of Halesowen his baptism is entered *as "child of George Casselon by Mary his wife." Tradition has it that the surname was*

Eight Point

CASLON'S WORK MARKS A DEFINITE TURNING-POINT in English type-founding. He was born in 1692 at Cradley, Worcestershire, near Halesowen in Shropshire, and in the parish register of *of Halesowen his baptism is entered as "child of George Casselon by Mary*

Ten Point

CASLON'S WORK MARKS A REAL TURNING-point in English type-founding. He was born in 1692 at Cradley, Worcestershire, near Halesowen in Shropshire, *and in the parish register of Halesowen his baptism is entered*

Twelve Point

CASLON'S WORK MARKS A REAL turning-point in English type-founding. He was born in 1692 at Cradley, Worcestershire *near Halesowen, Shropshire, and in the parish*

Fourteen Point

CASLON'S WORK MARKS A definite turning-point in English type-*founding. He was born in 1692 at Crad*

Eighteen Point

CASLON'S WORK MARKS a real turning-point in English *type-founding. He was born in*

American Caslon

Twenty-four Point

CASLON'S WORKS
mark a turning-point in
English type-founding.
He was born in 1692 at

Thirty Point

THE WORK OF
Caslon was a real
turning-point in Eng

Thirty-six Point

THE WORK
of Caslon was a
turning-point in

American Caslon

Forty-two Point

CASLON'S
work marks
the turning
point in type

Forty-eight Point

CASLON
type mark
a real turn

Caslon Condensed

Six Point

CASLON'S WORK MARKS A DEFINITE TURNING-POINT IN English type-founding. He was born in 1692 at Cradley, Worcestershire, near Halesowen in Shropshire, and in the parish register of Halesowen

Eight Point

CASLON'S WORK MARKS A DEFINITE TURNING-point in English type-founding. He was born in 1692 at Cradley, Worcestershire, near Halesowen in Shropshire, and

Ten Point

CASLON'S WORK MARKS THE DEFINITE turning-point in English type-founding. He was born in 1692 at Cradley, Worcestershire, near

Twelve Point

CASLON'S WORK MARKS A DEFINITE turning-point in English type-founding. He was born in 1692 at Cradley, Worcestershire

Fourteen Point

CASLON'S WORK MARKS THE definite turning-point in English

Eighteen Point

CASLON'S WORK MARKS the definite turning-point in

Twenty-four Point

CASLON'S WORK IS a definite turning-point

Caslon Condensed

Thirty Point

THE WORKS OF
Caslon were of real

Thirty-six Point

THE WORKS
of Caslon were a

Forty-two Point

THE WORK
of Caslon was

Forty-eight Point

CASLON'S
work mark

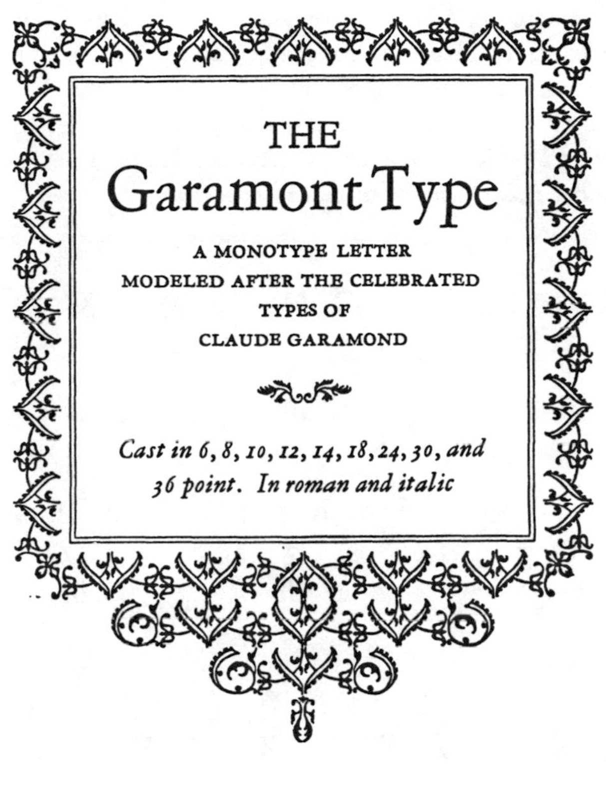

THE

Garamont Type

A MONOTYPE LETTER MODELED AFTER THE CELEBRATED TYPES OF CLAUDE GARAMOND

Cast in 6, 8, 10, 12, 14, 18, 24, 30, and 36 point. In roman and italic

HE GARAMONT TYPE is a version by Frederic W. Goudy of a letter attributed to the great type designer and punch-cutter, Claude Garamond, who flourished in France about 1510. It is one of the most beautiful of recent type designs and is particularly appropriate for such printing as books in de luxe editions, pamphlets, announcements, programs, etc.

The characters in the various fonts are illustrated by the following alphabets. All regular accents are available and, by special order, any desired special accents may be secured.

A B C D E F G H I J K L M N
O P Q R S T U V W X Y Z &

A B C D E F G H I J K L M N
O P Q R S T U V W X Y Z &

a b c d e f g h i j k l m n o
p q r s t u v w x y z 1 2 3
4 5 6 7 8 9 0 ff fl fi ffi ffl $

A A B B C D D E E F G G H
I J K L M M N N O P P Q R
R S T U V V W X Y Z &

a b c d e f g h i j k k l m n o p
q r s t u v v w x y z 1 2 3 4 5
6 7 8 9 0 ff fi fl ffi ffl ct st Qu $
a e ll m n

Swash letters available only in 14, 18, 24, 30, and 36 point — *Terminals in 14, 18, 24, 30, and 36 point*

Monotype Garamont

Six Point, One Point Leaded

OF CLAUDE GARAMOND, THE GREAT TYPE DESIGNER AND punch-cutter, very little seems to be known, the scant statements found in the various biographical dictionaries and in encyclopaedias merely repeating one another with such slight changes in phraseology as may be necessary to escape the penalties of the laws in regard to literary property. Mr. D. B. Updike in his recent book *Printing Types* has brought together more informa-*tion than is to be found elsewhere in English. There is no evidence to show when or where Garamond was born, but it seems to have been accepted that it was sometime*

Characters to square inch, 260; solid, 320

Eight Point, One Point Leaded

OF CLAUDE GARAMOND, THE GREAT TYPE DE-SIGNER AND PUNCH-CUTTER, VERY LITTLE SEEMS TO BE known, the scant statements found in the various bio-graphical dictionaries and in encyclopaedias merely re-*peating one another with such slight changes in phraseology as may be necessary to escape the penalties of the laws in regard to*

Characters to square inch, 168; solid, 188

Ten Point, Two Point Leaded

OF CLAUDE GARAMOND, THE GREAT TYPE DESIGNER AND PUNCH-CUTTER, VERY LIT-tle seems to be known, the scant statements found in the various biographical dictionaries *and in encyclopaedias merely repeating one another*

Characters to square inch, 105; solid, 125

Twelve Point, Two Point Leaded

OF CLAUDE GARAMOND, THE GREAT TYPE DESIGNER AND PUNCH-CUT-ter, very little seems to be known, the *scant statements found in the biographical*

Characters to square inch, 76; solid, 88

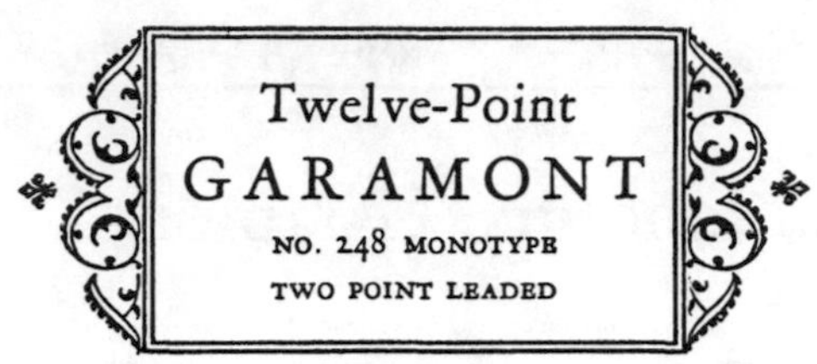

Twelve-Point
GARAMONT
NO. 248 MONOTYPE
TWO POINT LEADED

OF CLAUDE GARAMOND, the great type designer and punch-cutter, little seems to be known, the scant statements found in the various biographical dictionaries and encyclopaedias merely repeating one another with such slight changes in phraseology as may be necessary to escape the penalties of the laws in regard to literary property. Mr. D. B. Updike in his recent book *Printing Types* has brought together more information than is to be found elsewhere in English.

There is no evidence to show when or where Garamond was born, but it seems to have been accepted that it was sometime in the fifteenth century, a supposition probably based upon Lottin's unsupported statement that he was working (*exerce*) in 1510. The tradition that he was a pupil of Tory's is apparently based upon the Latin epitaph prepared for Tory long after his death by a certain Catherinot at the request and from material supplied by a Bourges printer named Jean Toubeau, who claimed descent from Tory on the female side. The text of this epitaph is given in full by Bernard in his study of Tory, and reads: *Et Garamundum calcographum principem edocuerit.*—W. M. Ivins, Jr., in *Monotype*.

Monotype Garamont

Fourteen Point, Two Point Leaded

OF CLAUDE GARAMOND, A GREAT TYPE DESIGNER AND PUNCH-cutter, little seems to be known, the scant statements found in the *various biographical dictionaries and*

Eighteen Point

CLAUDE GARAMOND, THE GREAT TYPE DESIGNER and punch-cutter, of whom little seems to be known, at *one time flourished in France*

Twenty-four Point

CLAUDE GARA-mond, the great type designer and punch-*cutter, of whom little is*

Monotype Garamont

Thirty Point

OF CLAUDE
Garamond, the
type designer &
punch-cutter, lit-
tle seems to be known

Thirty-six Point

OF CLAUDE
Garamond the
type designer
& punch-cutter

SCOTCH ROMAN

MONOTYPE NUMBER 36

A MODERNIZED OLD-STYLE TYPE
USEFUL FOR ALL CLASSES
OF GENERAL WORK

*Cast in 6, 8, 9, 10, 11, 12, 14, 18, 24, 30, 36
48, 60, and 72 point. Italic
in 6 to 30 point*

SCOTCH ROMAN is one of the well-known and much used type faces, and belongs in the large class of transitional or "modernized old-style" types. It is a strong, mannish letter, suitable for book and magazine work, and for general display composition where a bold, direct effect is sought.

The characters in the various fonts are shown in the following alphabets. All regular accents are available, and any special ones desired can be cut to order. The sizes up to 12 point are on the monotype machine; the larger sizes are foundry type.

A B C D E F G H I J
K L M N O P Q R S T
U V W X Y Z & Æ Œ

a b c d e f g h i j k l m n o
p q r s t u v w x y z 1 2 3 4
5 6 7 8 9 0 ff fi fl ffi ffl $ œ æ

A B C D E F G H I J
K L M N O P Q R S T
U V W X Y Z & Æ Œ

a b c d e f g h i j k l m n o
p q r s t u v w x y z 1 2 3 4
5 6 7 8 9 0 ff fi fl ffi ffl $ œ æ

Scotch Roman

Six Point, One Point Leaded

WHEN PRINTING WAS INVENTED THE FIRST TYPES USED WERE IMITATIONS OF THE CURRENT GOTHIC LETTERING, KNOWN TO US AS Black Letter, Old English, etc. A few years later, when typography was introduced into Italy, the types were cut in imitation of the lettering selected for use by the scribes of the Italian Renaissance, which lettering is familiarly known in our time as Roman. The capitals of *this Roman lettering are fashioned after those used in ancient Rome, and the small or lower-case letters are after the Roman writing known as the*

Characters to square inch, 250; solid, 290

Eight Point, One Point Leaded

WHEN PRINTING WAS INVENTED THE FIRST TYPES USED WERE IMITATIONS OF THE CURRENT GOTHIC lettering, known to us as Black Letter, Old English, etc. A few years later, when typography was introduced into *Italy, the types were cut in imitation of the lettering selected for use by the scribes of the Italian Renaissance, which lettering*

Characters to square inch, 163; solid, 180

Nine Point, Two Point Leaded

WHEN PRINTING WAS INVENTED THE FIRST TYPES USED WERE IMITATIONS OF THE CURrent Gothic lettering, known to us as Black Letter, Old English, etc. A few years later, when typogra*phy was introduced into Italy, the types were cut in imitation of the lettering selected for use by the scribes*

Characters to square inch, 125; solid, 150

Ten Point, Two Point Leaded

WHEN PRINTING WAS INVENTED THE FIRST TYPES USED WERE IMITATIONS OF THE current Gothic lettering, known to us as Black Letter, Old English, etc. A few years later, *when typography was introduced into Italy, the*

Characters to square inch, 100; solid, 120

ELEVEN-POINT MONOTYPE SCOTCH ROMAN

With Two Point Leads

WHEN printing was invented the first types used were imitations of the current Gothic lettering, known to us as Black Letter, Old English, etc. A few years later, when typography was introduced into Italy, the types were cut in imitation of the lettering selected for use by the scribes of the Italian Renaissance, which lettering is familiarly known in our time as Roman. The capitals of this Roman lettering are fashioned after those which were used in ancient Rome, and the small or lower-case letters are after the Roman writing known as *minuscule*, of the twelfth century.

The ancient Roman writing was all capitals, and as found on stamps and coins was of the character of the modern so-called "gothic" (plain strokes, without the small cross strokes known as serifs). The more carefully made Roman capitals, as carved on monuments and buildings, are not unlike the present type-faces known as Caslon and French old style.

The evolution of Roman capitals into the small or lower-case letters of the present day is traced in the writing called *uncial*, in which the letters A, D, E, H, M, Q are rounded and altered in appearance.—GRESS, *The Art and Practice of Typography*.

Scotch Roman

Eleven Point, Two Point Leaded

WHEN PRINTING WAS INVENTED THE FIRST TYPES USED WERE IMITATIONS OF the current Gothic lettering, known to us as Black Letter, Old English, etc. A few years later, when typography was intro- *duced into Italy, the types were cut in imitation of the lettering selected for use by the*

Characters to square inch, 83; solid, 100

Twelve Point, Two Point Leaded

WHEN PRINTING WAS INVENTED the first types used were imitations of the current Gothic lettering, known to us as Black Letter, Old English, etc. A few years later, when typography was *introduced into Italy, the types were cut in imitation of the lettering selected for the*

Characters to square inch, 74; solid, 82

Fourteen Point, Two Point Leaded

WHEN PRINTING WAS IN- vented the first types used were imitations of the current Gothic lettering, known to us as Black *Letter, Old English, etc. A few years later when movable types*

Scotch Roman

Eighteen Point

THE FIRST TYPES
to be used when printing
was invented were imita-
tions of the Gothic letter-
ing known to us as Black

Twenty-four Point

WHEN PRINT-
ing was invented the
types used were imi-
tations of the letter

Thirty Point

THE FIRST
types used when
printing was in-

Scotch Roman

Thirty-six Point

PRINTING when first invented was an imitation of a

Forty-eight Point

INVENT ion of the first types

Scotch Roman

Sixty Point

TYPE was invented

Seventy-two Point

THE invent

MODERN NUMBER EIGHT

A Modern Monotype letter particularly adapted to book and magazine work where sharpness of impression is desired
The equipment at the University Press includes all the regular and hundreds of special accents and characters, and any others can be furnished on order

CAST IN 4½, 6, 7, 8, 10, 11, AND 12 POINT
ROMAN AND ITALIC

Monotype Modern Number Eight

Four and One-half Point, Half-Point Leaded

WHATEVER WE MAY THINK of the various styles of ornament that have come down to us, it is impossible for us to ignore them altogether. They are the various languages in which the past has expressed itself, and unless we fancy in our foolishness that we can evolve from inner consciousness something at once independent of and superior to all that has been done before our time, we must begin by some study of the ancient principles and practice. It will save time in the end. Even those who flatter themselves that it will be easy for them to take one bound into successful originality, would do well to reflect that they are more likely to succeed by stepping back a pace or two for a spring than by "toeing the line."

If there were no other reason why we should know something of past styles, it would be sufficient that, in the absence of any marked national style among us at present, we have taken to "reviving' in succession all manner of bygone styles. The ornament of today is to so great an extent a reflection, in some instances a distortion of old work, that one cannot well discuss it without reference to its origin. These "revivals," irrational as they are in themselves, are not without good results. We have such a wealth of old work about us, accessible through modern facilities of travel, purchasable through modern processes of reproduction, brought to our notice by modern methods of publication, that we cannot escape their influence if we would; and the "revivals" have involved such a thorough study of the various styles that, when we shall have arrived at reason and begin to express ourselves naturally in the language of our own day, it will surely tell in our work to some purpose.—LEWIS F. DAY, in *Historic Design in Printing* by HENRY LEWIS JOHNSON.

Characters to square inch, 430

Six Point, One Point Leaded

NO TYPE-FOUNDER has changed the form and effect of roman letter more than Bodoni of Parma. His first specimen of 1771 shows that he had carefully studied the best French types of that period, but it shows also the hand of an innovator. He made his new faces rounder and lighter, and of great openness and delicacy. The round letters of the lower-case were unusually short for the body, with ascenders and descenders so long that the composed types had the appearance of leaded matter. Excessive care was given to the correct drawing of curves and ovals. Serifs were long and flat; hair-lines had unusual length and sharpness. He delighted in little graces which struck every reader by their novelty. These mannerisms prevented other founders from faithfully copying his forms, but all of them have been influenced by his style. He set the fashion for light-faces and round forms, and for that imitation of copperplate effects which has so seriously damaged the appearance of the books of this century.

Firmin-Didot of Paris, equally able as printer and type-founder, undertook the difficult task of making a bolder type with the round form, sharp lines, and true curves of Bodoni. His first face was an obese letter of harsh contrasts, for it opposed thick stems to feeble hair-lines and fragile serifs.—THEODORE LOWE DEVINNE, *The Practice of Typography.*

Characters to square inch, 240; solid, 275

Monotype Modern Number Eight

Seven Point, One Point Leaded

WHEN, WHERE AND BY WHOM was typography invented? It is surprising that there should be any real uncertainty about the facts connected with the invention of typography, but some uncertainty does exist, and various opinions and conclusions are set forth in books on the subject. The new method of printing was invented in the midst of indifference and ignorance, and for many years but few cared that it had come among them.

The inventor of typography, whether Coster or Gutenberg, was too modest to claim the credit in a substantial way, as he failed to print his name on the first books done by the new method.—E. G. GRESS, *The Art and Practice of Typography.*

Characters to square inch, 182; solid, 206

Eight Point, Two Point Leaded

ASIDE FROM TORY, Garamond worked with and for some of the most notable men in the history of printing. He was typefounder in the printing office of Simon de Colines, who for years was associated with the Estiennes and who later established his own business. Types especially designed by Garamond are said to have been used by Christopher Plantin, of Antwerp, for his immense Polyglot Bible.

In time Garamond established his own typefoundry, the first in the world, by the way, that was not an adjunct of a printing plant. Guillaume le Bé, an apprentice of Garamond's, started the second in Paris about 1552, to which he added many of Garamond's matrices upon the latter's death in 1561. —J. L. FRAZIER, *Inland Printer.*

Characters to square inch, 133; solid, 166

Monotype Modern Number Eight

Nine Point, Two Point Leaded

JOB PRINTING as a distinct department is of modern development. Typographers of old were primarily book and pamphlet printers, and in many cases interest was chiefly centered in publishing newspapers or almanacs; job printing was incidental. This caused similarity in the typography of newspaper, book and job work, a condition that today exists only in a small degree. Now these three classes of work are generally separated into departments, each with its own rules, styles and practices, job composition being less restrained by customs and rules than any of the other departments.

Attractiveness is as necessary to the typography of the general job of printing as dignity and legibility are to a law brief, but, endeavoring to get attractiveness into their work, job printers often go astray. They wrongly labor under the impression that to have a job distinctive it must be made freakish. Typography is not good unless based upon art foundations.

Ideas in plenty could have been plucked by the printer of the nineteenth century from old books, especially from those printed for religious organizations, such as the "Book of Common Prayer." A handsome edition of a book of this kind was printed in London by John Murray in 1814.—EDMUND G. GRESS, *The Art and Practice of Typography.*

Characters to square inch, 118; solid, 140

TEN POINT

MONOTYPE MODERN NUMBER EIGHT

with

POINTED HEBREW AND ARABIC

TWO POINT LEADED

We may accordingly render Job 4:12, וַתִּקַּח אָזְנִי שֵׁמֶץ מֶנְהוּ, "Mine ear received a small portion thereof" (cf. Targum, "Mine ear learned a fraction of what emanated from Him"); and Job 26:14, וּמַה שֵׁמֶץ דָּבָר נִשְׁמַע בּוֹ, "And how infinitesimal a part do we hear of Him!" (Targum קצת מלתיה). As for לְשִׁמְצָה, Exod. 32:25 (LXX presupposes לְשִׂמְחָה), BDB "(derisive) whisper, derision," the passage might be rendered, "For Aaron had let them loose to become insignificant with their enemies" (lit., an object of small size, something to be despised).

Eccles. 10:18, שִׁפְלוּת יָדַיִם. BDB: "sinking of hands," negligence. The word is thus connected with שָׁפֵל, "be low" (Arab. سَفُلَ). Ehrlich is no doubt right in identifying it with a root שפל which is found in RL and corresponds to Arab. ثَفَالٌ, "slow," used of a camel which is lazy and reluctant to rise (Lane). Cf., e.g., Pesaḥim 50*b*, יש זריז ונשכר ויש זריז ונפסד יש שפל ונשכר ויש שפל ונפסד, "There is a diligent man who gains profit and one who loses; there is an indolent man who gains profit and one who loses"; Giṭṭin 25*a*, בנות זריזות ובנים שפלים, "diligent daughters and lazy sons." Hence שִׁפְלוּת יָדַיִם should be translated "indolence."

מִשְׁלַחַת (1) Eccles. 8:8, "There is no discharge in war." (2) Ps. 78:49, "A deputation (or sending) of angels of evil."

Characters to square inch, 96; solid, 115

Monotype Modern Number Eight

Eleven Point, Two Point Leaded

English books between 1500 and 1800 are important to us as sources from which most of our present-day styles in printing are derived. The sixteenth century is an archaic period typographically in England, and its interest is mainly historical. While in the seventeenth century English books are less archaic, its traditions have but little effect on our printing to-day. But eighteenth century work, especially after the advent of Caslon, has a close connection with nineteenth and twentieth century printing; and the influence of its somewhat dubious taste is shown, in recent years, in American books and especially in ephemeral typography. The books used to illustrate the progression of English type-forms during these three centuries are chosen from the rank and file of volumes of their respective periods—although among them there are some remarkable specimens of book-making. —D. B. Updike, *Printing Types; Their History, Forms, and Use.*

Characters to square inch, 78; solid 94

Monotype Modern Number Eight

Twelve Point, Three Point Leaded

IT IS INTERESTING to note that the Printer's Mark preceded the introduction of the title-page by nearly twenty years, and that the first ornamental title known appeared in the "Calendar" of Regiomontanus, printed at Venice by Pictor, Loeslein and Ratdolt in 1476, in folio. Neither simple nor ornate title-pages secured an immediate or general popularity, and not for many years were they regarded as an essential feature of the printed volume. Their history is intimately associated with that of the Printer's Mark, and the progress of the one synchronizes up to a certain point with that of the other. In beauty of design and engraving, the Printer's Mark, like the title-page, attained its highest point of artistic excellence in the early part of the sixteenth century.—W. ROBERTS, in *Historic Design in Printing* by H. L. JOHNSON.

Characters to square inch, 63; two point leaded, 70; solid, 77

MONOTYPE BODONI BOOK

is shown in connection with the Modern Number Eight since it is especially fitted for the display pages of books set in the Number Eight

Cast in 14, 18, 24, 30, and 36 point Roman and italic

Monotype Bodoni Book

Fourteen Point

NO TYPE-FOUNDER HAS EVER changed the form and effect of roman letter more than Bodoni of *Parma. His first specimen of 1771 shows that he has made a careful*

Eighteen Point

TYPE-FOUNDERS HAVE never changed the form or effect of roman letter more *than Bodoni of Parma has. His first specimen of 1771*

Twenty-four Point

TYPE-FOUNDERS have never changed the form and effect of *the roman letter more*

Monotype Bodoni Book

Thirty Point

THE FORM OF
the roman letters
in general effect
and design have
never changed in

Thirty-six Point

THE ROMAN
letter has never
changed more
in form and in

FOREIGN TYPES

MONOTYPE GREEK
ANTIQUE GREEK
INSCRIPTION GREEK
HEBREW
NESTORIAN SYRIAC
ARABIC
ETHIOPIC
MONOTYPE RUTHENIAN
MONOTYPE GERMAN

Greek Alphabet

Α	α	alpha
Β	β	beta
Γ	γ	gamma
Δ	δ	delta
Ε	ϵ	epsilon
Ζ	ζ	zeta
Η	η	eta
Θ	θ	theta
Ι	ι	iota
Κ	κ	kappa
Λ	λ	lambda
Μ	μ	mu
Ν	ν	nu
Ξ	ξ	xi
Ο	ο	omicron
Π	π	pi
Ρ	ρ	rho
Σ	σ ς*	sigma
Τ	τ	tau
Υ	υ	upsilon
Φ	φ	phi
Χ	χ	chi
Ψ	ψ	psi
Ω	ω	omega

Hebrew Alphabet

א	älef
ב בּ	be̲th
ג גּ	gimel
ד דּ	däleth
ה	he̲
ו	waw (wow)
ז	zăyin
ח	ḥeth
ט	ṭeth
י	yōdh
ך* כ כּ	kăf
ל	lämedh
ם* מ	me̲m
ן* נ	nun (nōōn)
ס	sammeḥ
ע	ăyin
ף* פ פּ	pe̲
ץ* צ	sädhe̲
ק	kōf
ר	re̲sh
שׂ	sin
שׁ	shin
ת תּ	taw (tow)

* Final letters

Monotype Porson Greek

Six Point, Two Point Leaded

Τάδε δέ μοι πάντως, ἔφη, Κροῖσε, λέξον πῶς ἀποβέβηκε τὰ ἐκ τοῦ ἐν Δελφοῖς χρηστηρίου· σοὶ γὰρ δὴ λέγεται πάνυ γε τεθεραπεῦσθαι ὁ Ἀπόλλων καί σε πάντα ἐκείνῳ πειθόμενον πράττειν. Ἐβουλόμην ἄν, ὦ Κῦρε, οὕτως ἔχειν· νῦν δὲ πάντα τἀναντία εὐθὺς ἐξ ἀρχῆς πράττων προσηνέχθην τῷ Ἀπόλλωνι. Πῶς δέ; ἔφη ὁ Κῦρος· δίδασκε· πάνυ γὰρ παράδοξα λέγεις. Ὅτι πρῶτον μέν, ἔφη, ἀμελή

Eight Point, Two Point Leaded

Τάδε δέ μοι πάντως, ἔφη, Κροῖσε, λέξον πῶς ἀποβέβηκε τὰ ἐκ τοῦ ἐν Δελφοῖς χρηστηρίου· σοὶ γὰρ δὴ λέγεται πάνυ γε τεθεραπεῦσθαι ὁ Ἀπόλλων καί σε πάντα ἐκείνῳ πειθόμενον πράττειν. Ἐβουλόμην ἄν, ὦ Κῦρε, οὕτως ἔχε

Ten Point, Two Point Leaded
(Can be cast also on Nine Point)

Τάδε δέ μοι πάντως, ἔφη, Κροῖσε, λέξον πῶς ἀποβέβηκε τὰ ἐκ τοῦ ἐν Δελφοῖς χρηστηρίου· σοὶ γὰρ δὴ λέγεται πάνυ γε τεθεραπεῦσθαι ὁ Ἀπόλλων καί σε πάντα ἐκείνῳ πειθόμενον πράττειν. Ἐβου

Eleven Point, Two Point Leaded

Τάδε δέ μοι πάντως, ἔφη, Κροῖσε, λέξον πῶς ἀποβέβηκε τὰ ἐκ τοῦ ἐν Δελφοῖς χρηστηρίου· σοὶ γὰρ δὴ λέγεται πάνυ γε τεθερα

Twelve Point, Two Point Leaded
(Foundry Type)

Τάδε δέ μοι πάντως, ἔφη, Κροῖσε, λέξον πῶς ἀποβέβηκε τὰ ἐκ τοῦ ἐν Δελφοῖς χρηστηρίου· σοὶ γὰρ δὴ λέγε

Antique Greek

Eight Point, Two Point Leaded

Τάδε δέ μοι πάντως, ἔφη, Κροῖσε, λέξον πῶς ἀποβέβηκε τὰ ἐκ τοῦ ἐν Δελφοῖς χρηστηρίου· σοὶ γὰρ δὴ λέγεται πάνυ γε τεθεραπεῦσθαι ὁ Ἀπόλλων καί σε πάντα ἐκείνῳ πειθόμενον πράττειν. Ἐβουλόμην ἄν,

Eleven Point, Two Point Leaded

Τάδε δέ μοι πάντως, ἔφη, Κροῖσε, λέξον πῶς ἀποβέβηκε τὰ ἐκ τοῦ ἐν Δελφοῖς χρη-στηρίου· σοὶ γὰρ δὴ λέγεται πάνυ γε

Inscription Greek

Ten Point, Two Point Leaded

ΡΗΣΑΝΤΑ▨ΨΙ▨ΡΑΦΥΛΑΞΑΣΤΑ▨▨▨▨
ΠΑΝ▨ΑΓ▨▨ΨΡΑΦΥΔΑΞΝΤΑ▨▨▨▨▨
ΤΑΜΙΕΨΣΑΝΤΑΔΕΚΑΠ▨ΤΞΨΣΑΝΤΑ▨Ↄ
ϾΡΑΜΜΑΤΕΨΣΑΝΤΑΚΑΙΤΗΣΦΙΛΟΣΕΒΑΣ

Pointed Hebrew

Six Point, Two Point Leaded

מִשְׁלֵי שְׁלֹמֹה בֶן־דָּוִד מֶלֶךְ יִשְׂרָאֵל׃ לָדַעַת חָכְמָה וּמוּסָר לְהָבִין אִמְרֵי בִינָה׃ לָקַחַת מוּסַר הַשְׂכֵּל צֶדֶק וּמִשְׁפָּט וּמֵשָׁרִים׃ לָתֵת לִפְתָאיִם עָרְמָה לְנַעַר דַּעַת

Nine Point, Two Point Leaded

מִשְׁלֵי שְׁלֹמֹה בֶן־דָּוִד מֶלֶךְ יִשְׂרָאֵל׃ לָדַעַת חָכְמָה וּמוּסָר לְהָבִין אִמְרֵי בִינָה׃ לָקַחַת מוּסַר הַשְׂכֵּל צֶדֶק וּמִשְׁפָּט וּמֵשָׁרִים׃ לָתֵת

Nestorian Syriac

Nine Point

ܘܡܬܐܪܝܐ ܡܪܝ ܒܗܘܢ ܐܡܝܪܐ ܗ̄ ܥܒܕܐ. ܗܘܝܐ
ܗܘܡܬܐܝܗ. ܘܡܫܝܚܐ ܕܗܠܘ ܫܘܪܝܐ. ܘܡܗܡܢܢܐ ܡܪܝ
ܒܗܘܢ ܐܬܐܡܝܢ ܗ̄ ܡܢܬܗܫܢܝܐ. ܘܡܬܝܐ ܕܢܗܝܢ
ܡܫܪܝܗ ܘܚܕܡܟܐ ܟܠܐܪܐ ܗܘܝܐ ܠܒܪܐ. ܡܩܕܡܝܐ

Arabic

Nine Point

فقال العربُ تَنْسِبُ كلَّ خيرٍ الى اليمين
وكلَّ شرٍّ الى الشمال ولذلك قال اللّه عزّ
وجلّ فَأَمَّا مَنْ أُوتِيَ كِتَابَهُ بِيَمِينِهِ وأَمَّا مَنْ
أُوتِيَ كِتَابَهُ بِشِمَالِهِ فامّا الفِعْلُ فى مثل

Ethiopic

Nine Point

መጽሐፈ ፡ ጤቀላ ፡ ሕመ ፡ ይሰብክ ፡ ጳውሎስ ፡ ው
ስተ ፡ ዙሉ ፡ አህጉር ፡ ወበጽሐ ፡ መቄዶንያ ፡ ወኀደ
ረ ፡ ማኅደሮ ፡ ለታምሬኖስ ፡ ወይቤ ፡ እንዘ ፡ ይሜሀ
ር ፡ ወይጌሥጾሙ ፡ መጻእኒ ፡ ንሰብክ ፡ መንግሥተ ፡
ሰማያት ፡ በቃለ ፡ እግዚአብሔር ፡ ብፁዓን ፡ እለ ፡ የአ
ምኑ ፡ በልቦሙ ፡ በወልደ ፡ እግዚአብሔር ፡ እስመ ፡

Monotype Ruthenian

RUSSIAN ALPHABET

А	**а**	[a]	**Р**	**р**	[εr[
Б	**б**	[*b*ε]	**С**	**с**	[εs]
В	**в**	[*v*ε]	**Т**	**т**	[*t*ε]
Г	**г**	[*g*ε]	**У**	**у**	[u]
Д	**д**	[*d*ε]	**Ф**	**ф**	[εf]
Е	**е**	[jε]	**Х**	**х**	[xa]
Ж	**ж**	[žε]	**Ц**	**ц**	[tsε]
З	**з**	[*z*ε]	**Ч**	**ч**	[ča]
И	**и**	[i dvajnoj ε]	**Ш**	**ш**	[ša]
І	**і**	[i s točkoj]	**Щ**	**щ**	[šča]
Й	**й**	[i s kratkoj]	**Ъ**	**ъ**	[jεr]
К	**к**	[ka]	**Ы**	**ы**	[jirы]
Л	**л**	[εl]	**Ь**	**ь**	[je*r*]
М	**м**	[εm]	**Ѣ**	**ѣ**	[ja*t*‘]
Н	**н**	[εn]	**Э**	**э**	[ε abarotnaj ε]
О	**о**	[o]	**Ю**	**ю**	[ju]
П	**п**	[*p*ε]	**Я**	**я**	[ja]

Eight Point No. 308, Two Point Leaded

Въ гостиной принимаютъ гостей. Полъ ея устланъ коврами и на стѣнахъ висятъ прекрасныя картины. Спальни—комнаты, въ которыхъ спятъ люди; въ спальняхъ стоятъ кровати, комоды и высокіе шкапы. Въ кухнѣ приготовляютъ кушанье; съѣстные припасы хранятся въ кладовыхъ или въ погребахъ.

Столовая—комната, въ которой кушаютъ: завтракаютъ, обѣдаютъ и ужинаютъ. Въ столовой стоятъ большой, круглый столъ и высокій буфетъ. Около стола стоятъ нѣсколько стульевъ

Monotype Ruthenian

Ten Point No. 308, Two Point Leaded

Въ гостиной принимаютъ гостей. Полъ ея устланъ коврами, и на стѣнахъ висятъ прекрасныя картины. Спальни—комнаты, въ которыхъ спятъ люди; въ спальняхъ стоятъ кровати, комоды и высокіе шкапы. Въ кухнѣ приготовляютъ кушанье; съѣстные припасы хранятся въ кладовыхъ или въ погребахъ.

BOLD-FACE

Eight Point No. 318, Two Point Leaded

Въ гостиной принимаютъ гостей. Полъ ея устланъ коврами, и на стѣнахъ висятъ прекрасныя картины. Спальни—комнаты, въ которыхъ спятъ люди; въ спальняхъ стоятъ кровати, комоды и высокіе шкапы. Въ кухнѣ приготовляютъ кушанье; съѣстные припасы хранятся въ кладовыхъ или въ погребахъ.

Столовая—комната, въ которой кушаютъ: завтракаютъ, обѣдаютъ и ужинаютъ. Въ столо-

Ten Point No. 318, Two Point Leaded

Въ гостиной принимаютъ гостей. Полъ ея устланъ коврами, и на стѣнахъ висятъ прекрасныя картины. Спальни—комнаты, въ которыхъ спятъ люди; въ спальняхъ стоятъ кровати, комоды и высокіе шкапы. Въ кухнѣ приготовляютъ кушанье; съѣстные припасы хранятся въ кладовыхъ или въ погребахъ.

Monotype German

A B C D E F G H I K L M N O
P Q R S T U V W X Y Z Ä Ö Ü
a b c d e f g h i j k l m n o p q r ſ s
t u v w x y z $ 1 2 3 4 5 6 7 8 9 0
ä ö ü ſſ ſt ſi ll ß tz ck ch ff fl fi ꝛc.

Eight Point, Two Point Leaded

Die beſte Art von Originalität iſt diejenige, welche ſich nach einer gründlichen Lehrzeit fühlbar macht, eine ſolche,

Ten Point, Two Point Leaded

Die beſte Art von Originalität iſt diejenige, welche ſich nach einer gründlichen Lehrzeit fühlbar

Twelve Point, Two Point Leaded

Die beſte Art von Originalität iſt diejenige, welche ſich nach einer gründlichen

Eight Point, Bold

Die beſte Art von Originalität iſt diejenige, welche ſich nach einer gründlichen Lehrzeit fühlbar macht, eine

Ten Point, Bold

Die beſte Art von Originalität iſt diejenige, welche ſich nach einer gründlichen Lehrzeit

Twelve Point, Bold

Die beſte Art von Originalität iſt diejenige, welche ſich nach einer gründ-

Text Types

CHAUCER
In 14, 18, 24, 30, 36, and 48 point

CLOISTER
In 6, 8, 10, 12, 14, 18, 24, 30, 36, 42, and 48 point

TUDOR
In 6, 8, 10, 12, 18, 20, 24, and 36 point

BRADLEY
In 10, 12, 18, and 24 point

WEDDING
In 6, 8, 10, 12, 14, 18 point Nos. 1 and 2
24 point Nos. 1 and 2

TEXT LETTERS, in their many and various forms as used today, are outgrowths of the earliest types of Gutenberg and his contemporaries, which in themselves were the result of attempts to copy the hand-lettering of the earlier scribes. The fonts here shown have been selected as the best available for the class of work which a university press may be called upon to produce.

CHAUCER TEXT

A B C D E F G H I J K L M N
O P Q R S T U V W X Y Z &
a b c d e f g h i j k l m n o p q r s t
u v w x y z 1 2 3 4 5 6 7 8 9 0 $

CLOISTER TEXT

A B C D E F G H I J K L M N
O P Q R S T U V W X Y Z &
a b c d e f g h i j k l m n o p q r s t u
v w x y z 1 2 3 4 5 6 7 8 9 0 $ ä ll

TUDOR TEXT

A B C D E F G H I J K L M N
O P Q R S T U V W X Y Z &
a b c d e f g h i j k l m n o p q r s t u v
w x y z 1 2 3 4 5 6 7 8 9 0 $ ff fi fl ffi ffl

BRADLEY TEXT

A B C D E F G H I J K L M N
O P Q R S T U V W X Y Z &
a b c d e f g h i j k l m n o p q r s
t u v w x y z 1 2 3 4 5 6 7 8 9 0 $

WEDDING TEXT

A B C D E F G H I J K L M N
O P Q R S T U V W X Y Z &
a b c d e f g h i j k l m n o p q r s t u v
w x y z 1 2 3 4 5 6 7 8 9 0 $ nd rd st th

Chaucer Text

✣

Fourteen Point

Text Letters in their many and varied forms as used today, are outgrowths of the earliest

Eighteen Point

Text Letters in their various forms as used today, are the outgrowth of

Twenty-four Point

Text Letters, in their many and various forms as used

Thirty Point

Text Letters, in their

Thirty-six Point

Text Letters in the

Forty-eight Point

Text Letters,

Cloister Text

✦

Six Point

Text Letters, in their many and various forms as used today, are outgrowths of the earliest types of Gutenberg and his contemporaries, which in themselves were the results of attempts to copy hand-letter

Eight Point

Text Letters, in their many and various forms as used to-day, are outgrowths of the earliest types of Gutenberg and his contemporaries, which in themselves were the results of

Ten Point

Text Letters, in their many and various forms as used today, are outgrowths of the earliest types of Gutenberg and his contemporaries, of

Twelve Point

Text Letters, in their many and various forms as used today, are outgrowths of the earliest types of Gutenberg and his

Fourteen Point

Text Letters, in their many forms as used today, are the outgrowths of the earliest types of Gutenberg

Eighteen Point

Text Letters, in their many and various forms as used today, are outgrowths of the

Cloister Text

✣

Twenty-four Point

Text Letters, in their various forms are the

Thirty Point

Text Letters in the many and various

Thirty-six Point

Text Letters in their many and

Forty-two Point

Text Letters

Forty-eight Point

Text Type

Tudor Text

✠

Six Point

Text Letters, in their many and various forms as used today, are outgrowths of the earliest types of Gutenberg and his con-

Eight Point

Text Letters, in their many and various forms as used today, are outgrowths of the earliest

Ten Point

Text Letters, in their various forms as used today are outgrowths of the

Twelve Point

Text Letters, in their many and various forms as used today, are

Eighteen Point

Text Letters in the many forms as used today, are

Twenty-four Point

Text Letters, in the many forms as used

Thirty-six Point

Text Letters

Bradley Text

✣

Ten Point

Text Letters, in their many and various forms as used today, are outgrowths of the earliest types of Gutenberg and his contemporaries which in themselves were the results of attempts to copy

Twelve Point

Text Letters, in their many and various forms as used today, are outgrowths of the earliest types of Gutenberg and his contemporaries which in themselves were

Eighteen Point

Text, Letters in their many and various forms as used today, are outgrowths of the earliest types of Gutenberg and copy

Twenty-four Point

Text Types in the many forms as used today are outgrowths of the early

Wedding Text

+

Six Point

Text Letters, in their many and various forms as used today, are the outgrowths of the earliest types of Gutenberg and his contemporaries, which

Eight Point

Text Letters, in their many and various forms as used today, are outgrowths of the earliest types of Gutenberg and

Ten Point

Text Letters, in their many and various forms as used today, are outgrowths of the earliest type

Twelve Point

Text Letters in the many and various forms as used today, are outgrowths of the earliest

Fourteen Point

Text Letters, in their many and various forms as used today, are outgrowths of

Eighteen Point No. 1

Text Letters in their many and various forms as used today are the out-

Eighteen Point No. 2

Text Letters, in their many and

Twenty-four Point No. 1

Text Letters in their many and

Twenty-four Point No. 2

Text Letters in their many

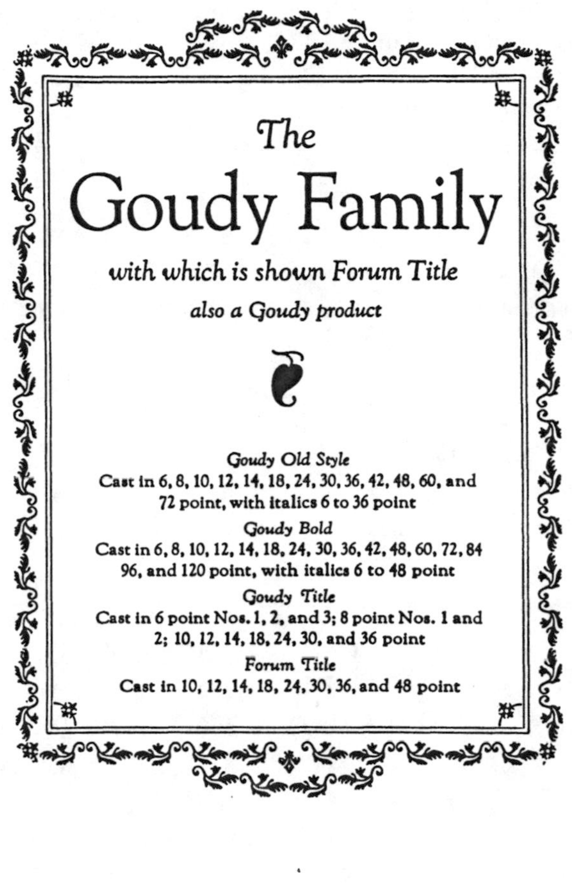

The

Goudy Family

with which is shown Forum Title

also a Goudy product

Goudy Old Style
Cast in 6, 8, 10, 12, 14, 18, 24, 30, 36, 42, 48, 60, and 72 point, with italics 6 to 36 point

Goudy Bold
Cast in 6, 8, 10, 12, 14, 18, 24, 30, 36, 42, 48, 60, 72, 84 96, and 120 point, with italics 6 to 48 point

Goudy Title
Cast in 6 point Nos. 1, 2, and 3; 8 point Nos. 1 and 2; 10, 12, 14, 18, 24, 30, and 36 point

Forum Title
Cast in 10, 12, 14, 18, 24, 30, 36, and 48 point

THE GOUDY FAMILY (with the exception of Goudy Bold, adapted by Morris Benton from Goudy Old Style) was designed by Frederic W. Goudy. The Old Style and the Bold are particularly good letters for general job advertising work, while the Title is well adapted for covers, title-pages, and headings. The following alphabets display the characters in the various fonts.

GOUDY OLD STYLE

A B C D E F G H I J K L M N
O P Q R S T U V W X Y Z &
ABCDEFGHIJKLMNOPQRSTUVWXYZ&
a b c d e f g h i j k l m n o p q r s t u v
w x y z 1 2 3 4 5 6 7 8 9 0 ct ff fi fl ffi ffl $
A B C D E F G H I J K L M N O
P Q Qu R S T T U V W X Y Z &
a b c d e f g h i j k l m n o p q r s t u v
w x y z 1 2 3 4 5 6 7 8 9 0 ct ff fi fl ffi ffl $

GOUDY BOLD

A B C D E F G H I J K L M N
O P Q R S T U V W X Y Z &
a b c d e f g h i j k l m n o p q r s t u
v w x y z ff fi fl ffi ffl 1 2 3 4 5 6 7 8 9 0 $
A B C D E F G H I J K L M N
O P Q R S T U V W X Y Z &
a b c d e f g h i j k l m n o p q r s t u
v w x y z 1 2 3 4 5 6 7 8 9 0 ff fi fl ffi ffl $

GOUDY TITLE

ABCDEFGHIJKLMNOPQRS
TUVWXYZ&1234567890$

Goudy Old Style

Six Point

THE GOUDY FAMILY OF TYPE FACES IS A RECENT PRODUCT OF THE DESIGNER WHOSE NAME IT BEARS, AND IS A WIDELY used and most popular medium for general printing of almost *every character. It is available only in hand type and therefore is not*

Eight Point

THE GOUDY FAMILY OF TYPE FACES IS A RECENT PRODUCT OF THE DESIGNER WHOSE NAME IT BEARS, and is a widely used and most popular medium for *general printing of almost every character. It is available*

Ten Point

THE GOUDY FAMILY OF TYPE FACES IS A RECENT PRODUCT OF THE DESIGNER WHOSE name it bears, and is a widely used and most *popular medium for general printing of almost*

Twelve Point

THE GOUDY FAMILY OF TYPE FACES IS A RECENT PRODUCT OF THE DESIGNER whose name it bears, and is a *widely used and most popular medium for*

Fourteen Point

THE GOUDY FAMILY OF type faces is a recent product of the designer whose name it bears *and is a widely used and popular*

Goudy Old Style

Eighteen Point

THE GOUDY FAMILY
of type faces is a product
of that great type designer
whose name it bears, and is

Twenty-four Point

GOUDY FAMILY
of type faces is a re-
cent product of that
great type designer and

Thirty Point

GOUDY TYPE
a product of the
great designer who

Goudy Old Style

Thirty-six Point

GOUDY IS
the product of
that great type

Forty-two Point

GOUDY IS
a product of

Forty-eight Point

GOUDY
family is a

Goudy Old Style

Sixty Point

TYPES
that can

Seventy-two Point

TYPE
of that

Goudy Bold

Six Point

THE GOUDY FAMILY OF TYPE FACES IS A RECENT product of the designer whose name it bears, and is a widely used and most popular medium for general printing of almost ***every character. It is available only in hand type and therefore***

Eight Point

THE GOUDY FAMILY OF TYPE FACES IS a recent product of the designer whose name it bears, and is a widely used and most popular ***medium for general printing of every description in***

Ten Point

THE GOUDY FAMILY OF TYPE faces is a recent product of the designer whose name it bears, and is a widely used ***and most popular medium for printing of***

Twelve Point

THE GOUDY FAMILY OF TYPE faces is a recent product of the designer whose name it bears, and is ***a widely used and popular medium***

Fourteen Point

THE GOUDY FAMILY OF type faces is a recent product of the designer whose name ***it bears, and is a widely used***

Goudy Bold

Eighteen Point

THE GOUDY FAMILY
of type faces is a recent
product of the designer
whose name it bears and

Twenty-four Point

GOUDY FAMILY
of type faces is a re-
cent product of the
great type designer

Thirty Point

THE GOUDY
family of type is
a recent product

Goudy Bold

Thirty-six Point

GOUDY IS
a product of
the great de-
signer whose

Forty-two Point

TYPES IN
the Goudy
family are
the product

Goudy Bold

Forty-eight Point

GOUDY family of *type faces*

Sixty Point

TYPE named

Goudy Bold, without italic, is also on hand in 72, 84, 96, and 120 point for large display

GOUDY TITLE

Six Point No. 1

THE GOUDY FAMILY OF TYPE FACES IS A RECENT PRODUCT OF THE DESIGNER WHOSE NAME IT BEARS, AND IS A WIDELY USED AND MOST POPULAR MEDIUM FOR PRINTING OF ALMOST EVERY CHARACTER AND

Six Point No. 2

THE GOUDY FAMILY OF TYPE FACES IS A RECENT PRODUCT OF THE DESIGNER WHOSE NAME IT BEARS, AND IS A MUCH USED AND POPULAR MEDIUM FOR GENERAL PRINTING OF

Six Point No. 3

THE GOUDY FAMILY OF TYPE FACES IS A RECENT PRODUCT. OF THE GREAT TYPE DESIGNER WHOSE NAME IT BEARS, AND IS A WIDELY USED AND A

Eight Point No. 1

THE GOUDY FAMILY OF TYPE FACES IS A RECENT PRODUCT OF THE DESIGNER WHOSE NAME IT BEARS, AND IS A WIDELY USED

Eight Point No. 2

THE GOUDY FAMILY OF TYPE FACES IS A RECENT PRODUCT OF THE DESIGNER WHOSE NAME IT BEARS, AND

Ten Point

THE GOUDY FAMILY OF TYPE FACES IS A RECENT PRODUCT OF THE GREAT DESIGNER IN

Twelve Point

THE GOUDY FAMILY OF TYPE FACES IS A RECENT PRODUCT OF THE MAN

GOUDY TITLE

Fourteen Point

THE GOUDY FAMILY
OF TYPE FACES IS A

Eighteen Point

GOUDY FAMILY
OF TYPE FACES IS

Twenty-four Point

THE GOUDY
TYPES HAVE

Thirty Point

GOUDY IS
A RECENT

Thirty-six Point

GOUDY

FORUM TITLE

THE FORUM TITLE was designed by Mr. Goudy from rubbings taken by him of inscriptions in the Roman Forum. It is cast in capitals only, and is an exceedingly useful face in connection with such old-style letters as Caslon, Bruce, Garamont, and Goudy.

A B C D E F G H I J K L
M N O P Q R S T U V W
X Y Z & ' 1 2 3 4 5 6 7 8 9 0

Ten Point

A THOUGHTFUL GREEK WHOSE

Twelve Point

THOUGHTFUL GREEK LIKE

Fourteen Point

WHEN THOUGHTFUL

Eighteen Point

GREEK THOUGHT

Twenty-four Point

GREEKS LIKE

FORUM TITLE

Thirty Point

GREEKS OF THOUGHT

Thirty-six Point

WHEN A GREEK IS

Forty-two Point

LIKE A GREEK

A TYPE WIDELY USED IN
ADVERTISEMENTS

Cheltenham Wide

Cast in 6, 8, 10, 12, 14, 18, 24, 30, 36, 42, and 48 point with italics 6 to 36 point

Cheltenham Bold

Cast in 6, 8, 10, 12, 14, 18, 24, 30, 36, 42, 48, 60, and 72 point, with italics 6 to 48 point

THE CHELTENHAM FAMILY is the largest of the type families produced to date, and because of the great variety of faces available is well adapted for advertisement composition. It has been produced in twenty-four different series. It was designed by Bertram G. Goodhue in collaboration with Ingalls Kimball. The following alphabets of the Wide and Bold series illustrate the characters in those fonts:

A B C D E F G H I J K L M N O P
Q Qu R S T U V W X Y Z & Æ Œ
a b c d e f g h i j k l m n o p q
r s t u v w x y z 1 2 3 4 5 6 7
8 9 0 ff fi fl ffl ffi $ æ œ ct st

A B B C D D E E F G H I J K L M N N
O P P Q Qu R S T T U V W X Y Z &
a b c d e f g h i j k l m n o p
q r s t u v w x y z 1 2 3 4 5
6 7 8 9 0 ff fi fl ffi ffl $ ct

A B C D E F G H I J K L M N
O P Q R S T U V W X Y Z &
a b c d e f g h i j k l m n o p q r s
t u v w x y z 1 2 3 4 5 6 7 8 9 0 $

A B C D E F G H I J K L M N
O P Q R S T U V W X Y Z &
a b c d e f g h i j k l m n o p q r s
t u v w x y z 1 2 3 4 5 6 7 8 9 0 $

Cheltenham Wide

Six Point

THE CHELTENHAM TYPES HAVE BEEN DEVELOPED in twenty-four series through various modifications, and are known in all countries of the civilized world. It has been largely ***used as an advertising letter, and was, for that purpose, a great improve-***

Eight Point

THE CHELTENHAM TYPES HAVE BEEN DEveloped in twenty-four series through various modifications, and are known in all countries of the civilized ***world. It has been largely used as an advertising letter, and***

Ten Point

THE CHELTENHAM SERIES OF TYPES have been developed in twenty-four series through various modifications, and is now *known in all countries of the civilized world. It is*

Twelve Point

THE CHELTENHAM TYPE HAS been developed in twenty-four series through various modifications, and is *known in all countries of the civilized world*

Fourteen Point

THE CHELTENHAM TYPE has been developed in twenty-four series through various modi-*fications, and is known everywhere*

Cheltenham Wide

Eighteen Point

THE CHELTENHAM type has been developed into a series of twenty-four *faces of various modification*

Twenty-four Point

THE CHELTEN-ham type has been developed in a series *of twenty-four faces of*

Thirty Point

A CHELTEN-ham type which *has been developed*

Cheltenham Wide

Thirty-six Point

THE CHEL
tenham types
were developed

Forty-two Point

CHELTEN
ham type is

Forty-eight Point

A TYPE
developed

Cheltenham Bold

Six Point

THE CHELTENHAM TYPES HAVE BEEN DEVELOPED in twenty-four series through various modifications, and are ***known in all countries of the civilized world. It has been***

Eight Point

THE CHELTENHAM TYPES HAVE BEEN DEveloped in twenty-four series through the various ***modifications and are known in all countries of the***

Ten Point

THE CHELTENHAM TYPES HAVE been developed in twenty-four series of ***various modifications and are known in***

Twelve Point

THE CHELTENHAM TYPE HAS been developed in twenty-four series ***through various modifications, and***

Fourteen Point

THE CHELTENHAM TYPE has been developed in twenty- ***four series through a various***

Eighteen Point

CHELTENHAM TYPE has been developed into ***a series of twenty-four***

Cheltenham Bold

Twenty-four Point

**THE CHELTEN-
ham type has been
*developed into the***

Thirty Point

**THE TYPE OF
cheltenham has
*been developed***

Thirty-six Point

**THE CHEL-
tenham type
*developed in***

Cheltenham Bold

Forty-two Point

CHELTEN ham types have been ***developed***

Forty-eight Point

A TYPE that was ***of recent***

Cheltenham Bold

Sixty Point

TYPES that are used on

Seventy-two Point

TYPE which

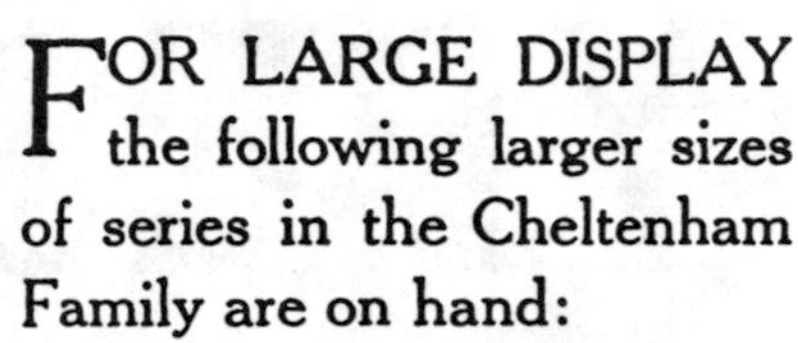

FOR LARGE DISPLAY the following larger sizes of series in the Cheltenham Family are on hand:

Cheltenham Bold Condensed in 72
96, 120, 144, 188, and
216 point

Cheltenham Bold Extra Condensed
in 72, 96, and 120 point

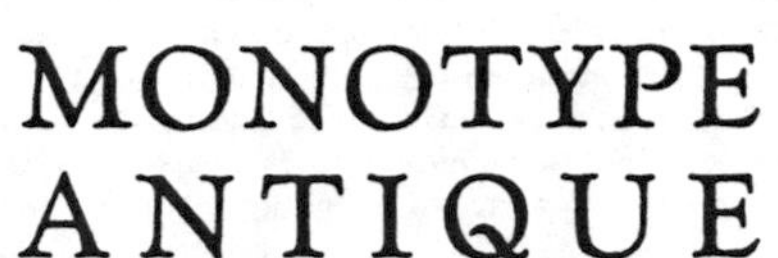

MONOTYPE ANTIQUE

NUMBER 25

A BOLDFACE ANTIQUE
SUITABLE FOR USE WITH
BRUCE OLD STYLE NO. 31
AND CASLON OLD STYLE

CAST IN 6, 7, 8, 9, 10, AND 11 POINT
WITH ITALIC IN 7, 8, 10, AND 12 POINT

Monotype Antique No. 25

Six Point, Two Point Leaded

JOB PRINTING AS A DISTINCT DEPARTMENT IS OF MODERN DEVELOPMENT. TYPOGRAPHERS OF OLD WERE primarily book and pamphlet printers, and in many cases interest was chiefly centered in publishing newspapers or almanacs; job printing was incidental. This caused similarity in the typography of newspaper, book, and job work, a condition that today exists only in a small degree. Now these three classes of work are generally separated into several

Seven Point, Two Point Leaded

JOB PRINTING AS A DISTINCT DEPARTMENT IS OF MODERN DEVELOPMENT. TYPOGRAPHERS OF OLD were primarily book and pamphlet printers, and in many cases interest was chiefly centered in publishing newspapers or almanacs; job printing was incidental. This caused similarity in the typography of newspaper, book, and job work, a condition

Eight Point, Two Point Leaded

JOB PRINTING AS A DISTINCT DEPARTMENT IS OF MODERN DEVELOPMENT. TYPOGRAPHERS of old were primarily book and pamphlet printers, and in many cases interest was chiefly centered in publishing newspapers or almanacs; job printing was incidental. This caused similarity in the typography of newspaper, book, and

Nine Point, Two Point Leaded

JOB PRINTING AS A DISTINCT DEPARTMENT IS OF MODERN DEVELOPMENT. PRINTERS of old were primarily book and pamphlet printers, and in many cases interest was chiefly centered in publishing newspapers or almanacs; job printing was

Ten Point, Two Point Leaded

JOB PRINTING AS A SEPARATE AND DISTINCT DEPARTMENT IS OF MODERN development. Typographers of old were primarily book and pamphlet printers, and in many cases interest was chiefly centered in publishing news

Monotype Antique No. 25

Eleven Point, Two Point Leaded

JOB PRINTING AS A SEPARATE AND DISTINCT DEPARTMENT IS OF RE-cent development. Typographers of old were primarily book and pamphlet printers, and in

Seven Point Italic, Two Point Leaded

Job Printing as a distinct department is of modern develop-ment. Typographers of old were primarily book and pamphlet printers, and in many cases interest was chiefly centered in publishing newspapers or almanacs; job printing was inciden-tal. This caused similarity in the typography of newspaper, book, and job work, a condition that today exists only in a few

Eight Point Italic, Two Point Leaded

Job Printing as a distinct department is of modern develop-ment. Typographers of old were primarily book and pamph-let printers, and in many cases interest was chiefly centered in publishing newspapers or almanacs; job printing was incidental. This caused similarity in the typography of newspaper, book, and job work, a condition that today exist

Ten Point Italic, Two Point Leaded

Job Printing as a distinct department is of modern development. Typographers of old were primarily book and pamphlet printers, and in many case in-terest was chiefly centered in publishing newspapers or almanacs; job printing was incidental. This cause

Twelve Point Italic, Two Point Leaded

Job Printing as a distinct department is of modern development. Typographers of old were primarily book and pamphlet printers and in many cases interest was chiefly on

MONOTYPE ANTIQUE NO. 25
WITH BRUCE OLD STYLE

Eight Point, Two Point Leaded
With Nine-Point Bruce Old Style

THUS in the foregoing example **takaku** and **samuku** must be translated by the English present indicative, because of the final adjective **sukunashi** makes a general assertion, and may therefore be considered to be in the present tense. Again, take the example: **Toshi wakaku, karada mo tsuyokereba gunjin ni teki su-beshi,** "Being young and strong, he will be suitable for a soldier." Here the intervention of the adjective **tsuyokereba** in the conditional mood at the end of the succeeding clause shows that **wakaku** also must be construed as a conditional (**wakakereba**). The construction is often a little more complicated. Thus: **Fune aredomo hito naku: hito aru mo kikai nakariki,** "We had ships, but no men; and even if we had had the men, we had no machinery." Here the rhythm of the sentence shows that we must go to the end of the clause **hito aru mo, kikai nakariki** to find the adjective (verb) corresponding to **naku.** The **aru** of the second clause has to be passed over.

98. The conclusive form, which is obtained by adding **shi** to the stem. It is used only as a predicative, as in the case of **sukunashi** in the first example given in the preceding paragraph. Those adjectives whose stem ends in **shi** or **ji** do not add another **shi** to form the conclusive, the one **shi** being held to suffice. Thus: **mezurashiku,** conclusive **mezurashi,** "strange"; **arumajiku,** conclusive **aru-maji,** "should not be." This exception is sometimes disregarded by ignorant writers; and such ungrammatical forms as **ashishi** (for **ashi**), "bad," are therefore occasionally met with.

99. The attributive form, which is obtained by adding **ki** to the stem. It is used in three distinct manners.

GOTHIC TYPES

NEWS

IN 6, 8, 10, 12, 14, 18, AND 24 POINT

COPPERPLATE

IN 6 POINT NOS. 1 TO 4; 12 POINT NOS. 1 TO 4
AND 18 POINT NOS. 1 AND 2

INTERCHANGEABLE

IN 6 POINT NOS. 1 TO 5; 8, 10, 12, 18
AND 24 POINT

THESE TYPES ARE SHOWN BECAUSE OF THEIR
EXTENSIVE USE IN LETTERING
SCIENTIFIC DRAWINGS

News Gothic

Six Point

ADVERTISING TYPOGRAPHY IS NOT A SEPARATE AND PECU-liar art, but the natural and simple principles of typography applied to advertising purposes. Remember that we put words

Eight Point

ADVERTISING TYPOGRAPHY IS NOT A SEPARATE AND peculiar art, but the natural principles of typography applied to advertising purposes. Remember that we

Ten Point

ADVERTISING TYPOGRAPHY IS NOT A SEPA-rate and peculiar art, but a natural and simple principle of typography applied to advertising

Twelve Point

ADVERTISING TYPOGRAPHY IS NOT A separate and peculiar art, but the natural and simple principles of typography that

Fourteen Point

ADVERTISING TYPOGRAPHY IS A natural and simple principle in the

Eighteen Point

THE TYPOGRAPHY OF AD-vertisements is the natural

Twenty-four Point

ADVERTISING TYPOG-raphy is a natural and

COPPERPLATE GOTHIC

Six Point No. 1

ADVERTISING TYPOGRAPHY IS NOT A SEPARATE AND PECULIAR ART, BUT THE NATURAL AND SIMPLE PRINCIPLES OF TYPOGRAPHY WHICH IS APPLIED

Six Point No. 2

ADVERTISING TYPOGRAPHY IS NOT A SEPARATE AND PECULIAR ART, BUT THE NATURAL AND SIMPLE PRINCIPLES OF TYPOGRAPHY

Six Point No. 3

ADVERTISING TYPOGRAPHY IS NOT A SEPARATE AND PECULIAR ART, BUT THE NATURAL AND SIMPLE PRINCI-

Six Point No. 4

ADVERTISING TYPOGRAPHY IS NOT A SEPARATE AND PECULIAR ART, BUT THE NATURAL AND

Twelve Point No. 1

ADVERTISING TYPOGRAPHY IS NOT A SEPARATE AND PECULIAR ART BUT IS

Twelve Point No. 2

ADVERTISING TYPOGRAPHY IS A NATURAL & SIMPLE PRINCIPLE

Twelve Point No. 3

ADVERTISING TYPOGRA-PHY IS NOT A SEPARATE

Twelve Point No. 4

SIMPLE PRINCIPLES OF ADVERTISEMENT

Eighteen Point No. 1

ADVERTISING IS

Eighteen Point No. 2

TYPOGRAPHY

INTERCHANGEABLE GOTHIC

Six Point No. 1

ADVERTISING TYPOGRAPHY IS NOT A SEPARATE AND PECULIAR ART, BUT THE NATURAL AND SIMPLE PRINCIPLES OF TYPOGRAPHY APPLIED TO ADVERTISING

Six Point No. 2

ADVERTISING TYPOGRAPHY IS NOT A SEPARATE AND PECULIAR ART, BUT THE NATURAL AND SIMPLE PRINCIPLES OF TYPOGRAPHY AS APPLIED TO

Six Point No. 3

ADVERTISING TYPOGRAPHY IS NOT A SEPARATE AND PECULIAR ART, BUT THE NATURAL AND SIMPLE PRINCIPLES OF

Six Point No. 4

ADVERTISING TYPOGRAPHY IS NOT A SEPARATE AND PECULIAR ART BUT THE NATURAL AND SIMPLE PRIN-

Six Point No. 5

ADVERTISING TYPOGRAPHY IS NOT A SEPARATE AND PECULIAR ART BUT THE NATURAL

Eight Point

ADVERTISING TYPOGRAPHY IS NOT A SEPARATE AND PECULIAR ART BUT A

Ten Point

ADVERTISING TYPOGRAPHY IS NOT A SEPARATE ART, BUT IS

Twelve Point

A SIMPLE AND NATURAL PRINCIPLE OF THE ART

Eighteen Point

ADVERTISING IS

Twenty-four Point

ADVERTISE

MISCELLANEOUS TYPE FACES

Modern No. 527

(Foundry)

Five Point, One Point Leaded

MEMORIES OF THINGS that have deeply stirred the imagination are the seeds from which invention springs. The art of printing from movable types was foreshadowed by the brick stamps of the ancient Babylonians, yet it is none the less honor to Gutenberg, who conceived the invention and made the first practical application of the principle, that some germ of the principle itself was known and in use centuries before him.

To present ideas visibly, that is, to exhibit conceptions of the mind by the use of written or printed characters that represent spoken sounds expressing those conceptions, has been deemed the noblest and most beneficial invention of human ingenuity. "With the art of writing," said Carlisle, " . . . . of which printing is a simple, an inevitable, comparatively insignificant corollary, the true reign of miracles for mankind commenced."

From the far-off hieroglyphs of the ancient Egyptians down to the almost perfect characters of the Renaissance, letters have been in the making. In the days before printing the scribe was born into a tradition; forms that he used without conscious thought were already universal and fundamental, and actually in the process of growth and development under the hand of each writer who used them.—FREDERIC W. GOUDY, *Monotype*.

EFFECTS IN TYPE DISPLAY, which are consistent and productive of good results, come as a rule from avoiding and not from attempting the execution of difficult and time consuming problems.

It is in an attention to little things and not by striving for big things that one can accomplish that which is truly worth while.—WILL BRADLEY, in the *American Chap-Book*.

Characters to square inch, 325; solid, 415

Modern No. 1

(Monotype)

Six Point, Two Point Leaded

THE TITLE-PAGE, besides fulfilling its function of announcing the subject or name of the work and its author, gives to the book the general tone of its typographical treatment. When a lover of books handles a new volume he instinctively opens it at the title-page, ready to receive a sensation of delight or a sense of disappointment. Imagine a day in which there was no such thing as a title-page! Yet the earliest printed books were without them.

The earliest printers slavishly followed the traditions of the scribes and calligraphers in the detailed arrangement of the book's text. The scribe took his quire of paper or vellum, wrote the name of the book on the cover, and, leaving the first leaf blank, straightway began writing at the top of the second leaf, thus keeping his text clean. Indeed, when the name of the book had been written on the cover of the vellum, there seemed no need to repeat it inside in the form of a full page. The scribe began his copy with either a preliminary paragraph, which contained the name of the book or section thereof, or else he began straightway with the text. The latter course was the more usual, since the author generally added a colophon at the end of his work, giving a few details as to the nature of the work and the date and place of its completion, which in its turn was copied by the calligraphers, and later by the printers.—OLIVER SIMON, *The Fleuron*.

Characters to square inch, 250; solid, 335

CENTURY EXPANDED

Six Point

THE TITLE-PAGE, BESIDES FULFILLING ITS FUNCTION OF ANNOUNCING THE SUBJECT OR NAME OF THE WORK A

Eight Point

THE TITLE-PAGE, BESIDES FULFILLING ITS FUNCTION OF ANNOUNCING THE SUBJECT OR

Ten Point

THE TITLE-PAGE BESIDES FULFILLING ITS FUNCTION OF ANNOUNCING THE

Eleven Point

A TITLE-PAGE, BESIDES FULFILLING ITS FUNCTION OF ANNOUNCING THE

Twelve Point

A TITLE-PAGE, BESIDES FULFILL-ING ITS FUNCTION TO ANNOUNCE

Fourteen Point

A TITLE-PAGE ANNOUNCES

Eighteen Point

TITLE-PAGES, BESIDES

Twenty-four Point

THE TITLE-PAGE

Thirty Point

A TITLE-PAGE

Goudy Open

Eighteen Point

THE TITLE-PAGE, BESIDES fulfilling its function of announcing the subject or name of the work and its author, *gives to the book the general tone of its typographical treatment. When a lover of books*

Twenty-four Point

A TITLE-PAGE, BEsides fulfilling its function of announcing the subject or name of the *work and author, gives to the book the general tone of its typography*

Goudy Open

Thirty Point

A TITLE-PAGE besides fulfilling its function of an- *nouncing the sub- ject or name of the*

Thirty-six Point

TITLE-PAGES besides fulfilling their function of *announcing the*

Original Old Style

Eighteen Point

THE TITLE-PAGE, BESIDES FULFILLING ITS FUNCTION OF ANNOUNCING the subject or name of the work and its author, gives to the book the general tone of its typographical treatment. When a lover of books handles a new volume he instinctively opens it at the title-page, ready to receive a sensation of delight or a sense of disappointment. Imagine a day in which there was no such thing as a title-page! Yet the earliest printed books were without them.

The earliest printers slavishly followed the traditions of the scribes and calligraphers in the detailed arrangement of the book's text. The scribe took

French Old Style

Six Point

THE TITLE-PAGE, BESIDES FULFILLING ITS FUNCTION OF ANnouncing the subject or name of the work and its author, gives to the book

Eight Point

THE TITLE-PAGE, BESIDES FULFILLING ITS FUNCTION of announcing the subject or name of the work and its author,

Nine Point

A TITLE-PAGE, BESIDES FULFILLING ITS FUNCtion of announcing the subject or the name of the work and

Ten Point

THE TITLE-PAGE, BESIDES FULFILLING ITS function of announcing the subject or the name of

Twelve Point

THE TITLE-PAGE, BESIDES FULFILling its function of announcing the subject

Eighteen Point

TITLE-PAGES, BESIDES FULfilling their function of announc-

Twenty Point

THE TITLE-PAGE, BEsides fulfilling its function of announcing the name

French Old Style

Twenty-four Point

A TITLE-PAGE AN-
nounces the subject

Thirty Point

A TITLE-PAGE,
besides fulfilling

Thirty-six Point

TITLE-PAGE
announces its

Forty-eight Point

BESIDES
fulfilling its

Tiffany Script

Fourteen Point

A Title-Page besides fulfilling its function of announcing the subject or name of the work and its author, gives the book the general tone of its typographical treatment. When a lover of books handles a new volume he instinct

Eighteen Point

A Title-Page, besides fulfilling its function of announcing the subject or name of the work and its author, gives to the book the general

Twenty-four Point

The Title=Page, besides fulfilling its function of announcing the subject or name of the work and its author, it

Thirty Point

A Title=Page besides fulfilling its function of announcing the subjects or name of the work

Tiffany Upright

Twelve Point

A Title-Page, besides fulfilling its function of announcing the subject or name of the work and its author, gives the book

Fourteen Point

A Title-Page, besides fulfilling its function of announc-ing the subject or name of the work and its authors,

Eighteen Point

A Title-Page, besides fulfilling its function of announcing the subject or name of the

Twenty-four Point No. 1

The Title-Page, besides fulfilling its function of announcing the subjects

Twenty-four Point No. 2

A Title-Page, besides fulfilling its function of announcing its subject

Thirty Point

The Title-Page, besides its function of announcing its

Borders
Ornaments
Initials
&c.

PRINTERS' FLOWERS

WRITING of Caslon's ornaments or flowers, Mr. W. A. Dwiggins says: "To a designer's eyes they have taken as individual patterns an inevitable quality, a finality of right construction that baffles any attempt to change or improve. . . . . Excellent as single spots, the Caslon flowers multiply their beauties when composed in bands or borders as ornamentation for letterpress. They then become a true flowering of the letter forms—as though particular groups of words had been told off for special ornamental duty and had blossomed at command into intricate, but always typographical patterns. This faculty possessed by the Caslon ornaments of keeping an unmistakable type quality through all their graceful evolutions sets them apart from the innumerable offerings of the type founders' craft as a unique group. . . . . From the point of view of the pressman, as practical working types for impressing ink into paper, they may be claimed to be better, so far as English and American designs are concerned, than any type-flowers produced since their period. The proportion of printing surface to open paper . . . . is excellently adapted for the purposes of clean, sharp impression. Certain ones have elements broken by the tint-lines into a clear-printing gray, and it will be also observed that this tint is not the gray of copper-plate, but has the weight and solidity of a printing surface backed by metal."

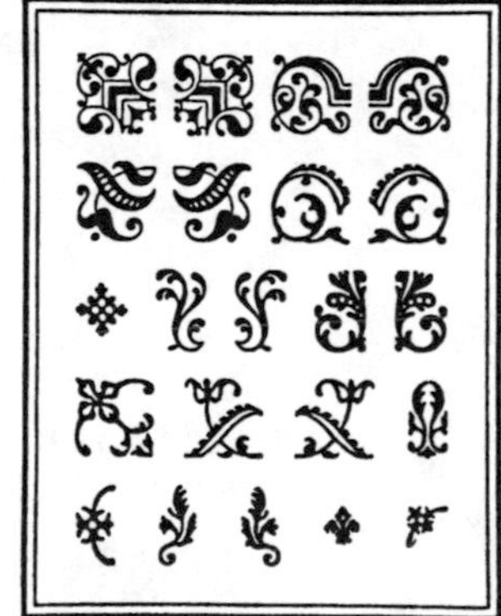

Combinations of Flowers

Combination Flower Borders

No. 1—Monotype

No. 2—Monotype

No. 3—Monotype

No. 4—Foundry

No. 5—Foundry

No. 6—Monotype

No. 7—Monotype

No. 8—Monotype

No. 9—Monotype

No. 10—Foundry

No. 11—Monotype

No. 12—Foundry

Combination Flower Borders

No. 13—Monotype

No. 14—Monotype

No. 15—Monotype

No. 16—Monotype

No. 17—Monotype

No. 18—Monotype

No. 19—Monotype

No. 20—Monotype

No. 21—Monotype

No. 22—Foundry

No. 23—Foundry

Combination Flower Borders

No. 24—Monotype

No. 25—Monotype

No. 26—Monotype

No. 27—Foundry

No. 28—Foundry

No. 29—Monotype

No. 30—Monotype

Borders

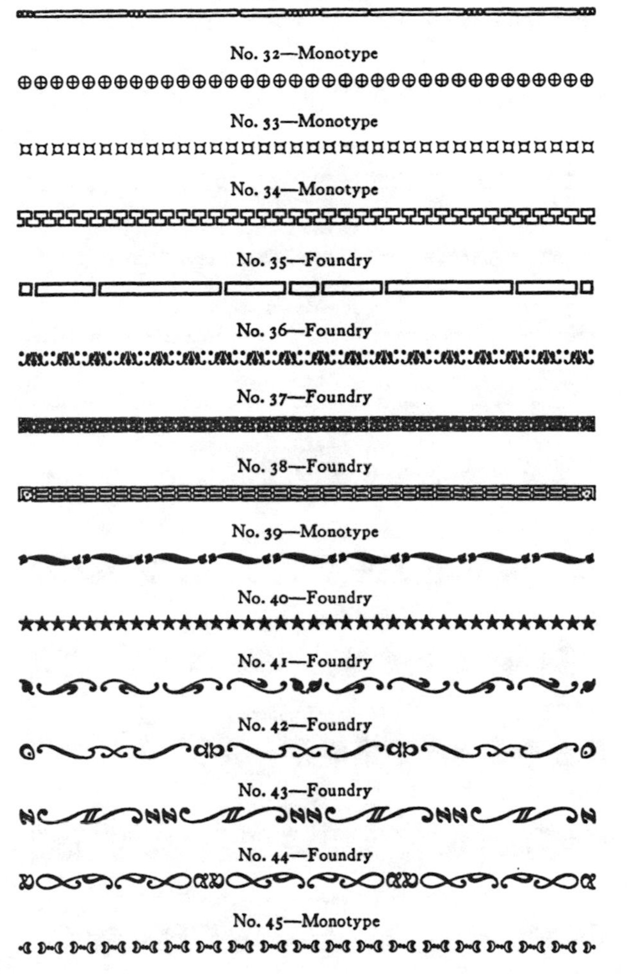
No. 31—Foundry
No. 32—Monotype
No. 33—Monotype
No. 34—Monotype
No. 35—Foundry
No. 36—Foundry
No. 37—Foundry
No. 38—Foundry
No. 39—Monotype
No. 40—Foundry
No. 41—Foundry
No. 42—Foundry
No. 43—Foundry
No. 44—Foundry
No. 45—Monotype

Borders

No. 46—Foundry

No. 47—Foundry

No. 48—Monotype

No. 49—Monotype

No. 50—Monotype

No. 51—Monotype

No. 52—Monotype

No. 53—Foundry

No. 54—Foundry—Two colors

No. 55—Foundry

No. 56—Foundry

No. 57—Foundry—Two colors

Borders

No. 58—Foundry

No. 59—Foundry

No. 60—Foundry

No. 61—Foundry

No. 62—Foundry

No. 63—Foundry—Two colors

No. 64—Foundry

Borders

No. 65—Foundry

No. 66—Foundry

No. 67—Foundry

No. 68—Foundry

No. 69—Foundry

No. 70—Foundry

No. 71—Foundry

No. 72—Foundry

No. 73—Foundry

No. 74—Foundry

No. 75—Foundry

No. 76—Foundry

No. 77—Foundry

No. 78—Foundry

Borders

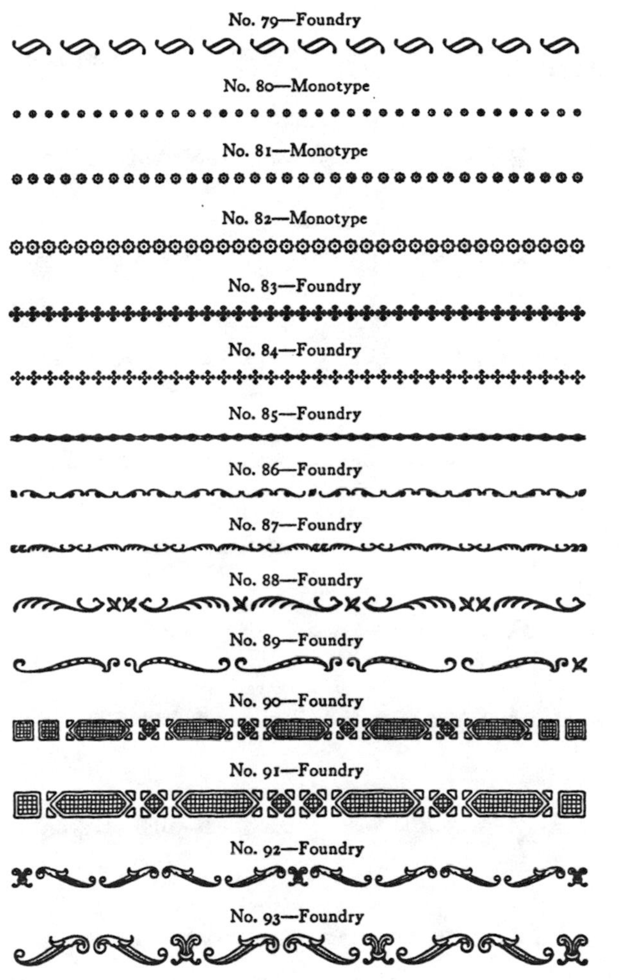
No. 79—Foundry
No. 80—Monotype
No. 81—Monotype
No. 82—Monotype
No. 83—Foundry
No. 84—Foundry
No. 85—Foundry
No. 86—Foundry
No. 87—Foundry
No. 88—Foundry
No. 89—Foundry
No. 90—Foundry
No. 91—Foundry
No. 92—Foundry
No. 93—Foundry

Borders

No. 94—Foundry

No. 95—Foundry

No. 96—Monotype

No. 97—Monotype

No. 98—Monotype

No. 99—Monotype

No. 100—Monotype

No. 101—Monotype

No. 102—Monotype

No. 103—Monotype

Borders

No. 104—Monotype

No. 105—Monotype

No. 106—Monotype

No. 107—Monotype

No. 108—Monotype

No. 109—Foundry

No. 110—Foundry

No. 111—Foundry

No. 112—Monotype

No. 113—Foundry

Nos. 114, 115, 116—Monotype

Cochin Borders

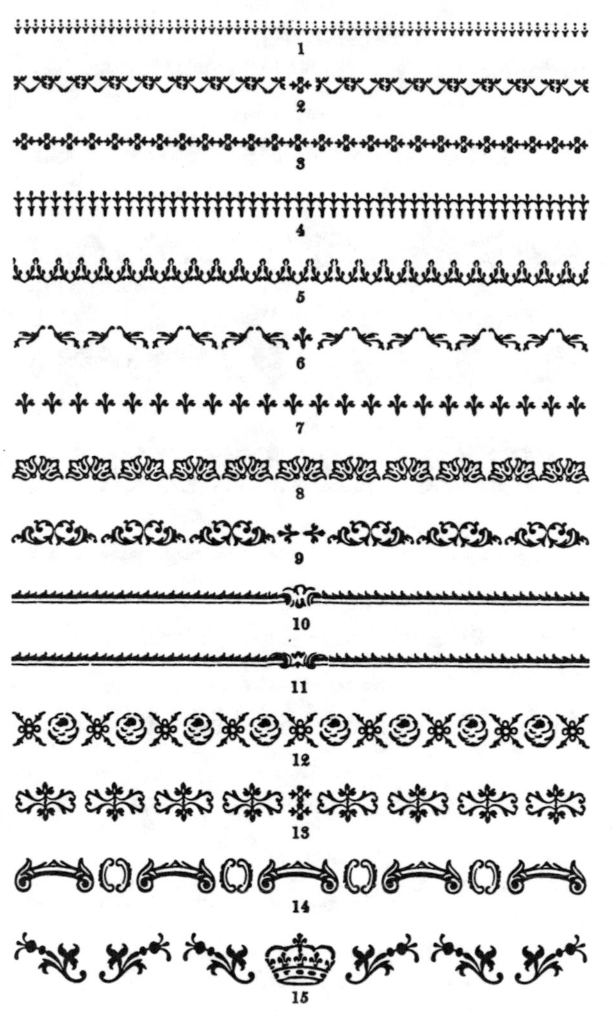

Cochin Borders

16

17

18

19

20

21

22

23

24

25

Ornaments

1 2 3 4 5 6 7 8 9 10 11 12 13
14 15 16 17 18 19 20 21 22 23
24 25 26 27 28 29 30 31 32
33 34 35 36 37 38 39 40 41
42 43 44 45 46 47
48 49 50 51 52 53 54
55 56 57 58 59 60
61 62 63 64 65
66 67 67 68
69 70 71 72
73 74 75 76

Ornaments

77
78
79
80
81
82
83
84
85
86
87
88
89
90
91
92
93
94
95
96
97
98
99
100
101

Ornaments

102
103
104
105
106
107
108
109
110
111
112
113
114
115
116
117
118
119
120

Ornaments

121

122

123

124

125

126

127

128

129

130

Ornaments

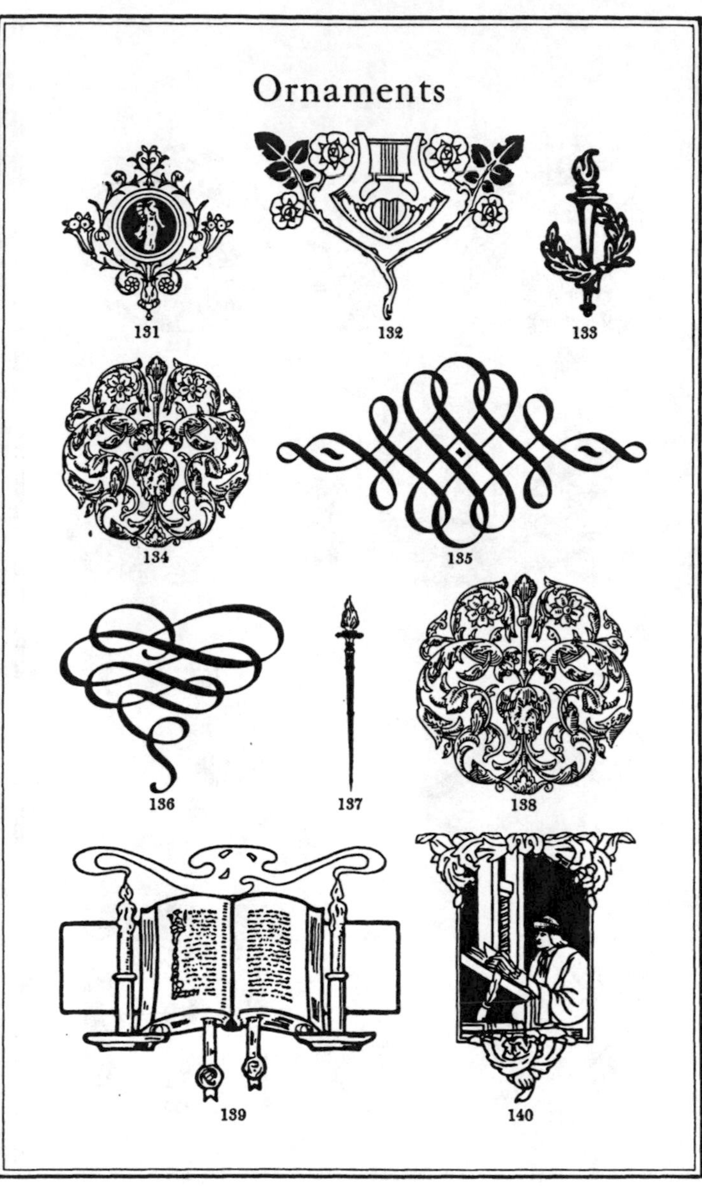

Ornaments

Ornaments

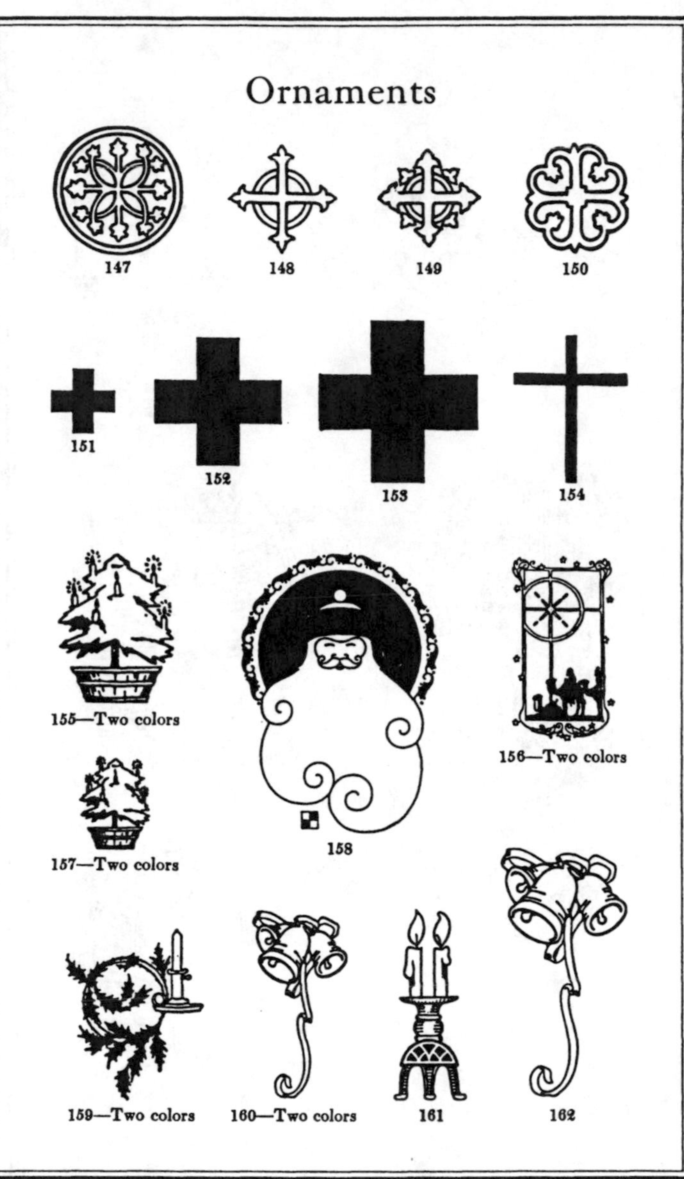
147
148
149
150
151
152
153
154
155—Two colors
156—Two colors
157—Two colors
158
159—Two colors
160—Two colors
161
162

Ornaments

163 164 165

166 167 168

169 170

171

Ornaments

No. 172—Linotype Dash

No. 173—Linotype Dash

No. 174—Brass German Dash
Also available in 3, 5, 7, 9, 11, 13, 17, 21, 25, 29, and 33 picas

No. 175

No. 176

No. 177

No. 178

No. 179

No. 180

No. 181

Headbands and Tailpieces

1

2

3

4

5

Headbands and Tailpieces

6

7

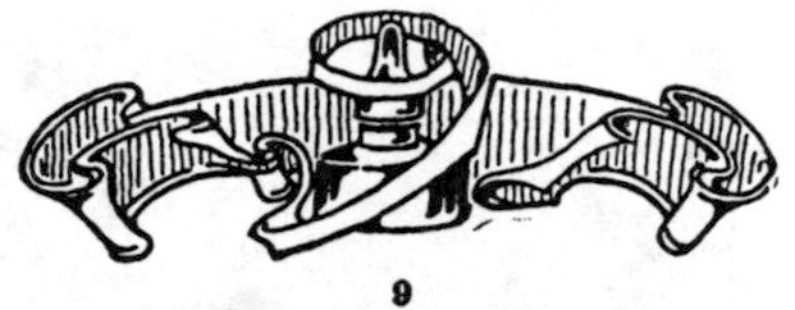

8

9

10

Monotype Rules

No. 65—Hairline

No. 66—Hairline Parallel

No. 67—One-half Point

No. 68—One-half Point Parallel

No. 69—One-half Point Parallel

No. 70—Parallel

No. 71—Parallel

No. 72—Parallel

No. 73—One Point

No. 74—Two Point

No. 75—Three Point

No. 76—Six Point

No. 77—Twelve Point

Brass Rules

No. 78—Dotted

No. 79—Linear

No. 80—Linear

Brass Rules

No. 81—Hairline Wave

No. 82—Two-point Wave Rule

No. 83—One-point Antique

No. 84—Antique Parallel

No. 85—Antique Parallel

No. 86—Antique Parallel

No. 87—Antique Parallel

No. 88—Antique Parallel

No. 89—Four-point Ornamental

No. 90—Six-point Ornamental

No. 91—Four-point Ornamental

No. 92—Six-point Ornamental

No. 93—Six-point Ornamental

Paragraph Signs and Dashes

1 2 3 4 5 6 7 8 9 10 11 12 13

14 15 16 17 18 19 20 21 22

23 24 25 26 27 28 29 30

31 32 33 34 35 36 37 38

39 40 41 42 43 44

45 46 47 48

49 50 51 52

53 54 55 56 57 58 59 60 61

62 63 64 65

Brackets

(*No. 41 also available in 120 point. Nos. 2, 4, 5, 7, 8, 9, 11, 12 13, 15, 18, 20, 22, and 24, are cast in monotype*)

[ ] {} [ ] {} [ ] [ ] {} [ ] [ ] [ ] {}
1 2-565 3 4-565 5-562 6 7-565 8-268 9-562 10 11-565

12-562 13-268 14 15-565 16 17 18-565 19 20-565

21 22-565 23 24-565 25 26

27 28 29 30 31 32

33 34 35 36 37

38 39 40 41

The University of Chicago Coat-of-Arms

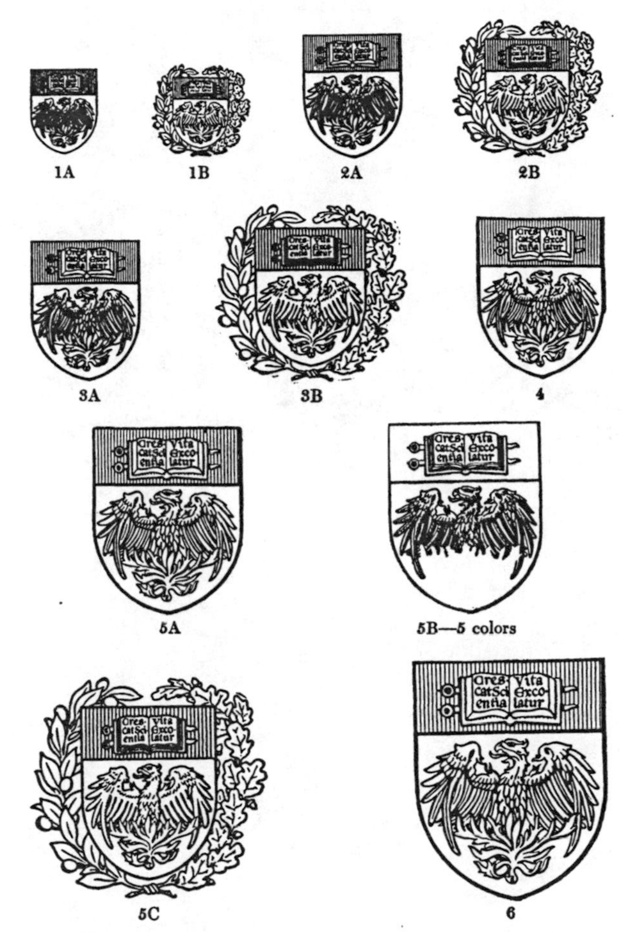

Cuts of all three series are on hand in several larger sizes

Press Seals

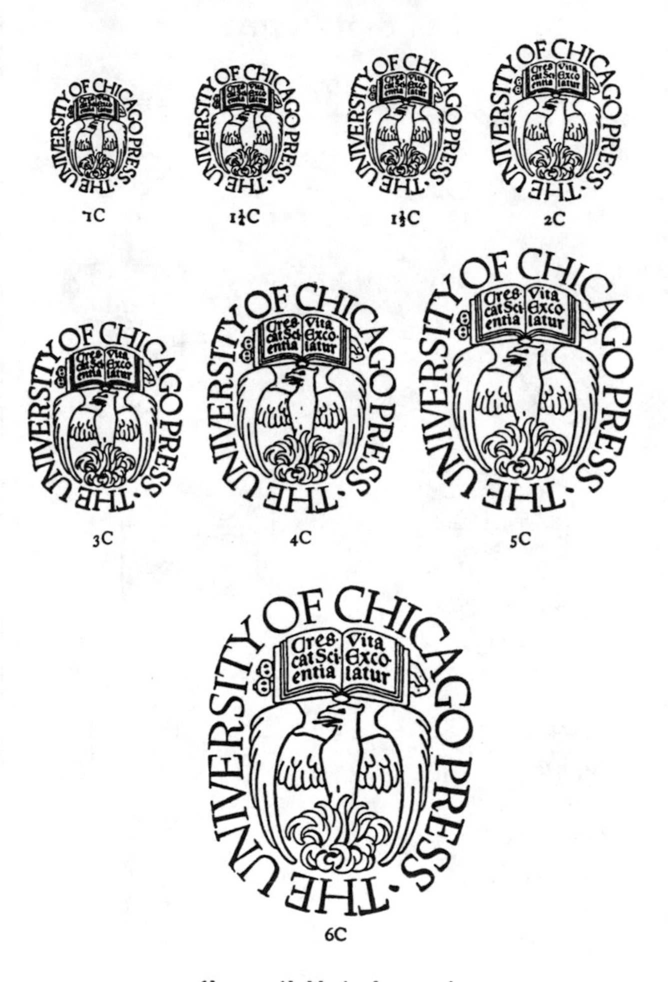

Also available in larger size

Initial Letters

(*Complete Alphabets*)

1 2 3 4 5 6

7

8

9

10 11

12

13

14

15

16

17 18

19

20

21

22

23

24

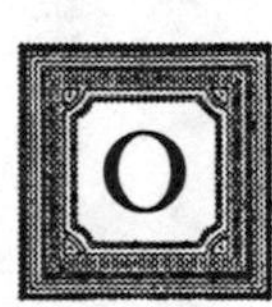

25

26—With tint block

Initial Letters

27

28

29

30

31—With tint block

32

33

34

35

36

37

38

Initials

39—With tint block

40

41

42

43

44—With tint block

45

46

47

Initials

48

49

50

51

52

Special Characters

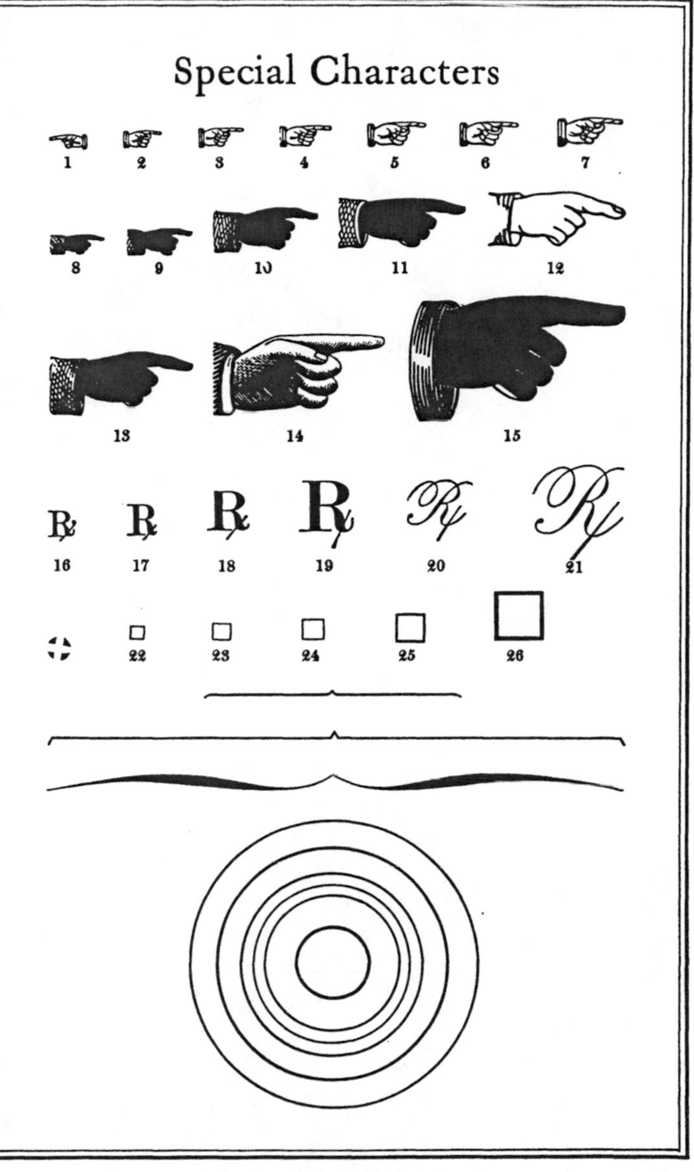

INDEXES

GENERAL INDEX

[Reference figures in italics are to page numbers; those in roman refer to section numbers. *Exc.* = Exception. n. = Footnotes.]

GENERAL INDEX

GENERAL INDEX

INDEX TO SPECIMENS OF TYPE

[References are to page numbers only.]

INDEX TO SPECIMENS OF TYPE

[PRINTED IN U·S·A·]

Printed in the United States
103204LV00001B/14/A

9 789562 913966